DATE DUE

A CRITIQUE OF NEOCLASSICAL MACROECONOMICS

Also by John Weeks

CAPITAL AND EXPLOITATION
THE LIMITS TO CAPITALIST DEVELOPMENT: The Industrialization of Peru,
1950–1980
THE ECONOMIES OF CENTRAL AMERICA

A Critique of Neoclassical Macroeconomics

John Weeks

Professor of International Politics and Economics
Middlebury College, Middlebury, Vermont

St. Martin's Press   New York

First published in the United States of America in 1989

Printed in Hong Kong

ISBN 0–312–03470–9

Library of Congress Cataloging-in-Publication Data
Weeks, John, 1941–
A critique of neoclassical macroeconomics/by John Weeks.
p. cm.
Bibliography: p.
Includes index.
ISBN 0–312–03470–9: $45.00 (est.)
1. Neoclassical school of economics.   2. Keynesian economics.
3. Macroeconomics.   I. Title.
HB98.2.W44   1989
339—dc19
89–10140
CIP

For Ben Fine

Contents

List of Tables and Figures

Tables

Figures

Preface and Acknowledgements

This book grows out of an attempt to specify the differences between the approach to aggregate economic analysis in the neoclassical and Marxian traditions. Early in the inquiry I decided that no serious progress could be made in this task without first investigating the essential features of the neoclassical approach. Therefore, this volume represents the critical prelude to a development of Marxian (and to a degree, Ricardian) macroeconomics.

The book was written over a period over three years, during which I benefited from the help of a large number of people. The research to prepare for writing was largely carried out while I held a research fellowship at the Université Catholique de Louvain-la-Nueve during 1985. During that fellowship period I received invaluable help from Michel Devroey, Phillipe deVille, and Jacque Grouvnuer, all part of the Economie et Société group at the university. Following my stay in Belgium, I spent a year as visiting professor at the University of Leeds, and was fortunate to participate in a project to turn out a volume of essays marking the fiftieth anniversary of *The General Theory*. During the year at Leeds I had stimulating formal and informal discussions about macroeconomics which manifest themselves throughout the book. My thanks go to John Brothwell, John Hillard, and John Bowers for their interest, and in the case of the former for reading an early draft. Also while I was in Great Britain I was fortunate to exchange ideas with Victoria Cheik, Geoffrey Harcourt and Laurence Harris, who took time to read draft chapters.

Upon returning to the United States in August 1986, I discovered how lucky I was to be at the American University, for my department included two distinguished authors of macroeconomics textbooks, Thomas Dernburg and Nancy Barrett (the text of the latter unfortunately is out of print). I thank them for their help, particularly Nancy who provided extensive comments on the inflation chapters. My good fortune continued at Middlebury College, where constructive doubts about some of my arguments were prompted through discussions with David Colander, whose excellent textbook (*Macroeconomics*, Scott, Foresman, 1986) is to be highly recommended. Thanks go also to Richard Cornwall who clarified issues relating to general equili-

xiv   *Preface and Acknowledgements*

brium theory. Were all macro texts similar to David Colander's, the book which follows would be considerably less relevant. I also wish to thank Paul Sweezy, John Kenneth Galbraith, and Ed Nell for both their suggestions and honouring me with jacket endorsements. Finally, thanks go to Keith Povey, whose careful work of editing improved the manuscript immeasurably.

Greatest thanks go to my wife Elizabeth Dore and to Ben Fine. Through discussions with Elizabeth at an early stage in my work I was able to clarify my overall purpose. Ben, whose book with Andy Murfin in part inspired my own (*Macroeconomics and Monopoly Capitalism*, Wheatsheaf Books, 1984), read the entire manuscript. Without his help this book would not have been written, and for that reason it is dedicated to him.

JOHN WEEKS

Introduction

The purpose of this book is to provide a critique of the neoclassical approach to the analysis of aggregate economic activity – what is called in modern, mainstream economics, 'macroeconomic' theory. While this volume stands on its own, it is also the preface to a reconstruction of aggregate economic analysis based upon the work of Marx, which is developed in a second book.[1] One can identify two broad approaches to aggregate economic analysis, that of Marx and that of Keynes. What these two traditions have in common is that both consider aggregate economic relations with concepts developed at the aggregate level; i.e., their aggregates are not merely the summation of behaviour at the microeconomic level. In this regard, neither tradition is 'neoclassical'.[2] The primacy of aggregate behaviour over the activity of individual economic agents is explicit in Marx, but also a fundamental characteristic of Keynes's analysis in *The General Theory of Employment, Interest, and Money* (1936). This distinction, between aggregates derived from accumulating the reactions of individuals and aggregates that are in the first instance 'macro' relations, is one whose significance will emerge as the analysis in this book proceeds.

Having stated the broad purpose of the book, we should identify its intended audience. While some of the issues of theory we deal with are complex ones, often restricted to advanced treatments of economic theory (when treated at all), the presentation is designed to be comprehensible to someone who has taken an introductory course in economics. Certainly the 'income–expenditure' model we begin with will be quickly recognised by a first year student of economics. One need not be a specialist in economic theory to read this book, only a student of economic theory. The book is intended to be a complement to a standard textbook on undergraduate macroeconomics. Much of the book runs parallel to such a text, though the emphasis is different and the reader will find critiques that few undergraduates would encounter in their careers. The intention is to make these critiques as understandable as is the orthodox model presented at the advanced undergraduate level. Written for students, the book critiques neoclassical macroeconomics *as it is taught*, and the reader will find many reference to standard macroeconomic textbooks past and current.

This book is inspired by two convictions. The first of these convictions is that in most textbooks used in undergraduate courses there are theoretical errors and misrepresentations of considerable significance, errors and misrepresentations that have strong ideological implications. The second conviction is more fundamental: that the strictly 'macro' aspects of the theories of both Marx and Keynes have largely slipped from sight. Each the foremost theorist of his century, both men have spawned schools that claim the heritage of the master; but what makes the analysis aggregate in both cases has largely been abandoned. In the course of this book it shall be argued that the loss of what is essentially macro in Keynes is the result of a preference for some form of equilibrium analysis. In the case of Marx's work, emphasis upon this theory of exploitation, and from this the tendency to stress class struggle as the immediate cause of capitalism's difficulties, led to an almost complete neglect of his treatment of the aggregate demand and aggregate supply of commodities.[3]

In the case of Keynes, the essentially aggregate character of his 'revolution' has not survived the 'neoclassical synthesis'. Here the loss of the macroeconomic element is closely related to what Leijonhufvud identifies as the implicit bargain struck between the defenders of pre-Keynesian theory and the Keynesians: that the latter would accept the abstract validity of the automatically-adjusting, general equilibrium view of a capitalist economy if the former would concede its limited applicability in practice.[4] In light of the resurgence of the pre-Keynesian theory in the form of 'the new classical economics', the implicit compromise has proved a disastrous one for the synthesis Keynesians, who can no longer claim as theirs the mainstream of economics after dominating it for three decades.

Macroeconomics can be conveniently divided into three areas of inquiry – the analysis of aggregate reproduction, the analysis of cycles, and the analysis of growth or expansion of the economic system. Here we deal almost exclusively with the first, which in neoclassical theory is referred to as static equilibrium analysis. Marx, however, was not an equilibrium theorist, so to consider macroeconomics to include both Keynes and Marx the more general term 'aggregate reproduction' needs to be used. By this term we mean the analysis of the level of aggregate economic activity in the absence of certain qualitative changes or disturbances, the most important of these being technological change. Textbooks on neoclassical macroeconomics deal with technical change hardly at all, and since the purpose of this book is to provide a critique of the internal logic of mainstream theory the effects of technical change will not be considered.

Developing a theory of aggregate reproduction does not necessarily imply equilibrium analysis, though this is a central characteristic of the neoclassical synthesis approach to macroeconomics. Aggregate analysis must, however, incorporate the fact that capitalist economies are not for the most part racked by continuous and violent fluctuations. The extreme manner by which to do this is to begin with a model of aggregate reproduction which is not only relatively stable in that it does not tend to extreme values, but absolutely so, such that it has no tendency to move from a position uniquely determined by certain exogenous factors ('parameters') in the absence of changes in those factors. An approach such as this involves an equilibrium model. When there are a number of variables and relationships which are determined simultaneously, the result is a model of general equilibrium.

General equilibrium is the point of departure of the neoclassical macroeconomic model, with the added characteristic that the stable position is also one of full and efficient utilisation of all economic resources. Investigation of the neoclassical general equilibrium macroeconomic model is the subject of this book. Chapter 1 presents the basic model without money, a method of presentation which allows one to emphasize the dominance of the pre-Keynesian influence in neoclassical macroeconomic theory. First, we consider what is commonly called the 'income–expenditure' model, without a 'supply side'. It is from this restricted version of the model that one obtains the condition that aggregate economic activity is in equilibrium if 'saving equals investment' (in the simplest case), a condition well known to first year students of economies.

The next step is to fill in a supply side (Chapter 2), with the purpose of providing the model with a theory of wages and employment, rather than to treat the production of commodities as such. By giving the income–expenditure model a neoclassical labour market, one can derive the basic conclusions (or 'parables' as some have called them) about the tendency towards full employment of resources and the restricted possibility or equilibrium with unemployed resources. The presentation here has two purposes: first, to provide a clear exposition of the neoclassical model, comparable but also complementary to that found in standard textbooks; and second, to emphasise certain aspects of the model in anticipation of the mainstream critiques presented in Part II of the book.

Introduction of money into the neoclassical model, which allows for the standard distinction between 'real' and 'nominal' variables, creates a number of complications. Among these is the process of equilibration, involving general equilibrium solutions. Chapter 3 develops the concept of market clearing, particularly with regard to Walras' Law, which will prove omnipresent in subsequent discussion. The 'real/nominal' distinction is frequently referred to as the 'classical dichotomy', though as we shall see as it is neoclassical also. This dichotomy leads us to the famous 'neutrality' of money argument, which plays a central role in the debate over the uniqueness and stability of the neoclassical general equilibrium model when at full employment of resources. Particularly at issue here is the role of 'Walras Law' as the mechanism for automatic self-adjustment of the system, and its compatibility with the quantity theory of money. The concept of money itself comes under close scrutiny in Chapter 4, where the famous quantity theory is introduced.

Chapters 5 to 7 explore in considerable detail variations of the neoclassical model with interactive labour commodity and money markets. The presentation is similar to what one would find in a standard textbook, though the emphasis is different. The purpose here is to demonstrate the extremely restrictive assumptions required in order to construct an internally consistent macro model which tends automatically (without state intervention) to full employment. In Chapter 7 the discussion goes beyond that found in most standard textbooks by treating in detail the impact of aggregate wealth on the commodity and money markets.

These seven chapters provide what might be called an 'internal' critique of the synthesis model, pointing out contradictions and inconsistencies when all of its assumptions are granted. Because much ground is covered in these chapters, it is useful to pause and summarise the critique, as well as to extend it along lines only briefly considered during presentation of the models. Summary and elaboration is done in four chapters, 8 to 11, each of which considers a particular aspect of the conclusion that capitalist economies tend automatically to full employment. In earlier chapters a particular property of most neoclassical models, the 'neutrality' of money, was discussed in some detail. Chapter 8 explores the relationship between the theory of money and full employment, particularly the implications of presuming money to be 'neutral'. The argument is that this property of models is as ideologically important as the allegation of automatically-adjusting full employment. Chapter 9 turns to the neoclassical treatment of the expectations by agents of the future. For Keynes and those who follow his lead, expectations are a source of instability in the economic system. In contrast the tendency in neoclassical theory has been to introduce expectations into the analysis in a manner which makes models more stable. The extreme form of this (*reductio ad absurdum* one might say) is the use of the rational expectations hypothesis by the new classical economics.

In an excursion that is somewhat unusual for a book on short-run macroeconomic models, Chapter 10 presents the argument over the relevance of the aggregate production function. The critique of this function, which calls into question the entire supply side of the synthesis model, goes back to the early 1950s and Joan Robinson. Our interest is in the implications for labour market adjustment in the short-run neoclassical model. From the Capital Controversy we turn in Chapter 11 to the work of the 'disequilibrium Keynesians' (primarily Clower and Leijonhufvud), with the emphasis upon the methodological and analytical inadequacies of Walras' Law as an equilibrium mechanism. This, in turn, is closely related to the division of the model between real and monetary sectors, a basic division which the disequilibrium Keynesians reject. A centre-piece of their school is the attack upon the neoclassical formulation of the market for labour services, itself an extension of the critique of the real/ monetary distinction.

Throughout the first eleven chapters the emphasis has been upon the neoclassical conclusion that smoothly functioning markets will bring about full employment of resources. In Chapters 12 to 15 the critique turns to neoclassical inflation theory as it has come to be presented in standard textbooks. Chapters 12 and 13 dissect in detail the dubious practice of constructing aggregate supply and aggregate demand curves with 'the price level' on the vertical axis. The next chapter, 14, combines these curves to tell neoclassical inflation stories, which invariably involve some variant of the hypothesis that capitalist economies are characterised by a 'natural' rate of unemployment (a concept introduced in Chapter 9). In Chapter 15 the critique of neoclassical inflation theory is completed, with the argument that clinging to the neutrality of money renders the analysis largely trivial. With this chapter behind us, we have treated the two most basic issues of aggregate economic theory and policy, unemployment and inflation.

Finally, in Chapter 16 the various points made throughout the book are brought together, with emphasis placed upon four crucial and theoretically unsatisfactory elements in synthesis macroeconomics: (1) treating aggregate reproduction in terms of value added instead of commodities; (2) analysing production in a one-commodity framework; (3) formulating monetary theory with valueless money; and (4) integrating different markets through general equilibrium theory. In this final chapter most attention is directed to the first two of these. We argue that the simplification to value added categories and one commodity reflects an attempt to resolve what is perhaps the principal analytical problem involved in formulating a theory of capitalist economies. This, we argue, is the problem of relating the value of commodities to the material output of the commodities arising from actual production processes. Solution to this problem defied Keynes and is rendered trivial by the neoclassical one commodity model. Not since Ricardo and Marx has any major economic theorist seriously attacked the problem of relating values to material production.

Before proceeding to the analysis, a comment by way of disclaimer is necessary. Practitioners of the synthesis model might maintain that many of the arguments found in this book are based not upon the neoclassical macroeconomic model in its most sophisticated form, but rather upon a 'strawman', chosen for its simplicity and vulnerability to theoretical attack. Two points can be made in anticipation of such a defence of neoclassical macroeconomic theory. First, at many points the argument considers the more sophisticated defences of the model, so we do not restrict ourselves to simplistic formulations. It is worth adding, however, that in all economic theory, it is the analysis in its simplest form which is most representative, or best encapsulates the basic insights of the discipline. While increasing sophistication enhances the theory, this is frequently at the cost of losing the fundamental vision in a wealth of exceptions and special cases. Second, and more important, the objective reader would do well to refer to any standard textbook on neoclassical macroeconomics, whether at the undergraduate or graduate level. There he or she will find that the version of the synthesis model presented in Chapters 5 to 7 is true to what is offered as the summarised and synthesised wisdom of the mainstream of the economics profession.

Finally, it should be noted that the simple form of the model, on which we spend considerable time, provides the basis for many recommendations for economic policy. To take but one example, it is common for neoclassical economists (and non-economists who hold to neoclassical parables), to argue that lower wages, 'other things equal', will result in more employment of labour.[5] This conclusion derives from the neoclassical model in its simplest form. One of the main purposes of this book is to investigate conclusions of this type, usually derived from the basic neoclassical model. Those who make such assertions rarely have anything but the simplest theoretical formulations in mind.

I hope that the reader who completes this book will, if nothing else, emerge at the end with sufficient scepticism about the neoclassical model to be open to an alternative vision of aggregate economic theory, and to accept at least in principle that the model which has dominated the economics profession since the 1930s (since Adam Smith in fact) is not necessarily the source of all insight.[6]

Part I

The Neoclassical Macro Model

1 The Demand Side of the Neoclassical Model

1.1 INTRODUCTION

Economics is a discipline whose scientific development has closely reflected the political temper of the times. One would expect this from a subject intimately involved in the welfare of people. As a separate, clearly-defined field of study, economics emerged in the eighteenth century, and from that point until the late nineteenth century was usually called 'political economy'. The first great figure in political economy was Adam Smith, and all economists from Smith to J. S. Mill (who wrote about ninety years later) are referred to collectively as the 'classical' economists. This group of writers had an important common characteristic from the point of view of those that superseded: they all incorporated in their analysis a value theory based upon the labour content in commodities.

The classical school dissolved before the analytical onslaught of the 'marginalists'. This name derives from their theory of value, based upon subjective utility and substitution among what they defined as 'factors of production'. By the end of the nineteenth century, the marginalists held the mainstream of economic theory virtually without challenge. Modern microeconomics derives from the marginalists with little fundamental alteration, only elaboration. It was members of the marginalist school that Keynes took as his strawmen, though he confused terminology by referring to them as the 'classicals'.

Keynes took the method of his contemporaries as his point of critical (and frequently polemical) departure. Basic to his critique of the marginalist school was the argument that a capitalist economy had no automatic tendency towards full employment of resources, while such a full employment equilibrium had been the hallmark of pre-Keynesian analysis (rejuvenated today in the 'new classical economics'). After the Second World War there emerged a movement in economics to reconcile Keynes's insights with what had gone before. This reconciliation emerged as the orthodoxy in the profession, and is referred to as the 'neoclassical synthesis'. 'Classical' here comes from Keynes's use of the term, and 'synthesis' refers to the alleged reconciliation of the analysis of *The General Theory* with what that work

3

had sought to replace. In this chapter we are not interested in what was synthesised, but in the result of that synthesis for the analysis of aggregate economic relations. In what follows, the terms 'neoclassical model' and 'synthesis model' will be used interchangeably.

1.2 THE CIRCULAR FLOW AND ITS AGGREGATES

The neoclassical formulation of aggregate behaviour begins with a particular specification of the circulation of money and commodities, called *the circular flow of income*. This provides the basis for the subsequent treatment of aggregate variables. By breaking into the circuit at an arbitrary point, one can follow the process of circulation. In the circular flow the emphasis is upon the flow of income rather than on commodities as such. The economic system is conceived of as incorporating two types of 'agents', households, which sell services[1] of various types, and businesses which purchase these services. In addition, consumer commodities are destined for households, and investment commodities for businesses. Businesses derive their revenues from the sale of produced commodities, then distribute these revenues as payments for services. This interpretation of aggregate circulation is shown in Figure 1.1, taken from a widely-used textbook on macroeconomics.

It is important to realise that this is an interpretation or theoretical presentation of the circulation of commodities, not an empirical representation as such. Nor is it a simplification, if by that term one means the schematic representation of the most important aspects of an actual system. The counter-intuitive character of the circular flow diagram becomes obvious upon inspection. At the top of the diagram, all commodities[2] and services are represented as sold to households. This is not true for an actual economy. Many and perhaps a majority of commodities (in terms of money value) are bought and sold among businesses, never reaching households. First, there are the commodities which are consumed in the process of producing other commodities, what neoclassical economists call 'intermediate' products or commodities. Second, there are the commodities that are used as instruments to produce other commodities, machinery, plant, etc. The elimination of the former from the circular flow (and from all analysis in the synthesis model) is justified on the grounds of avoiding 'double-counting'. Perhaps more surprising than the omission of intermediate commodities is the apparent inclusion of expen-

Figure 1.1 The neoclassical circular flow of income

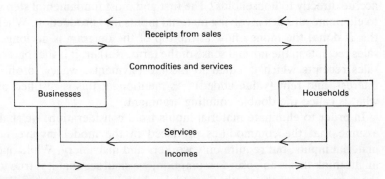

Source: William H. Branson, *Macroeconomic Theory and Policy* (New York: Harper & Row, 1972) p. 16.

diture upon machinery and plant in the flow from businesses to households, for this is a category which the model subsequently analyses in some detail.

Treating investment in this way can be understood by looking at the flow of services and incomes. At the top, 'services' included activities such as haircuts, banking, etc. At the bottom 'services' refer to factors of production: the renting of land, selling of labouring activity, lending of money, and holding of equities in businesses. These are activities that result in the payment of rent, wages and salaries, interest, and profits, which together constitute income (lowest line). The model implicit in the standard circular flow is one in which all of these categories of income are regarded as payments to individuals. By definition these payments are in return for something those individuals sell, which are called services of various types.

The diagram can and in some textbooks is expanded to take account of the exchange of investment commodities within the business sector (though it is never expanded to include the exchange of material inputs to production). This addition would enable the diagram to describe more correctly the way by which exchanges actually occur. However, the purpose at this point is to understand the synthesis model, not actual economies. The very simple version of the circular flow shown in Figure 1.1 is a true representation of the formal synthesis model, as will be seen in the next section.

How is one to rationalise a schema in which all sales of commodities are from businesses to households, and all income payments accrue directly to households? The first and most fundamental step is to eliminate all sales involving material inputs into production. When this is done, the money flow at the top of the diagram is no longer sales receipts in the normal sense of the term. Rather, it is that part of sales receipts which is equal to income payments, wages, profits, interest, and rent (value added). As mentioned, this is justified by what is called the double-counting argument.

In order to eliminate material inputs from consideration, we shall assume that the commodities produced in the model involve no material inputs, but require only workers and machinery. While one might think this is an absurd assumption, we shall see that it is true to the supply side of the synthesis model, which involves what is called an aggregate production function. Alternatively, we could assume that the circulating commodities represent a stock at the beginning of the period, and the only economic activity which engages capital and labour is their distribution. This also may seem a strange assumption, that commodities appear magically at the outset in fixed supply. It will prove consistent with the manner in which markets equilibrate in the neoclassical general equilibrium model (Walras' Law).

To justify the inclusion of expenditure upon plant and machinery in the exchange between businesses and households requires a more involved and subtle set of assumptions. The argument begins at the bottom of the diagram, where it is assumed that all business receipts accrue to households. This implies that there are no retained profits by businesses. In effect business enterprises are treated as conduits, the passive intermediaries between sales receipts and income payments. Individuals receive income payments by virtue of property relations, or to use the neoclassical term, their endowments. For reasons incidental to the model, some people own land, hold corporate assets, or lend money, while others derive the vast majority, if not all, of their incomes from working for employers. Each of these is treated in the model as providing a service – landlords supply the services of land, stockholders the services of plant and machinery (capital), lenders the service of postponing consumption, employees labour services. Each type of income payment is the reward for the relevant service. The assumption of no retained corporate profits now presents itself as logical. Since profits are the payment for a service rendered, they can be treated analytically as accruing to households even if they never leave corporate balance sheets, as this merely reflects the manner in which households chose to hold them.

This view of income as payment for services clarifies the treatment of investment expenditure in the diagram.

When all income accrues to households, then businesses cannot make the decision to purchase anything. What appeared as common sense and obvious (businesses buy machines), is rejected in the model in favour of an esoteric relation (households buy machines) which is implied by the passive role played by business enterprises in neoclassical theory. The exchange relationships are the following: some households are net savers, and these receive interest payments; others are net borrowers, making investment purchases for which they receive profits in return for the sale of the services of capital. As contrary to common sense as this may be, few indeed are the economists, conservative, liberal, or radical, who have expressed any doubts about the descriptive validity of the circular flow on income model.[3]

1.3 THE INCOME–EXPENDITURE MODEL (DEMAND SIDE)

The circular flow takes a particular view about the way in which commodity exchange occurs, and this is formalised and made explicit in the income–expenditure model. At this point we consider the demand side only, introducing the supply side in the following chapter. Consideration of aggregate demand first is not just a convenience of exposition, but corresponds to the emphasis of a school of macroeconomists, usually referred to simply as 'Keynesians'. Since most of these 'demand-siders' operate within the framework of the synthesis model, they shall be called 'Keynesian Neoclassicals' or 'Neoclassical Keynesians' in our discussion.[4]

The basis of the demand side of the model is certain aggregates, which must be defined and clarified prior to developing the mechanics of the model. The method of aggregation, in terms of abstract constructs and their relationship to reality, is central to theory.[5] Assuming no role for government and no foreign trade, the model has the following aggregates: income, consumption, investment and savings. The aggregate demand for commodities is by definition consumption plus investment, and the income of households is divided between consumption and saving.

Consumption refers to the expenditure of households on commodities which are not used to produce other commodities, though their usefulness need not be exhausted with the period that the expenditure is made. Commodities whose useful life coincides with the expenditure period are 'non-durables' and those with a longer life are referred to as 'durables'. While this distinction is of considerable importance in empirical work, it plays no role in the basic model. Expenditure on commodities which go to produce other commodities is called investment. It is necessary, however, to define investment in such a way that materials used up in production are excluded. This is not as straightforward as it may seem. Since over time the value of machinery is passed on to the produced commodity, it could be argued that machines represent an intermediate cost no less than more short–lived inputs such as electricity and iron ore.

Formally, this ambiguity has been avoided by the assumption in the previous section that commodities are not produced, but only distributed with no material inputs except machinery. While this eliminates the problem of distinguishing between different types of inputs, it does not explain why plant and machinery are not treated as intermediate. Basically, the justification is one of practice handed down by generations of economists. Also, if investment were treated as intermediate, then aggregate demand (then reduced to consumption only) would not be equal to income. This equality is the equilibrium condition for the commodities market (see below). In keeping with common practice, investment is defined as expenditure upon means of production which last longer than one time period.

Consumption and investment together are by definition expenditure upon 'final commodities'. The validity of this last category is taken as given, and discussion of it postponed to the end of the book. Corresponding to aggregate demand $(C + I)$ is aggregate income (Y), which represents the total receipts of businesses from the sale of final commodities. This total is completely disbursed to households, becoming disposable income in the absence of any taxes, as $Y(d)$. Household disposable income is either spent upon consumption commodities or saved, so $Y(d) = C + S$. Before going any further, it can be noted that all final commodities in stock at any period will be sold if $C + I = C + S$ (assuming at this point no inventories are held). Since the model has only one period, this condition reduces to $I = S$, the well-known statement that the commodity market is in equilibrium, sales tending neither to expand nor to contract, when household savings equals expenditure on investment commodities.

At this early stage in the argument, it remains only to specify two further relationships. Investment expenditure is taken to be independent of the current level of income (though perhaps as function of levels in the past and expected levels in the future). To use a word common in the literature, it is treated as 'exogenous' with regard to the other variables in the model. Following Keynes, consumption expenditure is specified as a function of the level of current income itself, which we can write as $C = C(Y)$. The rate of change of consumption expenditure with respect to household income (dC/dY) is the marginal propensity to consume (MPC), presumed to be greater than zero and less than one. In the simplest case, the MPC is assumed constant over the relevant range of income levels in the short run. Since what is not spent on consumption is saved, it follows that $Y = C(Y) + S(Y)$, and the sum of the marginal propensity to consume and marginal propensity to save is one. Then the equilibrium condition becomes the following.

$$Y = C(Y) + I$$

or

$$S(Y) = I$$

The mechanics of this simple model are easily seen. A given level of investment expenditure generates a level of income such that the associated level of savings is brought into equality with the exogenous investment. Assuming no other exogenous elements of aggregate demand, the equilibrium level of income associated with a given investment expenditure is determined by the size of the parameter relating consumption to income (or saving to income). This ratio at the margin (dY/dI) is called the investment multiplier, or more generally the autonomous expenditure multiplier. If the MPC is constant, the multiplier is easily derived by simple algebra to be $1/[1 - MPC]$ (or 1/MPS).

Since the simple model with which we are dealing has no time dimension, its consideration out of equilibrium is meaningless. For disequilibrium considerations to be relevant, we would need to incorporate some sort of explicit adjustment behaviour that corresponds to situations in which saving and investment are not equal. As is common in standard textbooks, let us suspend the restrictions of equilibrium analysis to follow a stylised version of how investment generates income. Assume that, from an initial position of equilibrium, investment rises. The result of this is a situation in which aggregate demand exceeds income (value added). Since income equals the value of final commodities, there is excess demand for commodities. The excess demand calls forth a greater value of sales, to which there corresponds an increase in income payments. Part of this increase in income payments is saved, dropping out of the circular flow. The other part, consumption expenditure, adds a further increment to aggregate demand, which calls forth more sales and generates further income payments. This process continues until the newly-generated income is sufficient to create an increase in savings equal to the initial increase in investment.

There is one obvious difficulty with this argument: an increase in aggregate demand may result either in increased prices or an increased volume of commodities in circulation. In some manner the model must be specified to enable one to distinguish between price changes and quantity changes. This is done by distinguishing between the 'real' and 'nominal' values of the variables so far treated. It should be noted that Keynes rejected this dichotomy, arguing that the concept of 'real' variables has no scientific content (see appendix on Keynes).

The problem would seem to have a simple solution – to measure the variables in terms of constant prices drawn from some reference period. This is what is done in all empirical work, for the simple reason that there is no alternative. It is however an ideal measure, not a measure of what anyone can directly observe. While commodities exist and their prices exist, commodities at constant prices aggregated over time do not exist. Neoclassical theory has devoted considerable attention to this problem, under the rubric of the 'index number problem'. The problem in question is that consumer theory tells us that households should change their consumption patterns in response to changes in relative prices, and one cannot assume that a generalised increase in prices (inflation) will leave relative prices unchanged. On the other hand, the theory of aggregation tells one that measures of the type necessary for the income-expenditure model are consistent only if the weights used to combine the commodities into an aggregate do not change. Theoretically, one is at an impasse – consumer theory and aggregation theory are in conflict. In empirical work the conflict may be of little practical importance, for there one seeks specific results whose reliability has internal and external checks. For purposes of theorising, the aggregation problem is quite important, for theory reaches for general conclusions based upon logic.

The difficulty can be shown by reference to the income-expenditure model in the simple form presented above. Assume an increase in investment. The initial consequence of this will be an increase in the demand for investment commodities relatively to consumption commodities. The microeconomic theory of market behaviour predicts that in such a case the price of investment commodities should rise relatively to the price of consumer commodities, which is the signal for resources to shift. If this does occur, then within the model itself a change is required which contradicts the basis upon which the real variables are constructed: the model is specified in terms of constant relative prices, but changes in the level of aggregate demand result in relative price shifts.

Keynesian neoclassicals argue that this contradiction arises only when the model is very close to its maximum real output position (full employment of resources). When there is unemployed labour and unutilised plant, they argue, supply of all commodities can be treated as forthcoming at constant prices. Whether this is correct or not is an empirical question, but it is certainly a useful working hypothesis. On the basis of this hypothesis, one can reformulate the multiplier process sketched out above. If the model is initially at less than full employment with no scarcities of complementary inputs, an increase in investment expenditure will result in falling inventories of investment commodities (or a rise in production for order), inducing businesses to increase capacity utilisation and hire more workers. As a result, payments of wages and profits will increase, raising household incomes. Part of the increase will be spent by households on consumer commodities, inducing greater capacity utilisation and employment in that sector. The feedback process continues until new saving is generated equal to the initial increase in investment spending.

The above parable is the essence of the Keynesian neoclassical view of aggregate circulation, in which autonomous expenditure determines the level of income subject to certain key parameters, such as the marginal propensity to consume. From such an argument flow the policy prescriptions associated with Keynesian neoclassicals, which are characterised by their emphasis upon fiscal policy – government expenditure and taxation. If government expenditure is treated as exogenous, then its role is completely analogous to that of investment in determining aggregate demand, and increases in government expenditure call forth increases in income. If taxes are specified in the model as in part induced by income, then the multiplier is no longer the simple expression, $1/[1 - \text{MPC}]$, but the principle is the same. Should the model be at a position in which resources are not fully utilised (with no bottlenecks), it can reach the full employment level by appropriate selection of an expenditure and tax package. It is useful at this point to present the model in algebraic form, with all variables measured in current prices.

Y = national income
C = consumption expenditure
I = investment expenditure
S = income not spent
G = government expenditure
T = tax revenue of government

Identities:[6]

$Y = C + I + G$ (aggregate demand)
$Y = C + S + T$ (aggregate supply)

The only new element in the model is the description of $(C + S + T)$ as 'aggregate supply', which means that this income flow is taken to be equal to the total value of final commodities (consumer commodities plus investment commodities). It should be noted that this treatment of the income paid out by businesses skips the step in which it appears as the functional distribution among classes – wages, profits, rent and interest. This is consistent with treating all income payments as going to an undifferentiated household sector. This omission is formally rectified when the supply side of the model is introduced. The demand-side model is completed by specifying what are called the behavioural relationships.[7]

$C = C* + aY(d),$

where $Y(d) = Y - T$

$T = hY$
$I = I*$ and $G = G*$

The stars indicate that the variables are exogenous, of given values. Through substitution, one gets the following.

$$Y = C* + a[Y - hY] + I* + G*$$
$$Y[1 - a + ah] = C* + I* + G*$$
$$Y = \frac{[C* + I* + G*]}{[1 - a + ah]}$$

or

$$Y = \frac{[C* + I* + G*]}{\{1 - a[1 - h]\}}$$

Increases in government expenditure result in an increase in the equilibrium level of income via the feedback of induced consumption, though the multiplier is less than in the previous case because of the dampening effect of induced taxes. This typical presentation of the model is one of static equilibrium in which there is no time dimension. Strictly speaking only equilibrium values of the variables are consistent with the model's logic. An excess of aggregate demand over aggregate supply involves a logical contradiction. It implies that the sales of commodities exceed the supply of commodities. This in turn implies that the value added in these commodities (Y) is less than what is required to generate the consumption which is part of the aggregate demand with which one began.

In describing the feedback mechanism of the multiplier we implicitly introduced time (adjustments were not instantaneous). The simplest way to formalise this is to specify time lags: for example, to make consumption in the current period a function of income in a previous period or periods. One possibility is $C = C(Y(t - 1))$. Similarly, one can introduce a lag between aggregate demand and the level of production; e.g., that businesses set their output level in the current period equal to sales in the previous period.[8] The first type of lag has been called the Robertsonian lag and the second the Lundbergian lag, though these terms have largely fallen out of use. A unique equilibrium solution remains once lags are introduced, but the values of the variables are no longer defined for equilibrium positions alone. Econometric aggregate models are specified in terms of such lags.

Discussion of lags indicates a fundamental feature of the synthesis model as a whole and the demand side of it in particular: namely that there is no treatment of production. A third potential lag in this simple system is that between the moment when inputs are gathered in readiness for production and the subsequent moment when the completed commodities flow off the assembly line. So little is this possible lag treated that unlike the other two it has no specific name. In almost every textbook treatment of macroeconomics it is asserted that sales receipts from final commodities and value added are equal by definition, so a lag is impossible.[9] Keynes explicitly rejected this view.

It is to be remembered that the above model was rendered into an analysis in terms of quantity changes by assuming unemployed resources, so that increases in the demand for consumption and investment commodities could be met by expansion of production at constant prices. The view that changes in demand are accommodated by quantity adjustment rather than price adjustments is the central characteristic of the demand side model, based implicitly or explicitly upon the assumption that businesses set their prices by a given markup over unit costs which are constant up to the region of full employment.[10] Within the context of a model with no material inputs, constant unit cost implies a given money wage and constant marginal productivity in the use of labour services.

In the full synthesis model the fixed price assumption is rejected in favour of the opposite extreme, that prices adjust instantaneously to clear markets (Walrasian general equilibrium). In the 1950s and 1960s the quantity-adjustment view was tolerated as a first approximation for empirical work. More recently the new classical economics school has shown no such tolerance, arguing that the perfectly-flexible-price model is suited to reality. In the next chapter we introduce the supply side of the synthesis model, which provides the rationale for the belief that capitalist economies tend automatically to adjust to a position of full employment stability.

2 The Neoclassical Model with a Supply Side

2.1 AGGREGATE ONE COMMODITY PRODUCTION

The supply side of the synthesis model involves the introduction of an aggregate relationship between factor inputs and output. For those who believe that *The General Theory* achieved its claim of generality by focusing analysis upon a capitalist economy under conditions of less than full employment of resources, this relation, 'the aggregate production function' is an anathema, a Trojan Horse which dominates the entire synthesis model and undermines all of Keynes's insights. The full implications of the aggregate production function will be explored in Chapter 10. At this point we show that it becomes the keystone of the model, establishing the equilibrium solution to the system.

If we accept that the value of final commodities equals the value added generated in production, then the aggregate supply of final commodities is simultaneously income to households. Ignoring any material inputs, production (income) is a function of currently expended labour and the means of production used by that labour, with these means referred to as 'capital'. The output of this labour and capital must be measured in units which are unaffected by absolute or relative changes in prices (labour and capital produce commodities, not the market value of commodities). The expedient used in the previous section (assuming constant costs at less than full employment) will not serve. To make this explicit, we change our notation, now using lower-case letters to indicate 'real' variables. In its most general form, the aggregate production function is written as follows.

$$y = y(k, l), \quad y'(l) \text{ and } y'(k) > 0$$
$$y''(l) \text{ and } y''(k) < 0$$

The functions noted with a single prime are the marginal products of labour and capital, and are constrained to be greater than zero (more of either input results in more output/income). The functions with double primes are the second derivatives of income with respect to labour and capital, respectively. That they are less than zero indicates that the aggregate production function obeys the law of

15

diminishing returns to the variable input. This familiar law of marginal productivity theory states that, when one factor of production is held fixed and the other increases, output/income increases but at a diminishing rate. Following common practice, we assume *constant returns to scale*, implying that equal proportionate increases in both factors result in an equal proportionate increase in output/income.

The introduction of this aggregate function places severe restrictions upon the model. Presumably what makes commodities different is that they are produced under different processes. In the current context, that means with different combinations of capital and labour. If we accept this reasonable definition of why commodities differ, then it follows that when the commodity composition of a given level of y changes, the k and l necessary to produce the different combinations also changes. Therefore, presuming that the prices of commodities are constant is no longer a sufficient basis for aggregating income. It does not ensure that y is unique for a given combination of capital and labour. If all production can be summarised by this single function, then for every value of y all commodities must be produced in the same proportions. It is for this reason that the term 'composite commodity' is frequently used in the context of the aggregate production function.

But a constant composition of production is inconsistent with the demand side. On the demand side of the model we have two types of expenditure, for consumption commodities and investment commodities. In general, shifts in the parameters of the model will result in changes in the ratio of these expenditures. The equilibrium condition that aggregate demand be equal to aggregate supply now is complicated by the further condition that consumption expenditure be equal to the production of consumer commodities, and investment expenditure be equal to the production of investment commodities. These conditions cannot hold if commodities are always produced in the same proportions. The solution to this difficulty is to assume that only one commodity is produced. Operating in a single commodity world tremendously simplifies the model as well as removing potential internal contractions (though creating others). An irony of the synthesis model is that its practitioners claim that one of its strengths is its ability to analyse the role of the prices. In fact, with regard to *commodities*, the assumptions of the model eliminate the problem of relative prices at a stroke.

For the reasons given above and more technical ones pursued in Chapter 10, the aggregate production function necessarily involves

the extremely restrictive assumption that the economy being modelled produces only one commodity. Startlingly enough, this fundamental characteristic of the neoclassical macro model goes
unmentioned in most of the standard macroeconomic textbooks,
coming as a revelation to the student who continues on to higher
study in the discipline. Gordon, for example, in his widely-used text,
writes,[1]

> The firm . . . has a positively sloped supply curve [due to dimin-
> ishing returns to labour] even though it pays a fixed wage. . . . In
> the same way, the economy as a whole would have a positively
> sloped aggregate supply curve. . . . The aggregate supply curve is
> just the horizontal sum of the supply curves for the individual
> firms.

One does not have to know much economics to see that this
statement is wrong. Consider an economy with two commodities,
apples and oranges. When one moves to sum the supply of apples and
oranges, in what units will output be measured on the horizontal
axis? No such units exist which make economic sense. Sadly, casual
treatment of aggregate supply is common in macroeconomic texts, so
it is unfair to single out Gordon.[2]

Not to point out the single-commodity character of the neoclassical
macro model is no minor omission. It is this characteristic of the
synthesis model that renders it incapable of dealing with certain
categories of economic relationships. At this point we can identify
two: the process by which the demand for different commodities is
matched with their supply in an aggregate context;[3] and lags and
changes associated with the production process, occurring between
the sale of one period's output and the subsequent manufacture of
the next set of commodities. Since there is only one commodity in the
system, the price adjustments which play such a central role in the
neoclassical model must do their work outside of the market for
commodities.

But before turning to the role of prices, it is necessary to reassess
the variables of the model presented in the last section in light of the
aggregate production function. Income is now measured in units of a
single commodity which serves both as an article of consumption and
is accumulated as the capital stock. Since income is the sum of
consumption and investment (and consumption and saving), these
variables must also be measured in units of the single commodity. If

government enters, its expenditure and tax revenue are also denominated in units of the single commodity.

The model has taken its user a long way from the economy one observes. First, commodities are produced with material inputs (other commodities) as well as labour, and their prices are the sum of materials costs and value added. This characteristic of commodities is rejected in favour of an abstraction that production occurs with fixed capital and labour alone, and that prices are the sum of the components of value added. Second, many if not most exchanges are among businesses in a capitalist economy. In place of this, all exchanges are treated as sales from businesses to households. Third, every capitalist society is characterised by a multitude of products, each achieving its uniqueness by virtue of the specific labour process from which it arises. The neoclassical macroeconomic model simplifies to a one commodity world. This vision of commodity producing and exchanging societies is sufficiently at variance with reality that it is questionable whether it can be called a mere simplification of the complexities of the real world.

Broadly speaking, there are two methods of model construction. The first we shall call 'abstract-simplified', in which the theorist begins with concrete reality as it appears and extracts what he or she judges (perhaps incorrectly) to be the most important aspects of reality, and on this basis reconstructs the actual economy in simplified form. The elaboration of this type of model involves moving closer to the complexity of the concrete by use of the initial elements of reality selected as fundamental. To an extent, this method has an internal check to its adequacy, for the initially-selected elements should be abandoned if they cannot be elaborated to incorporate the complexities which were at first ignored. A second method, that of the neoclassical school, we call 'abstract-ideal', though the synthesis literature prefers the term *a priori*. In this case, the model is constructed on the basis of components which directly contradict reality – e.g. the world of a single commodity – and elaboration involves developing the logical aspects of these components rather than approaching the concrete.

As we shall see, many of the theoretical difficulties of the synthesis model arise not from the confusing complexity of reality, but from the contradictions of the internal logic of the model. As a consequence, one tends to deal with purely theoretical problems; i.e. problems which arise because of the inadequacies of the model rather than because of the complexities of the phenomena to be explained.

This approach is called 'ideal' because the elements of the model arise from mental construction and their relationship to observed phenomena is not obvious. In this type of theorising, actual outcomes enter only at the end of the process, compared against the ideal constructions, usually in a statistical test.

2.2 CONSTRUCTING THE 'REAL' SYSTEM

In our discussion of the circular flow, the hypothetical neoclassiscal economy was one in which no commodities were produced, but only distributed. Now one can see the utility of this presumption. Assuming no production is an explicit recognition of the necessity of considering the world in terms of a single commodity which itself has no material inputs. Distributional services conform well to this condition, since it is not outrageous to treat their price as value added only. When one attempts to imagine what an economy would be like which corresponds to the neoclassical production function, an economy without commodities is the closest analogue. It would be more accurate to call $y = y(k, l)$ a *value added* function rather than a production function, since its characteristics conform more closely to $Y = $ (wages + profits) than to $Q = $ (some collection of commodities aggregated in some appropriate manner).

The synthesis model can now be specified with a supply side.

Commodity market:

(1) $y = c + i$ (aggregate demand)
(2) $y = c + s$ (aggregate supply)
(3) $c = c(y), s = s(y)$ (consumption and savings functions)
(4) $y = y(k, l)$ (aggregate production function)

Factor markets:

(5) $w = y'(l)$ or $l(d) = ld(w)$ (labour demand)
(6) $l(s) = ls(w)$ (labour supply)
(7) $r = y'(k)$
(8) $k = k*$
(9) $y = rk + wl$

Relationships (1)–(4) have been explained. The remaining five define the conditions for the markets for labour and capital. The symbols w and r refer to the wage and interest (profit) rate, respectively, and $k*$

indicates that the supply (stock) of capital is invariant during the period under review. A well-known conclusion of microeconomic theory tells one that under conditions of perfect competition, businesses will minimise their costs (employ factors most efficiently by economic criteria) when factors are paid according to their marginal products. This rule gives the demand schedules for factors, relations (5) and (7). The supply of labour is specified in terms of the wage, and presumably $l(s)$ is an increasing function of w in the vicinity of the prevailing w. The market for labour services is cleared when $ld = ls$. Since the capital stock is given, r is derivative from the wage that equilibrates the labour market.

The last relationship is the 'adding-up' equation. On the basis of previous assumptions (diminishing marginal productivity and perfect competition) adding the assumption of constant returns to scale gives the result, $y = rk + wl$. Constant returns to scale imply that proportional increases in factor inputs yield a proportional increase in output/income. Proof that this assures that output/income is exactly equal to factor payments (when factors are paid their marginal products) is part of what is called 'Euler's Theorem'.[4] However, when one writes by whatever assumptions,

$$y = y(k, l) = rk + wl$$

the result has a tautological aspect. On the one hand, money income is by definition equal to value added – wages plus profits in the simplest case. Indeed, money income is just another name for value added. The relationship, value added equals wages plus profits, remains a definition when measured in real terms, by whatever method of deflation. On the other hand, $y = rk + wl$ also holds by definition as a production relationship, since an 'assumption' (constant returns to scale) is one aspect of defining a function. There is an important difference between the two senses in which equality holds. In the first case, $y = rk + wl$ is a definition which carries with it no implications for the behaviour of the economy. In the second case, the same equality involves a very specific view of how the economy operates – the demand for factors is determined by a single-commodity production function, factor payments are set in perfectly competitive markets, and production of the single commodity is subject to constant returns to scale. The risk is that a non-behavioural identity might be taken as evidence that the behavioural relationship is valid.

Tautologies or definitions have a respectable position in all sciences, and in themselves are unobjectionable. The problem with $y = rk + wl$ is that there is no empirical way to distinguish the pure tautological character (value added) from its theoretic behavioural character (output of the single commodity). The basic difficulty – and source of endless confusion – is that in the synthesis model it is not possible to speak of income without simultaneously meaning output, for they are the same thing. Not even in theory can one separate the pure tautology from the theoretic behavioural definition. This limitation becomes even more serious further along in our investigation when we discover that the behavioural definition is consistent only in equilibrium. The result is an equilibrium solution in which the key behavioural relationship, the clearing of the labour market, is indistinguishable from a tautology. In the next section we investigate just how key this relationship is.

Prior to doing this, a further relationship must be added to the nine equation model presented above. In that system it is implicitly assumed that investment is exogenous, carrying forward the treatment from the earlier discussion of the demand-side model. With the introduction of the aggregate production function this will no longer do, for the model is now inconsistent. Assume some given rate, w, measured in terms of the single commodity. On the basis of this wage rate, the demand for labour is determined, and with k fixed at $k*$ the level of output/income is also determined. Via the consumption function (relation (3)), the level of income sets the level of savings. This level of savings, however, must be equal to the level of investment for commodity market equilibrium. If exogenous investment ($i*$) is above or below the level of savings implied by the assumed wage rate, a logical inconsistency results. Should it be that $i* > s$, then there is apparently excess demand, requiring an expansion of income to generate further savings.

The generation of income in disequilibrium is the multiplier process of the Keynesian neoclassicals. However, more income/output will only be produced, given $k*$ and the production function, if the wage falls (law of diminishing returns). What has changed compared with the demand-side model is the nature of the supply-side cost functions. The Keynesian neoclassicals proceeded with their multiplier mechanism on the presumption of constant unit costs up to the vicinity of full employment, so no wage adjustment, real or monetary was necessary for an expansion of employment. With the introduction of the aggregate production function (diminishing returns to labour) a fall in the wage rate (measured in the single commodity) must accompany any increase in employment. In the present context it is hard to see how an excess demand for commodities would bring such a fall. This inconsistent scenario indicates that the arguments of the demand siders have lost much of their force. With the introduction of the aggregate production function, it is no longer possible to contend that excess demand generates increases in output and employment in a model with only real variables.

The inconsistency does not arise when the consumption function and investment function are redefined to include the interest rate as a variable in each. The previous relationship (3) is replaced with

(3a) $c = c(y, r), s = s(y, r)$
(3b) $i = i(y, r)$

With the new consumption and investment functions all variables are endogenous. In the absence of assumptions that restrict variables, the labour market determines the general equilibrium solution for the system, with aggregate demand playing a purely passive role. When the wage measured in the single commodity equates the demand for and supply of labour, output/income is determined, by definition at its full employment (maximum) level. If at this level of income savings exceeds investment, then the interest rate falls, which induces a movement along the savings and investment schedules such that the former decreases and the latter increases. Since full employment was previously assured by the labour market equilibrium, an increase in investment induces no increase in output/income – the multiplier is zero. The only consequence of the increase in investment (prompted by a fall in the interest rate) is to reduce consumption by an amount equal to the increase in investment, for aggregate demand cannot change. Had one begun at any point in the story other than the labour market, the story must be retold if the level of output/income is not consistent with labour market equilibrium (full employment).

This particular characteristic of the 'real' system, that every variable's value turns out to be ultimately derivative from the equilibrium wage rate measured in the single commodity, indicates a surprising anomaly in the model: the supply and demand for labour are specified to be independent of the interest rate.[5] Consider only the supply of labour. For a theorist inspired by the pre-marginalist economists, most prominently Ricardo and Marx, the absence of the interest rate is reasonable. In the pre-marginalist tradition, economic society is viewed in terms of classes. Workers sell their labour services because they have no capital and no prospects of obtaining any. Thus, their income can be treated as wages only. Capitalists, on the other hand, are the owners of capital, and their incomes derive from profits and interest.

In neoclassical theory the population of economic agents is not divided on the basis of class. All agents have a certain 'endowment', and while this endowment varies across agents, there is nothing in the theory to suggest that the population is divided among those who have capital and those who do not. Capital is acquired in the neoclassical world by saving – deferring consumption. Neoclassical theory is quite clear in arguing that whether one is a capitalist or a worker has no impact on savings behaviour.[6] If workers save, then the model implies that they must also invest. If they invest, they must receive interest and profit payments. Since the supply of labour reflects the trade-off between leisure and income, it must logically be a function of the interest rate, which partly determines income.

Yet no common or influential rendition of the neoclassical labour market in a macro context includes the interest rate as an influence upon the supply of labour. This omission seems to have gone virtually unnoticed in the neoclassical literature. One can offer two explanations for this oversight. First, the neoclassical model in effect treats wages as a cost to the capitalist, a payment for a commodity like any other, and the worker as a commodity seller like any other. In so far as what workers sell is viewed as disembodied labour services, the interest rate is irrelevant. The rate of return on bonds, for example, does not in the short run have an impact upon how many apples a farmer sells on a given market day. Thus, the omission may arise from an analogy with commodity sellers in general, an issue pursued further in the next section. However, the analogy is false. If an apple farmer can use the same resources to grow pears, how many apples will be offered for sale will be determined by the relative price of apples to pears. Similarly, the seller of labour services is simultaneously a seller of 'capital services' if he or she saves. In a neoclassical world workers should determine their offers on the basis of the relative price of labour services and 'capital services'. But this does not show itself in the model.

A second possible explanation for the omission of the interest rate from the supply of labour function is that this is a rare case in which neoclassical theory begins not from an ideal abstraction, but from an abstraction drawn from the world as it is. The overwhelming proportion of households in all advanced capitalist countries derive no significant income from any source other than wages. When one presumes that the decision to work and how much to work is not influenced by the interest rate or profit rate, this is a quite reasonable and empirically valid simplification. But when one makes such an abstraction based upon the world as it is, the abstraction enters in an *ad hoc* manner into the neoclassical model, conflicting with the method of the theory. It should also be noted that treating the supply of labour as independent of the interest rate is an implicit acceptance of the pre-marginalist view that the population of economic agents is divided strictly between the owners of capital and those who have no source of income but the capacity to labour.

To return to the principal theme of this section, the introduction of the aggregate production function into the synthesis model apparently brings a total theoretical defeat of the argument that unemployment could result from insufficient expenditure ('effective demand' in Keynes's terminology). At this point the defeat is purely formal. It results from a system of simultaneous equations which yields a unique solution in which the components of aggregate demand are derivative from the determination of output/income in the labour market. We have not as yet discussed the behavioural adjustment process by which this formal solution is reached. But it should be stressed again that the Keynesian neoclassical story can no longer be told.

With the presence of a labour market without constraints upon the value of the wage measured in the single commodity, an increase in investment no longer generates an expansion of output/income and employment. One can go further and say that the specification of the labour market partitions the model between the market for labour services, which determines output and employment, and the savings-investment market, where the interest rate determines the composition of aggregate demand. This treatment is quite close to the pre-Keynesian view in which the two markets were completely separate. In the synthesis model there is a formal link, since savings, consumption, and perhaps investment are in part a function of the level of income. But this functional link between the labour market and the commodity market is of no significance, for income is held invariant at its full employment maximum, leaving only the interest rate to operate. The implications of this approach for the theory of aggregate employment is explored in the next section.

2.3   EQUILIBRIUM IN THE 'REAL' SYSTEM

Our next step is to consider the adjustment mechanism in the synthesis model by which one moves from a hypothetical situation in which the labour market is not in equilibrium to one in which it is inequilibrium. The argument is clarified if first one contrasts the variables used in the Keynesian neoclassical model to those in the pure neoclassical model. Superficially, the variables seem the same – income/output, consumption, investment, saving, labour and capital. And in both models the first four of these assume both 'real' and 'money' values, though we have yet to make the synthesis translation from the former to the latter. That is, in both models calculations of the type, $C = pc$, $c = C/p$, are made, where C is the money value of consumption expenditure, p a price deflator, and c the 'real' value.

The similarity is only apparent, however. In the case of the Keynesian neoclassicals, C is observed or directly measurable consumption expenditure, p an empirically derived price index (its weights justified by consumer budget studies), and c nothing more than the result one gets when C is divided by p. In this treatment, C, which we observe, is the independent category, and c exists only as a calculation. In the synthesis model, the reverse is the case: the consumption component of aggregate demand has no direct empirical or observable analogue. It is the non-saving of households measured in units of the single commodity, which is determined by income (also measured in the single commodity) and the interest rate. Theoretically, it exists prior to the determination of C, where the latter is merely the expression of an arbitrarily determined money supply (see Chapter 4). The same is true for savings, investment, and income itself in the synthesis model. This is another aspect of what we called the 'abstract-ideal' method of neoclassical theory. The basis of the model is a set of variables which are constructions of the theorist, rather than simplified expressions of what one observes.

In summary, the Keynesian neoclassicals define their model for nominal variables – to keep to the same example, consumption expenditure in money terms is a function of income in money terms. Price changes complicate this relationship, requiring some deflation procedure. Therefore, c, 'real' consumption expenditure, exists only as derivative from the empirical category, C, consumption expenditure in money terms. In the synthesis model, all flow variables are defined in terms of the single commodity, generated by the aggregate income/output function. In this case, money consumption exists only as a derivative of 'real' consumption. Here no deflation is involved as such, but rather a mere translation of units, from units of the single commodity to units of money (yet to be defined). This characteristic of the synthesis model, that its basic concepts are specified independently of money, is of particular importance to the analysis of labour market equilibrium. Indeed, the nature of the labour market in the neoclassical model cannot be fully appreciated without grasping this point.

In the Keynesian neoclassical model there could be a less than full employment equilibrium. In formal mathematical terms this is possible because the only equilibrium condition is that aggregate demand equal income/output. This equilibrium is based implicitly upon a presumption of constant costs in production. In the synthesis model such as equilibrium is excluded by the further equilibrium condition that the demand for labour equal the supply. Again, this is a formal mathematical condition, though it implies a vision of economic behaviour radically different from that of the neoclassical Keynesians. For Keynesians, economic agents are viewed as income-constrained. For households, this means that their incomes are given in the short run, and income constrains their consumption decisions. In the case of businesses, the decision to set the level of output is constrained by anticipated sales.

Implicit in the pure neoclassical specification of the labour market is a reversal of the Keynesian neoclassical constraint. For households, income is not given, but a decision variable. It is the wage that is given (measured in the single commodity), and on the basis of the wage households determine their optimal mix of work and leisure.[7] Analogously, businesses are presumed to believe that they can sell as much as they might wish at the prevailing price. On this basis – all agents are 'price-takers' – the demand and supply schedules for labour can be specified without reference to the price of the single commodity in monetary units. Some have called these 'notional' schedules, the quantities of labour demanded by businesses and supplied by households on the presumption expectations will be fulfilled and that all markets will be cleared (the commodity market being the only other one at this point).

In the context of a single commodity, the labour market is cleared through barter exchange. What is called the 'real wage' is actually a certain amount of the single commodity, for which workers barter their labour services. Treating the exchange between capital and labour as barter is central to the equilibrium solution, for it makes the calculations of both workers and capitalists extremely simple. The reward for work is a certain amount of the single commodity, and the cost of hiring labour is the same. Further, labour services are seen as being sold in a manner completely parallel to the way in which capitalists sell their produced commodities.

Consider a situation in which at the prevailing price the demand for a commodity is less than its supply. In such a situation, neoclassical theory has a particular story to tell. If the market for the commodity is a competitive one, sellers will respond to this situation by reducing their offer price. If the demand for the commodity is negatively related to price and the supply positively related, the consequence of reducing the offer price will be to eliminate the initial excess supply. This apparently simple adjustment process will be considered in more detail in the next two chapters with reference to Walras' Law.

In anticipation of that discussion, it can first be noted that the onus for adjustment falls upon the seller in the case of excess supply. We consider this in the context of Figure 2.1 which is a four-part diagrammatical presentation of the equilibrium solution of the model presented above.[8] The diagrams make only one simplifying change from the equations previously specified: in Figure 2.1 it is assumed that investment is a function of the interest rate only. Nothing significant is lost in the logic by making this simplification, as we shall see when we reach the discussion of parts (c) and (d) of Figure 2.1. The diagrammatic technique used is a common one, though here the labour market is presented first, at the top of the page, as opposed to last as is usually the case. Putting the labour market first is singularly appropriate, for its equilibrium condition determines all else. Indeed, the savings–investment relationship enters as little more than an afterthought.

Part (a) of the figure shows an equilibrium point A at which the supply of labour and the demand are equal. This determines the full employment level. It should be noted that, while there are points to the right of the employment level $l(e)$, and output levels above $y(e)$ in part (b), these do not exist even conceptually. Should the wage be above $w(e)$, employment is determined by the demand curve, for the aggregate optimising rule is, marginal product of labour = the wage. If the wage is below $w(e)$, the employment level is determined by the supply curve. Any wage, above or below the equilibrium, results in a level of employment and income/output less than the full employment level.

We have used the term 'wage' repeatedly, and it is incumbent upon

Figure 2.1   General equilibrium in a single commodity barter model

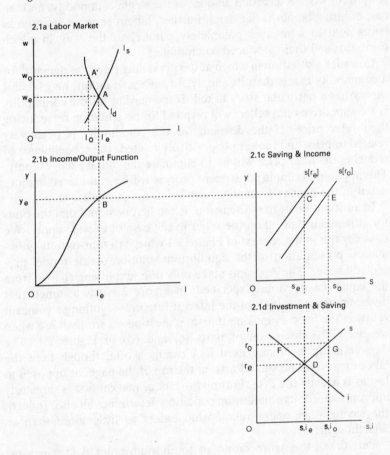

us to be precise about what is meant by it. Invariably in the context of the neoclassical model the variable on the vertical axis in Figure 2.1(a) is referred to as the 'real wage'. This is imprecise language, even misleading. Almost without exception, the neoclassical macro model involves only one commodity. Therefore, the variable w is necessarily measured in units of the single commodity, and is correctly referred to as the *commodity wage*. In the present context with no money, 'commodity wage' and 'wage' will be used interchangeably. When money is introduced this practice will not be justified.

With terms clear, consider the situation in which the commodity wage is momentarily above the equilibrium level, $w(o) > w(e)$. At such a wage the supply exceeds the demand, with employment set by the latter. Were this wage to prevail, y would be determined below $y(e)$, and the interest rate would adjust to equilibrate i and s. In the synthesis model, a situation in which $l(s) > l(d)$ results in a fall in the wage. The argument is as follows: workers have a commodity to sell, labour services; when they are unable to sell all the units of this commodity that they wish to sell at the prevailing price, they reduce the offer price until the amount they wish to sell can be sold. The analogy with a producer of commodities is clear: a farmer, for example, takes his or her potatoes to market and makes an offer; unable to sell all of the potatoes, he/she offers them at a lower price, and continues to reduce the offer price until all are sold. This behaviour forces other farmers to reduce their offer prices. Workers are presumed to act in the same fashion.[9]

There is a problem with the analogy, however. In the case of the farmer, assuming each to be alike with respect to production conditions and share of the market (infinitesimally small for perfect competition), each will be in the same situation: either all will find that they can sell all of their potatoes (market in equilibrium or in excess demand), or all will be burdened with potatoes they cannot sell. In this hypothetical situation, all will be motivated to do the same thing – reduce the offer price of potatoes. Or, at least, such behaviour is a logical possibility. However, not even hypothetically can one treat all workers as being in the same situation without additional assumptions. Even if all workers were alike, an excess supply of labour would be characterised by most workers successfully selling the amount of their labour services which they wish to sell, and only a minority of the labour force being unsuccessful in doing so.

While an excess supply of any non-labour commodity can reasonably imply disappointment on the part of the vast majority of sellers, an excess supply of labour services is consistent with contentment for the vast majority of sellers. Further, the equilibrating adjustment which would eliminate the excess supply of labour services, a lower wage measured in the single commodity, would leave the vast majority of satisfied sellers unambiguously worse off. This contrasts with the situation of the seller of a non-labour commodity, who, while losing from the fall in price, gains from the rise in quantity sold. No such gain goes to the worker, who sells his commodity in an all-or-nothing package.[10] A higher level of employment in general means more workers employed, or each worker employed for a longer time period but in this case at a *lower* wage. With these differences between workers and other commodity sellers in mind, why should the contented sellers of labour services lower the offer price which has secured them employment?

In order to achieve the clearing of the labour market, assumptions must be introduced which allow workers as sellers of their labour services to be treated identically to sellers of other commodities. At least two possibilities present themselves. First, one can contradict the real manner in which work is organised and contracted and assume that workers, like potato growers, sell their services bit-by-bit, so that a 10 per cent rate of unemployment, for example, can be viewed as each worker suffering from selling less than he/she wishes. Alternatively, and equally counter to reality, it can be presumed that employment contracts are for an extremely short period of time, coinciding with the market period. In this case, each market day dawns with all workers without jobs and all businesses without workers. The second is the ideal abstraction made in the synthesis model, and labour market equilibrium is dependent upon it. While post-Keynesians, Leijonhufvud for example, have sharply attacked the neoclassical treatment of the labour market on other grounds, they have implicitly or explicitly accepted this analogy between the sale of labour services and the sale of other commodities.

With the nature of employment redefined to conform with the needs of equilibrium, the schedules in Figure 2.1(a) take on particular meaning. If the prevailing wage is $w(o)$, the demand for labour is $l(o)$, corresponding to point A' on the demand schedule. This amount, $l(o)$, should not be thought of as the level of employment, but rather the job openings businesses would offer at such a wage. That is, it is not correct to interpret the horizontal distance to the demand curve as 'employment', and the horizontal distance from the demand curve on the supply curve as 'unemployment'. To use the term introduced earlier, these are *notional* offers, made in the context of a logically necessary equilibrium solution. Were it possible to treat point A' as the representation of an actual hiring process that left a certain number of workers disappointed, the logic of the equilibrium solution would have been contradicted.

Armed with equilibrium in the labour market, we move on. The full employment level of income/output implies a certain level of savings, given the interest rate (part (c)). If the interest rate is $r(o)$, then savings exceeds investment, by amount *FG* (part (d)). The excess supply of savings leads to a fall in the interest rate, which brings about $i = s$, and this has the effect of shifting the savings-income schedule to the left. The last two parts of Figure 2.1 clarify another characteristic of the synthesis macro model: the difference between consumption and investment is purely formal. Both are positive functions of income and negative functions of the interest rate (though the income influence on investment is not shown in Figure 2.1).

In the writings of Keynes and subsequent literature, consumption and investment expenditures are differentiated on a number of grounds. First, it is argued that the two types of expenditure are carried out by different agents, with different motivations and different purposes. This is completely eliminated by making both a function of the same variables, specified in general form.[11] Second, and on the basis of the first distinction, it was argued by Keynes and later writers that investment is more volatile than consumption, which justifies in part making investment expenditure key to the explanation of economic cycles. This also is lost when both are specified as functions of the same variables. And third, in the context of static equilibrium in which there is only one commodity, investment plays no role as a creator of productive capacity, its last claim to distinction once its role as an independent component of aggregate demand is abandoned.

The theoretical decision to drop any meaningful distinction between consumption and investment also implies dropping the distinction between consumption and saving, and saving and investment. In the Keynesian neoclassical model, saving is income not spent by households. In the strictly neoclassical treatment it becomes that portion of income spent under the name of investment. And investment expenditure itself merely represents the portion of the single commodity which is not consumed in this period but carried over into the next, where it is lost from view. In this context, r, the interest rate, has a very limited and restricted meaning. Since there is only one commodity in the model, variations in the interest rate by definition have no impact upon the composition of output.

The role of the interest rate, given output/income at its full employment level, is to set the division of income between consumption and savings, and the division of aggregate demand between consumption and investment. The latter division, however, is only semantic, two words for expenditure upon the same commodity or product. To the extent that these two words imply any theoretical difference, 'consumption' refers to expenditure which results in immediate use of the single commodity for personal (household) gratification, while 'investment' involves buying the same commodity but carrying it forward into another period. Since not consuming something in the current period means by definition to save it, investment and saving are exactly the same act in the model.

If this is the case, how does one justify having two words to describe the same act (not consuming now), and associating the two words with different mathematical functions, i.e. $s = s(r)$ and $i = (r)$? Indeed, this apparent redundancy is eliminated with the introduction of the IS function, as we shall see. The redundancy is justified in the present context by recalling our discussion of the circular flow. There we noted that some households are viewed as lending and others as borrowing. Since the equilibrium solution can be reached on the basis of 'real' variables, the borrowing and lending must be in the form of units of the single commodity. Borrowing involves some households deciding to consume more now and less later, while lending implies deferring some consumption to the future. Thus, the interest rate in the model serves merely to balance out the borrowers and the lenders. As Leijonhufvud argues, the interest rate plays no role in allocating resources between consumption commodities and investment commodities, for the two are the same. It is only the rate at which present consumption is transformed into future consumption (Leijonhufvud, 1968, p. 215).

In the neoclassical macroeconomic model the discussion of saving and investment can proceed with no reference to the capacity-expanding characteristic of the latter. In fact, the entire analysis can restrict itself to savings alone, and frequently does. Omitting reference to investment makes the model considerably more comprehensible, for it eliminates at least two nagging contradictions: how two different categories of expenditure (consumption and investment) could relate to the same commodity, and how a system could be in equilibrium with unchanging aggregate demand but expanding capacity. We see that another characteristic of the model is that it is equivalent to a circular flow with a consumption commodity only, analogous somewhat to a community of squirrels, which makes no investment but sets aside nuts for the future. The interest rate reflects the trade-off between nuts for the present and nuts for the future.

2.4   CLEARING AWAY THE FOG

It should be clear from the preceding discussion that unemployment in the usual sense of the term is impossible in the synthesis model. Appropriate assumptions are made to ensure that the labour market will automatically achieve equilibrium, which involves full employment by definition. If the wage measured in the single commodity rises above what had been its full employment value in a previous hypothetical exercise, the resulting fall in the level of employment would represent what is called 'voluntary' unemployment. The level of employment is determined by notional demand and supply curves, so a rise in the wage can only be the result of workers reducing their notional supply of labour (holding the notional demand curve constant).

This is a powerful political and ideological message: changes in the level of employment are the result of the work-leisure preferences of workers, not of any systemic malfunctions of the system of production and circulation. Such a conclusion is inherent in the one commodity model, and one needs none of the abstract-ideal assumptions governing the labour market to achieve it, nor any mathematical specifications of equilibrium conditions. These merely serve to give a non-exchange system the superficial facade of an exchange economy – and to ensure that the solution is an 'optimal' one as well as at full employment.

The term 'involuntary unemployment' would refer to a situation in which some members of the labour force seek jobs at prevailing wages or even lower than prevailing wages, but are unsuccessful in finding them. If workers are presumed to be in this situation – willing and able, but unsuccessful – then their failure to find jobs must be because employers are unwilling to offer work, again at prevailing or less than prevailing wage rates. Employers will be unwilling only if they believe that the output which additional workers would produce could not be sold profitably.

Such a condition is called a 'demand failure'. When a seller perceives a demand failure, the notional demand for labour curve upon which the neoclassical labour market equilibrium is based is no longer relevant. The necessary condition for a demand failure is that the producer must sell his or her commodity. Such a situation is ruled out of the neoclassical model by the nature of its assumptions – demand failures are not possible. Fundamentally, they are ruled out because the model involves no sale of the single commodity in the usual sense. One portion of the output of the single commodity is bartered directly with workers for their labour services. This is not a sale of the commodity, but a barter exchange for services rendered; it is inseparable from the decision which sets the producer's optimal level of employment. The producer can harbour no uncertainty about how much will be sold to workers, for the employment decision guarantees that amount. If for some reason, workers were to refuse an offer of output/income, this would simultaneously imply that it would not be produced.

Since there are only workers and profit receivers in the model, that proportion of output/income which does not go to workers is retained by the producer – not even bartered. Therefore, not only is there no lag between the circulation of the single commodity as an item of consumption (or investment) and its distribution, *there is no theoretical difference*. In this model, output is not bought and sold, but only divided into two forms of income – wages and profits. In a capitalist exchange economy, there are three distinct stages (or 'moments' Marx called them): production, when commodities are created; circulation, when these commodities are exchanged and reach their ultimate users; and distribution when that part of the money received in exchange corresponding to the value added in the commodities accrues to various categories of income recipients. In the neoclassical 'real' system, all of these stages are the same, not just because they are considered in timeless equilibrium, but also because no theoretical distinction is made among the three. The production function is simultaneously a value added function (production = distribution), and the exchange between capital and labour is simultaneously the sale of the product (distribution = circulation). An insufficiency of aggregate demand cannot present itself as a theoretical possibility in such a model.

The first necessary condition for demand failures to occur is that the exchange of the producer's product not be a direct act of distribution. The second necessary condition is that the producer's output not only be a vendible article,[12] but also that it *must* be disposed of by the sale of it. If the producer can keep the product for own use, then no demand failures are possible. In fact, except in the case of individual, self-employed producers who assemble their inputs without significant monetary exchange, the first condition implies the second. If employers of labour sell their product to anyone other than their own workers, those workers must be compensated for their work with something which will allow the workers to obtain the products of employers other than their own. This 'something', which represents a general medium of exchange for the products of sellers is, by definition, money. Once the employer of labour has paid out money to workers as a condition for achieving their cooperation in production, the employer must exchange the product for money, or cannot re-initiate the production cycle.

The necessary conditions for demand failures, and, therefore, for involuntary unemployment, are absent. The commodity is never sold – it never has to face the test of the market, lonely and uncertain without a guaranteed recipient. At this point, we can note that our terminology has been inaccurate, for we have used the term 'commodity' to refer to the single output of the synthesis model. In order that the words 'product' and 'commodity' not be synonymous, we shall make explicit definitions. A product is the result of a process of production. A commodity is a product which is produced for the purpose of selling it, and must be sold if the producer is to continue in his or her role as an economic agent.[13] This was the definition of a commodity used by the Classical economists (particularly Marx and Ricardo), and the usefulness of the definition should be clear. Fundamentally, the synthesis model precludes involuntary unemployment because it is a theoretical formulation without commodities. In the theory there is no difference between those products produced for self-consumption and those produced for the purpose of selling them, and the basic difference between private consumption and private production in a capitalist economy is obscured.

3 Comparative Statics and Equilibrium

3.1 STATICS, DYNAMICS AND GENERAL EQUILIBRIUM

In the previous chapters a simple definition of 'equilibrium' was used – markets were in equilibrium if there was neither unsatisfied demand nor unsold supply. In anticipation of the introduction of money into the analysis, a more precise definition is required. For the rest of this book, the following definition will be used:

A market or set of markets is in equilibrium if the agents participating in that (or those) market(s) have no cause to to alter their plans (how much they desire to buy and sell).

The analysis of this chapter and the next require a brief descussion of two related issues which presented themselves implicitly in the real solution to the synthesis model. The first of these is the distinction between models in which the variables reach steady-state values and models in which the variables are changing. Following convention, the former are referred to as static models and the latter as dynamic models.[1] The discussion of the preceding chapter involved static analysis, in which variables seek steady, unchanging values implied by a set of arbitrary parameters such as the production function, consumer utility functions, etc.

When one of the arbitrary parameters is assumed to change and the implications of this are pursued, one is indulging in *comparative static analysis*. The usual result of this analysis is the discovery of an equilibrium solution in which the variables are again at rest. Equilibria have three aspects – existence, uniqueness, and stability. The second two will not concern us in most of our discussion. It will be assumed that if an equilibrium solution exists, it is unique (there are no others for a given set of parameters). The stability of equilibria will also be presumed; given the parameters of the model, if a variable is 'disturbed' from its equilibrium value, it will return to it, not diverge further.

Discussions of equilibrium adjustment fall into two categories, *partial equilibrium* analysis and *general equilibrium* analysis. Vet-

erans of introductory and intermediate courses in economics would
be familiar almost exclusively with the former. The usual supply and
demand analysis involves consideration of a partial equilibrium solution. The demand curve for a particular commodity, for example, is
constructed on the assumption that the income of all consumers in
the market and prices of other commodities are fixed. These, along
with other assumptions, allow one to draw a curve in two dimensions,
in which quantity is a function of price. Maintaining these assumptions, one can deduce the new equilibrium price when the demand
curve is assumed to shift (as a result of a change in consumer income,
for example). The analysis is partial because the change in the price
of the commodity under consideration will affect the demand curves
for other commodities, which are constructed on the assumption that
the price of the first commodity is fixed. When these demand curves
shift, their change will feed back upon the demand curve for the first
commodity, resulting in a shift of price away from the partial (feedbacks ignored) equilibrium solution. Strictly speaking, partial equilibrium solutions are in general inconclusive even with regard to the
direction of movement of price and quantity.

An analysis which incorporates all of the feedback effects as they
ramify through all markets involves a general equilibrium solution. It
has its basis and inspiration in microeconomics, but plays an important role in the synthesis macroeconomic model. The synthesis model
is one of general equilibrium, in which there are feedbacks among
several markets, and analysis of any market taken alone is partial.
However, in considering the real system it was not necessary to
invoke general equilibrium analysis, Now that the distinction between partial and general equilibrium analysis has been made explicit, one can look back and see that the treatment of the real solution
involved an analysis of partial equilibrium. First, the labour market
was considered and equilibrium established there with no reference
to any other market. This was possible because no other variable
could feed back upon the labour market. Since the model had no
money, there was no price level (defined implicitly as unity), and,
therefore, no money wage which could be influenced by events in the
market for commodities.

This is the essence of what is called the *Classical dichotomy* – the
labour market stands alone, achieving solitary equilibrium, with the
price level of no significance. The absence of feedbacks from other
markets is the result of the complete dichotomisation of real and
nominal variables. Once money is introduced, it is no longer possible

to treat the labour market in isolation. The labour market remains the keystone of the model, however. With the introduction of money, the price level becomes a variable, and the real wage is not simply w, but W/p, where W is the money wage and P the price level (or, more precisely, the price of the single commodity). Disequilibrium in the labour market is not eliminated by a movement in the real wage as such, but by adjustment of W or p or both of these. With the introduction of money, the real wage does not exist independently of the two nominal variables W and p. As shall be clear later, the price level is determined by relationships which do not directly operate upon the labour market. In consequence, the synthesis model with money requires an explicit general equilibrium solution, in which the values of all variables are determined simultaneously, not sequentially as was the case in the previous chapter. While the labour market remains the basic determinant of the general equilibrium solution, it is not valid to consider it in isolation once one is dealing with nominal variables. It is for this reason that general equilibrium analysis is treated in some detail in Section 3.3. However, it is first necessary to deal with potential confusions arising from the relationship between equilibrium adjustment and the conceptual treatment of time in the neoclassical model.

3.2 CONFUSIONS OF LOGICAL AND CHRONOLOGICAL TIME

The distinction between the 'short run' and the 'long run' is commonly encountered in neoclassical economics, and can serve as a source of endless confusion unless clarified with some care. The precise meaning of these terms, and the only meaning which is free from serious ambiguities, derives from microeconomics. The short run is a period of time during which the capital stock is treated as given. This is the precise sense in which the macroeconomic model of the previous chapter can be defined as a short-run model, for in that real system it was assumed $k = k*$.

In microeconomics the *long run* is defined not as a period, but as a planning perspective. In the long-run perspective, the individual firm (and the personifying of an institution is usual) is presented with a range of alternative plant sizes, each of which is defined by a certain capital stock. The long-run analysis involves the theorist specifying the determinants of the decision as to which plant size to select. For this reason, the locus that traces out the minimum unit cost levels for each output is often (and most correctly) called a 'planning curve'. In textbooks on microeconomic theory it is common to encounter the statement that in the short run labour is variable and capital fixed, and in the long run both (or all) factors are variable. Strictly speaking, such a statement is incorrect or at best misleading, for it suggests that the two concepts, short run and long run, are both logical abstractions from chronological time, differing only in duration.

This not the case. The term 'long run' does not refer to time at all, but to alternative choices. The short run is a concept of time explicitly chronological in nature. Theoretical or hypothetical actions occur in the short run – the output decision is made by the firm, prices change, demand and supply curves shift, etc. In other words, the short run is a logical time period in which the actions of economic agents are carried out. In the long run, on the other hand, nothing can occur, for it is merely perception by agents of alternative short-run situations into which they can place themselves for action.

Strictly speaking there is no such thing as a static long-run model. If the capital stock is given, the analysis is short run. If the capital stock is changing, one is dealing with growth theory, where the terms short run and long run have no meaning. The short-run/long-run distinction refers to *static* analysis, and all static equilibrium models are short-run models. What, then, is one to make of a statement of the following type:[2]

> The neoclassical full [employment] equilibrium is a useful reference point for the study of more realistic descriptions of macroeconomics. We should expect to converge to the neoclassical equilibrium in the long run.

This is an example of loose use of precise terms that results in considerable confusion. Along the same line, one frequently encounters the judgement that 'the Quantity Theory is a long-run relationship'. Such statements have no theoretical status and fall into the category of what Leijonhufvud calls a 'fudge-phrase' – vague use of precise terms is employed to gloss over points at which the analysis becomes sticky and problematical. On the basis of the generally agreed precise meaning of short run and long run, nothing can converge in the long run, since events occur only in the short run by definition. If a statement like the one above refers to real time – i.e., it is an empirical assertion – then it is unacceptably simplistic. The neoclassical full employment equilibrium (to take the example in the quotation) is based upon an analysis in which there are no technical changes, no uncertainty, no change in consumer tastes, and no random shocks. It is simplistic indeed to argue that a model which excludes these yields such a definitive prediction (full employment stability) about the actual course of fluctuations in the real world over a given period of time.

There is a third interpretation of this type of use of the terms short run and long run. Neither an empirical prediction nor a rigorous theoretical statement, it could be taken to refer to what happens in a successive series of short-run situations after a parameter change such as an increase in the money supply has caused a deviation from equilibrium. In other words, after the 'shock', the model seeks equilibrium again when everything has 'shaken down' and sorted itself out. This, indeed, would seem to be the implication intended by authors of such statements. However, such an implication is invalid, indicating an attempt at spurious realism.[3] Short-run static models exhibit their equilibriating tendency in a single instantaneous short-run moment or not at all. To hold the capital stock and other parameters constant, then to refer to 'long-run' tendencies is to mix an abstract theoretical process with real world processes that contradict the assumptions of the model. The result is an inconsistent statement that has no theoretical or empirical content.

For this reason, there will be no reference to the 'long run' in the subsequent discussion of the synthesis model, except in the precise sense in which it is used in microeconomic theory. Our concern is not whether the neoclassical model tends to full employment in some vaguely specified 'long run', but whether given its assumptions, it tends towards such an equilibrium at all. This allows for a strict separation of theoretical generalisations and empirical predictions. In the previous section the nature of equilibrium solutions and adjustments was clarified, and in this section it has been argued that static equilibrium solutions are by their nature short run. The process of equilibrium adjustment itself can now be treated.

3.3 EQUILIBRATION OF MARKETS

Prior to introducing money into the synthesis model, it is necessary to pursue further the process of general equilibrium adjustment. In Chapter 2 we reached an equilibrium solution for the real system, and it appeared only necessary to transform its values into nominal terms. The stage seemed set for the entry of the quantity theory of money or some variant thereof to provide a facsimile of a monetary economy. Most textbooks would do so at this point and quickly transform real into money variables. However, as argued in this chapter, the introduction of money implies that a new method of solution is necessary, which treats all markets simultaneously – general equilibrium.

The first step in converting from partial to general equilibrium analysis is to consider why money need be introduced into the analysis at all, since the entry of money is what requires one to abandon the simple sequential treatment of market clearing. It is to be recalled that the solution to the model in the previous chapter was derivative from the labour market. If the labour market is considered in isolation, no concept of money is necessary. In a one commodity world, employers barter directly the output of their enterprises to the workers who along with the fixed endowment of capital produce that output. In this context, money plays no role. While it is true that actual commodity exchanging economies invariably involve money, this is not a theoretical justification for introducing the concept. Actual economies possess many characteristics which the neoclassical macro model never incorporates, such as intermediate inputs. These are excluded on the grounds that they are not relevant to the problem at hand. Why, then, is it relevant to introduce money? What theoretical problem is raised which leads one to consideration of the role of money?[4]

To answer that question, recall that the real system has two markets. First, there is the labour market, which we have treated in detail. Second, there is the market for the single commodity, which includes the determination of the distribution of the single commodity between consumption now and consumption in the future by the interest rate. If one allows for disequilibrium states, it is apparently possible for both or just one of the markets not to clear.[5] In such hypothetical circumstances, some agents (buyers and sellers) are disappointed. If a seller is disappointed, this takes the form of commodities in hand, unsold. If buyers are disappointed, this can take no form at all without a concept of money. Disappointed buyers are agents with money that they wish to spend but cannot.[6]

That money is necessary to accommodate the possibility of disappointed buyers (and, therefore, disequilibrium in general) is an indication of the limited content of labour market equilibrium in the real system. Since that market was analysed in terms of a barter exchange, it is not possible in a meaningful way to consider disequilibrium adjustments when more than one market is not cleared. Once disequilibrium conditions are allowed and the model confronts the need to introduce some concept of money, one is led logically to Walrasian General Equilibrium Adjustment and Walras' Law, which we now consider.

Before defining these terms, let us indicate the problem which Walrasian market analysis is designed to resolve. Consider a situation in which workers have a notional supply of their services, and they face employers with a notional demand for those services. Assume, for some reason, a portion of the potential workforce enters into a bargain with the employers at a money wage which is not the market clearing full employment equilibrium wage. When the contract is implemented, workers must formulate their expenditure decision on the basis of their negotiated incomes, which are now decision parameters. The resultant expenditure will generate an aggregate demand which is less than employers' notional offer of sales. This in turn will induce employers to cut back hiring. What we have described is, of course, the Keynesian multiplier process. The multiplier process can be interpreted as the quantity adjustments resulting from trades negotiated at disequilibrium prices (sometimes called 'false' prices).[7] If some trades occur at disequilibrium prices, there is no guarantee that full employment equilibrium will be achieved.

The implication of disequilibrium exchanges, in which 'false' trading results in prices of some commodities becoming parameters in markets for other commodities rather than market-clearing variables, implies that equilibrium full employment solutions require *simultaneous* clearing of all markets, not sequential clearing. 'Simultaneous' is the key and precise word here, and more euphemistic terms such as 'continuous market clearing'[8] are misleading attempts at spurious realism. It is not sufficient that disequilibrium trades converge toward equilibrium prices in some or most markets. Achieving the equilibrium solution requires that *no disequilibrium trades occur*. All markets must clear instantaneously and simultaneously, if permanent divergence from the full employment equilibrium is not to occur.

To ensure simultaneous clearing markets are constructed in accordance with the principles of Walras. Walrasian general equilibrium models presume no production, and the analysis is confined to an instantaneous market day. All agents arrive on the market day in possession of a bundle of commodities, often called their 'endowments'. Their purpose in the market is to maximise their utility through trading. The market operates under rules that forbid any disequilibrium trading, so the result is that all agents emerge satisfied – all markets are cleared with no excess supplies or excess demands for commodities.

In order that Walrasian models involve not merely the assumption of market clearing in other words, two elements are added: the Walrasian auctioneer and Walras' Law. The 'auctioneer' plays a role which we implicitly invoked in the previous chapter. Standing at the centre of all traders, the auctioneer hears alternative offers and is vested with the power to seek accomodation of all notional demands and supplies and to prohibit any trades at non-equilibrium prices. With the omniscience to divine when each and every trader is content or disappointed, the auctioneer aids the market participants in groping for the set of prices which will clear all markets simultaneously. The process is called by the French word *tâtonnement*. The auctioneer follows the rule of calling out lower prices when he perceives a market with excess supply and higher prices when excess demand is perceived. It is to be noted that the auctioneer cannot directly observe these (perhaps not a serious drawback since the auctioneer herself is imaginary), for with a prohibition against disequilibrium trading excess supplies and demands cannot manifest themselves in exchanges.

Of course, actual markets do not have auctioneers except in very specialised circumstances. And real auctioneers do not behave in the Walrasian manner. Where auctioneers exist, they serve to facilitate whatever trades agents momentarily agree upon, not only equilibrium trades. Further, markets are not in practice cleared simultaneously, but sequentially, with or without an auctioneer. The Walrasian rules of market clearing are another example of what we called in the previous chapter 'abstract-ideal' theorising. Nothing remotely resembling a Walrasian market exists in any exchange economy, yet such markets are taken as the basis of neoclassical general equilibrium models. The functional role of Walrasian markets in neoclassical theory is clear: these ideal assumptions serve as a superficial justification for the view that economic agents operate with perfect knowledge and foresight of market conditions. In effect, Walrasian markets eliminate the possibility of any disruptions due to unforeseen circumstances. Since disequilibrium trades are excluded by assumption, general equilibrium is established by assumption. An initially implausible idea – equilibrium in all markets for all traders –

is justified by an even more implausible (and more complicated) mechanism, the Walrasian auctioneer.

It is an interesting sociological phenomenon that such a patently absurd view of market operation should be incorporated into mainstream economics and generally accepted. But perhaps more interesting is that the absurd is formulated as the norm and what actually occurs as the deviation from the norm that must be justified. Since the 1930s, exchanges at prices other than the general equilibrium set have been referred to as 'false trading'.[9] This terminology is quite extraordinary – what real buyers and sellers actually do is 'false', and what imaginary buyers and sellers do under stylised circumstances which could never be approached in practice is 'true'.

Here one has entered into a quasi-religious realm, in which the observed world is judged in reference to an ideal construction of the mind. How powerful is the influence of the ideal we shall see as the analysis proceeds. The theoretical implication of Walrasian markets is that prices adjust with 'perfect flexibility' to excess demand and excess supply. A school of economists called the post-Keynesians has focused attack upon this treatment of market adjustment. It might seem that reference to the actual workings of markets lends strength to their arguments. But one discovers that the entire burden of proof is placed upon the post-Keynesian critics to demonstrate that prices do not adjust instantaneously, with the Walrasian position taken as established. Leijonhufvud has called such an inversion of reality an example of a 'tribal myth' of the economics profession.[10] Placing the burden of proof upon the critics of neoclassical market theory is reminiscent of the position of the Catholic Church during the Copernican revolution. While direct observation made it obvious that heavenly bodies did not move around the earth in perfectly circular orbits, all burden of proof fell upon the critics to show why a geocentric theory was not valid.[11]

In a Walrasian market excess demands and excess supplies are subject to Walras' Law. Walras' Law states that the sum of all excess demands and excess supplies over all commodities *including money* must be zero. It is to be noted that the Law does not require each commodity to have an excess demand of zero, a result that holds only in general equilibrium. Rather, the Law states that the sum of all positive excess demands will be exactly matched by the sum of all negative excess demands. It provides us with a simple relationship between commodities and money. If the sum of all excess demands is zero, then any excess demand for all commodities taken together must be exactly equal to an excess demand for money. Thus, by Walras' Law, where XD stands for excess demand in money units (price times quantity),

$$(XD \text{ for commodities}) = -(XD \text{ for money})$$

The mathematics of the Law are not difficult,[12] and are unnecessary for our purpose. The Law can be easily grasped in terms of the nature of a general equilibrium solution. Consider a static situation in which there is excess supply in the market for a particular commodity (implying excess demand elsewhere). For this market to clear, the price of the commodity in question must change. When the price of that commodity changes, the trading situation in other markets will be upset – price will rise for some of these commodities and fall for others. If the market for the first commodity is cleared, this is only achieved by creating repercussions in other markets. However, whatever repercussions occur, Walras' Law ensures that overall, the degree to which sellers cannot sell what they wish to sell will exactly be matched by the degree to which buyers cannot buy what they wish to buy. The importance of Walras' Law in neoclassical economic theory cannot be stressed too much. Even if one never allows disequilibrium to manifest itself by always considering only *notional* disequilibrium,[13] Walras' Law is a necessary element. While disequilibrium models are constructed in which Walras' Law does not hold, (see Harris, 1981, pp. 283–5), general equilibrium models are never without the Law or some variant of it.

The equality between the excess demand for commodities and the excess demand for money appears reasonable enough. Under certain circumstances, this could be taken as a tautology. If commodities go unsold, then someone must have failed to buy them. The money value of the unsold commodities for the seller must be equal to the money value of those commodities for the non-buyer, since the two amounts are the same thing. However, considerably more than this is involved, for the Law is defined for *notional* demands and supplies and over all markets. The equality represents an assertion that for every disappointed seller there is simultaneously a disappointed buyer, and the two are anxiously awaiting the call of the auctioneer to reconcile their differences. An excess supply of commodities is not balanced by a mere sum of unused money, but by a sum of money in the hands of a potential buyer actively seeking to trade. The implication is that a general 'glut' of commodities over all markets taken together cannot persist if prices are flexible in the Walrasian sense.

The potential to eliminate such a glut is always present, awaiting only the smooth functioning of the pricing mechanism.[14]

The reader familiar with microeconomics will have realised that Walrasian general equilibrium is the precise formulation of what is usually called 'perfectly competitive equilibrium'. Usually when that concept is introduced to the student of economics, he or she is told that such an equilibrium arises when there are a large number of buyers and sellers of homogenous products and producer cost curves are appropriately shaped. Alternatively, it is said that perfect competition results when buyers and sellers are 'price takers' (i.e., they presume that they can buy or sell any amount they desire at the prevailing price). Now one sees that 'perfect competition' is a considerably more problematical concept than as it is usually presented. Buyers and sellers will only be price takers if there is an auctioneer. In the absence of an auctioneer, agents must on their own initiative adjust prices if they cannot buy or sell the amount they desire. But once agents act in this way, they become 'price setters', and by definition one no longer has perfect competition but some variant of imperfect competition. Despite what one might read in standard textbooks, a large number of buyers and sellers is not a sufficient condition for perfect competition (even given the appropriate cost curves), and references to actual markets such as those for agricultural products are fallacious. Perfect competition is in fact an ideal construction, involving a mythological auctioneer, with no real world counterpart past or present. Though seldom made explicit, the fact that all perfectly competitive parables require the presence of what does not exist in any market – a Walrasian auctioneer – is well-recognised in the literature on general equilibrium theory (see Hahn, 1984).

We have argued that Walras' Law is a necessary element in a money economy in order that disequilibrium in hypothetical markets yield a general equilibrium across all of those markets. The purpose of considering general equilibrium adjustment in such detail has been to demonstrate the fragile theoretical basis upon which it is constructed. However consistent may be the mathematics of the solution, it is clear that the desired result – simultaneous clearing of all markets at prices which leave all traders content – occurs even in theory only under extremely restrictive assumptions, such as the *ex machina* auctioneer. It is not by choice that a market-clearing vehicle as bizarre as that suggested by Walras has persisted in models for almost a century. It is because no one has been able to come up with a better explanation for how general equilibrium might be achieved.

We have spent so long on Walras' Law and general equilibrium analysis because of the important role it will play in subsequent chapters. The critique of general equilibrium theory would not be complete, however, without at least brief reference to one of its distinguished practitioners and most eloquent defenders, Frank Hahn. In a series of carefully-argued papers,[15] Hahn has provided a sophisticated and compelling defence of general equilibrium theory. Three aspects of his argument are relevant for the present discussion. He first argues that constructing hypothetical models in which markets are all cleared and agents have no motivation to change their plans (because their notional demands and supplies have been realised) does not imply that any real world situation corresponds to such a model. Second, he argues that the usefulness of the model is that it serves as an organising structure for identifying systematic behavioural relationships, which then might be investigated for their real world analogues. And third, by specifying the extremely restrictive conditions necessary to achieve general equilibrium, one can better understand why the real world is so different from the ideal model and beset with maladies such as unemployment and inflation. He further argues that the very concept of equilibrium should be treated elastically (though rigorously), and all equilibria need not be defined as Walrasian in character.[16]

If all neoclassical economists emulated Hahn's careful attention to detail and theoretical rigor, one would be left with little to object about in general equilibrium theory, except on broad issues of methodological approach. In particular, many of the objections raised in this and the following chapters would be moot points, because Hahn makes no claim that general equilibrium theory describes real world processes, nor does he suggest that it provides a guide to policy (Hahn, 1984, p. 123). The unfortunate reality is that not even an economist as prestigious as Hahn has been successful in inspiring in the economics profession a careful and rigorous application of general equilibrium theory in macroeconomics, as Hahn himself decries in his writings. It is certainly true that in the high theory of Arrow, Debreu, and Hahn one does not find sanguine conclusions about how a free market economy tends to automatically achieve full employment equilibrium with optimum use of resources.[17] It is also true that such judgements are common in textbooks and journal articles, and even more frequently encountered in journalistic writings of economists, which have such great impact upon the consciousness of the public and the policies of governments. In the chapters which follow, our critique of general equilibrium theory is based upon that theory as it is used by the vast majority of economists, not with general equilibrium analysis as employed in the realm of high theory by those who know its limitations and are scrupulously honest in pointing them out.[18]

3.4   THE HOMOGENEITY POSTULATE

Before leaving Walras' Law it is necessary to point out an apparently narrow technical implication of it, what is called the homogeneity postulate. In most general form, the postulate states that an economic agent's demand for commodities and services (including 'leisure') is independent of the absolute price level.[19] At this point the postulate will seem of limited interest, but it shall return to haunt the analysis when considering the quantity theory of money. The postulate is commonly invoked in economic theory, independent of any explicit consideration of Warlas' Law.[20] Most of the microeconomic analysis of consumer and business behaviour is predicated on it.

The postulate is frequently illustrated by the following type of hypothetical example: were all prices and incomes to double, the decision by economic agents of how much of each commodity to buy and to sell would be unaffected. Since in the synthesis model price is composed of income payments only (wages plus profits or interest in the present context), a general rise in prices implies an equal proportionate rise in income. Therefore, at the aggregate level, it is redundant to include incomes in stating the postulate, and one can merely say that trading decisions are independent of the general price level, determined by relative commodity prices only.

The presence of the homogeneity postulate has an important implication for the excess demand identity derived from Walras' Law. As we saw, the excess demand for commodities is identically equal to the excess supply of money. According to the postulate, if commodity prices were to double, the quantities of commodities demanded and supplied would not change (these are independent of the absolute price level). With quantities unchanged and all prices twice as great, the excess demand for commodities doubles, and so must the excess supply of money. Walras' Law with the homogeneity postulate implies that the excess demand for money changes proportionately with the price level. This will be the source of some complications in the next section.

Walrasian markets armed with Walras' Law provide for market clearing in the neoclassical macroeconomic model, though at the cost of considerable 'willing suspension of disbelief',[21] to use Coleridge's famous phrase about how the contented reader treats fictional literature. It does so by providing a mathematically consistent solution to the set of relative prices in the system. It does not provide a theory of the price level, however. A solution for the general price level requires a theory of money, not just a theory of trading.

4 Money in the Neoclassical Model

4.1 INTRODUCTION

In Chapter 2 we presented the basic neoclassical macroeconomic model as a 'real' system, treating all variables measured in terms of the single product. It might be thought that this presentation was of a strawman, for the analysis of monetary relationships is apparently a central characteristic of the neoclassical school. Indeed, the term 'monetarist' refers to the most orthodox of the neoclassicists. However, this partitioning of economic analysis between the real system and the system in its monetary (or nominal) form is a fundamental trademark of the synthesis school, as inspection of any standard textbook will show.

This trademark manifests itself in a particular attribute which the neoclassical school claims for its theory of aggregate economic behaviour, the *neutrality of money*. The precise definition of this term is as follows:[1]

> Money is neutral if, following a disturbance to initial full employment equilibrium caused by a change in the nominal money supply, a new equilibrium is reached in which all real variables have the same values as before the change in the money supply.

In other words, in the standard presentation the equilibrium full employment solution to the synthesis model is independent of the amount of money available for circulating commodities. As we shall see, this implies the crude quantity theory of money deduction that a change in the money supply results in a proportionate change in the price level. It is necessary to qualify our statement with 'in the standard presentation', because in not all versions of the neoclassical macro model does money play a neutral role. However, the exceptions to neutrality are usually presented as the preserve of specialised and esoteric theory. The typical student of economics would have to pursue his or her studies with exceptional zealousness to encounter models in which money plays a non-neutral role.

It is to be noted that the definition of neutrality refers to positions of full employment general equilibrium. Were one to introduce arbitrary assumptions to create a hypothetical situation in which the model produced stable values for variables at less than full employment, then changes in the money supply could result in changes in real variables. This we consider in our treatment of 'rigid' money wages. However, at the moment our interest is in the workings of the the pure, unadulterated neoclassical system. Why and under what conditions money might be neutral is analysed below in some detail. But first, the implications of a money-neutral model must be made explicit.

If one confines the analysis to unconstrained equilibrium states, the neutrality of money implies that there is no fundamental difference between the barter-exchange model of Chapter 2 and a model involving money exchanges. Given the parameters of the barter-exchange model, all real variables are determined. The neutrality of money implies that none of these can change as a result of moving to monetary exchange. The money economy of the model is merely a transformation of the real system into nominal values, more of a 'tidying-up' exercise in which minor loose ends such as the price level are sorted out than a further development of theoretical analysis. However, it could be argued that except for the analysis of the labour market, all theorising involved in the synthesis macro model is a 'tidying-up' exercise, for it is there that the general equilibrium solution is born, like Venus, fully mature, lacking only the veils of consumption, investment, and finally, money.

In this and subsequent chapters money is introduced into the synthesis model. The discussion of a neoclassical money economy will become quite involved, with numerous qualifications and complications besetting the analysis. Therefore, it is useful to anticipate the discussion by clearly stating the general conclusion to be reached. It shall be shown that the static model in its full form can *either retain neutrality as a logical property or display an unqualified tendency to full employment equilibrium, but cannot in general enjoy both of these characteristics*. In other words, if the model is to claim an unambiguous full employment solution, the values of the real variables in that solution are not unique with respect to the nominal money supply. Alternatively, if the real variables are to be unique at full employment equilibrium with respect to changes in the money supply, then there are logically unavoidable circumstances in which that full employment equilibrium cannot be reached. To use a common metaphor referred to below, money is a mere 'veil' over the real system only when full employment equilibrium is not assured by the logic of the model. If the full employment solution is logically guaranteed, then nominal variables such as the money supply and the price level assume a status in causality equal to their real analogues. The implication of the model losing its automatic full employment guarantee should be obvious – the unregulated working of a capitalist economy is consistent with extensive unemployment and human misery even in theory. The loss of the neutrality of money by the model also has serious consequences, though these cannot be developed prior to considering the operation of the model as a system involving monetary exchanges.

4.2 NEOCLASSICAL MONEY

The first task in developing a theory of money is to define the concept. Definition involves two levels – first there is the abstract definition (what it is), and second the form it takes. Following on from the tradition of the American monetary economist Irving Fisher, neoclassical theory defines money in terms of exchanges: money is anything generally accepted as medium of exchange.[2] Following this definition, Johnson writes that money is anything acceptable 'as such', where 'as such' refers to the property of general exchangeability.[3] The 'acceptability' criterion is not without serious ambiguities, for what may be acceptable for one purpose may be totally unacceptable for another. To take an obvious example, one can purchase a meal with a credit card, but cannot use that credit card to cancel the bill received from the credit card company. But at this point the neoclassical argument that money can be anything is accepted.

If money can be anything, then it serves merely as a symbol of wealth in general, with no intrinsic value of its own; i.e., it is not a produced commodity and has no significant resource cost. While one can define money to be anything, a theory of money cannot be constructed on this basis. If money can be anything, then it cannot be isolated for analysis. A necessary step, then, is to provide an analysis to restrict the *forms* which valueless money can take. As we shall see, the neoclassical approach to money presumes the existence of something called the 'money supply', which as a first approximation is treated as exogenously given. This view of the money supply implies money is not 'anything' even in theory, but something very specific and restricted.

Neoclassical writers have for the most part resolved this problem – in principle money can be anything, but for rigorous theory it must be something quite specific – by reference to practice. In fact, anything does not serve as money. By some process commodity producing societies sort out a limited number of things to serve as money. Neoclassical textbook writers are content to leave the issues as settled: anything can be money, but in practice only a few things are; custom and history have resolved the indeterminancy. On this basis theory proceeds upon the assumption of a determinate definition of money and a supply of money exogenous with respect to the level of economic activity.

This is not a satisfactory approach. First, one is offered a definition – anything can serve as money. This theoretical generalisation proves to be absolutely central to the theory, for it is the ultimate defence of the argument that money has no value. Further, this generalisation creates a potential analytical problem of major importance – how are limits to be set on the definition of money so that the supply of money can be treated as exogenous? Second, one discovers that the theoretical prediction ('anything can be money') is refuted in practice (very few things serve as money). Then, third, the empirical rejection of the definition is taken as the vehicle to solve the major analytical problem created by the definition of money as potentially 'anything'. In brief, empirical rejection of the definition is used to reconcile its own contradictory nature.

What is required even at this early stage of the neoclassical theory of money is an explanation of why money in the theoretical analysis and in practice assumes limited forms when money was defined to suggest otherwise. Doing so is not merely a question of tidying up logic. Later in this chapter we shall see that the failure of neoclassical theory to resolve explicitly the contradiction, between money as anything in principle and something very specific in theoretical models, leaves the entire concept of 'the money supply' open to attack from within the synthesis school itself.

Rather than seeking to resolve the contradiction between definition of money and the use of the concept in practice, we shall ignore the definition and go straight to the theoretical treatment of money. We define M as a valueless commodity (i.e. it has no cost of production), whose unit price is one (unity), and whose supply is determined by what we shall call the 'monetary authorities'. The monetary authorities are presumed to leave the money supply unchanged until they are summoned to act by the theorist. In other words, the money supply is given until the model builder decides to change it.

It is worth stating explicitly that no such money supply exists in reality. The assertion common to neoclassical monetary theory that there exists a determinate money supply over which the monetary authorities have monopoly and control is a fiction. Not even neoclassical writers would argue that this is anything but a convenient assumption. The only part of the money supply over which a hypothetical monetary authority might have direct control is coin and paper notes, which account for a tiny portion of the total money supply in a developed capitalist economy. Further, coins and notes are frequently ignored in modern theoretical modelling, with the money supply defined as 'demand deposits'. Demand deposits can at this point be defined as ledger entries of certain institutions which individuals and businesses can draw upon to make purchases. The institutions which are the repositories of these ledger entries will be called banks. Banks can act to expand and contract the total value of these ledger entries by making new loans or calling in old loans. Thus, banks are the immediate creators of money when money is defined as demand deposits.

The monetary authorities influence (*not control*) the supply of money to the extent that they can influence the behaviour of banks. Integral to neoclassical monetary analysis is a *theory of bank behaviour* in which the action of banks with regard to credit creation or contraction is in systematic response to decisions by the monetary authorities. The assumption of a given money supply cannot otherwise be justified. On this point there is no controversy.[4] Notwithstanding the central role an analysis of bank behaviour plays in the assumption of a given money supply, such a theory is rarely treated in detail in neoclassical macroeconomic textbooks. The student is left to take an autonomous money supply as proved, with elaboration relegated to specialised courses in monetary economics.[5]

As a consequence, the student of macroeconomics can easily emerge from his or her studies unaware that the assumption of a money supply fixed with respect to the other variables in the neoclassical model is subject of extreme controversy, and that quite prominent and respectable economists reject the the assumption altogether.[6] We pursue this issue after investigating the theoretical role of a fixed supply of valueless money. The purpose of this section has been to clarify the concept of money which will be employed in the neoclassical model. The result of the discussion is somewhat inconclusive, for it has been demonstrated that there is an apparent inconsistency between the abstract definition of money on the one hand and its manifestation in the model as a parameter and variable for analysis.

4.3 MONEY AND THE PRICE LEVEL

We are now able to present the basic essentials of the role of money in the neoclassical macroeconomic model. Previously we defined y to be the output/income of the system measured in the single commodity. In addition, let p be the price of the single commodity, or the 'absolute price level'. The value of output/income in money units is, therefore, py. It is to be recalled that the neoclassical model is one of timeless equilibrium, and in keeping with the operation of Walrasian markets, all exchanges occur simultaneously once the equilibrium trading position has been established in all markets. Money is used only once in the Walrasian market day, so the amount of money necessary to trade y amount of the single commodity at price p is py.

However, the analysis of the determination of the price level abandons this timeless context. Breaking with the treatment of exchanges occurring in some instantaneous market period, it is now assumed that trading takes place over a period of time, and during this time period the same representation of money serves to realise a number of trades. If the supply of money (as defined in the previous section) is M^*, then one can define $1/v = py/M*$. The symbol $1/v$ in this equality is called *the velocity of money*, and measures the average number of times a representative unit of money in involved in a trade. Since output/income (y) is a flow per unit of time in the model, $1/v$ is defined for some hypothetical time period. By rearranging the definition, one gets, $M* = vpy$. The inverse of the velocity of money, v, can be interpreted as the average proportion of the money supply held idle at any moment by traders in anticipation of impending exchanges.

This relationship is true by definition – the inverse of the velocity of money is calculated by dividing the money value of output/income by the potential money supply. It is also an empirically measurable definition, though the specific value of v obtained depends upon one's operational definition of $M*$. Were it the case that the velocity of money and the level of output/income were fixed, the presumption of $M*$ as exogenous yields a determinate price for the single commodity (the 'price level'). Further, since $M* = vpy$ is homogenous, a change in the money supply as a result of action by the monetary authorities would result in a proportionate change in the price of the single commodity. This one-to-one proportional relationship between the money supply and price(s) is commonly interpreted as a central message of the quantity theory of money (see e.g. Shapiro, 1974, pp. 268–71).

A number of authors have gone back to the writings of the pre-Keynesian monetary theorists to demonstrate that attributing to them a crude proportional relationship between $M*^*$ and p is a complete misrepresentation of their work (Harris, 1981; ch. 6). True though this defence of the pre-Keynesians may be, the fact remains that the thrust of modern monetary theory is to demonstrate that under conditions of full employment general equilibrium, the elasticity of the price level with respect to the money supply is unity. That is, under such conditions a doubling of the money supply results in a doubling of the price level with all other variables left unchanged.[7] The crude quantity of money equation, $M* = vpy$ (with v and y fixed), is the simplest expression of the neutrality of money. The essence of the interaction of real and nominal values in the neoclassical model (e.g., y and py) is captured by using the quantity theory, for all of its simplicity.

At this point we are only interested in the explanation of the price level in full employment equilibrium, since we have yet to discover any circumstances in which the labour market does not clear (the necessary condition for a less than full employment equilibrium). If the Walrasian markets behave as they are designed to do, then output/income is determined at its maximum value on the basis of the wage measured in units of the single commodity. It remains only to establish that v (the inverse of the velocity of money) is constant with respect to the other variables in the model. As mentioned above, v can be interpreted as reflecting the proportion of money or nominal income which economic agents wish to hold as money balances at any moment in time. Since this holding of money is in anticipation of coming transactions, it is called the *transactions demand for money*, written as $M(td) = vpy$. The quantity equation now becomes an explicit equilibrium theory. In Chapter 2, the neoclassical 'real' system was set out in behavioural and definitional equations covering the markets for labour and the single commodity and the equilibrium of saving and investment. Now, three more equations can be added to cover the money market. At a later point the demand function will be expanded.

$$(10) \quad M(s) = M* \qquad \text{(autonomous money supply)}$$
$$(11) \quad M(td) = vpy \qquad \text{(demand for money)}$$
$$(12) \quad M(td) = M* \qquad \text{(money market equilibrium)}$$

The essential characteristic of this treatment of the money market is the presumption that the demand for and supply of money are independent of each other. Independence in this formulation is achieved in a very crude way – the supply of money is treated as autonomous, and the demand for money apparently arises only from the need to purchase output. As the money market is treated with more sophistication, this independence must be retained at all costs, for it is the necessary condition for a consistent theory of valueless money.[8]

At this point it is worth stressing that the history of economic thought offers only two 'mutually incompatible' ways by which to resolve the indeterminacy of the absolute price level. If money is valueless, then the price level is determinant if and only if the availability of money is independent of the demand for money, where the major determinant of the latter is the level of economic activity. Alternatively, money can be analysed as a produced commodity, in which case the absolute price level is strictly related to the inverse of the cost of producing the money commodity.[9] It is unlikely that a third alternative exists which does not beg the basic issues of monetary theory.

Pre-Keynesian writers devoted considerable attention to the determination of the parameter v, particularly with regard to its stability over various theoretical time periods. Since Keynes the debate over the stability of the velocity of money has involved different issues, particularly the impact of the interest rate. Since we have yet to introduce an interest rate-related demand for money, it is most convenient at this point to simply assume the velocity of money to be constant without justification.

Armed with a given money supply and a constant velocity, the determination of the price level would seem to be an easy task. Let us invoke the Walrasian labour market, cleared by movement in the wage measured in the single commodity. This yields full employment of labour, which implies a determinate level of output/income. The price level then 'falls out' of relationship (12) as $p = M*/v[y(e)]$, where y is full employment income. This is what was earlier called the 'classical dichotomy', in which the equilibrium solution of the real variables is established through a Walrasian general equilibrium model in which only relative prices are relevant variables, and the price level set by the quantity equation. As tempting as this procedure is, it is invalid. The dichotomy is false. The real variables cannot be determined in general equilibrium without some explicit reference to the money supply. The model cannot be strictly partitioned between real and nominal variables.

4.4   WALRAS' LAW AND THE QUANTITY THEORY

The simple application of the quantity theory to the real system is invalid because of a contradiction between Walras' Law and the quantity equation. It will be recalled from an earlier section that Walras' Law requires that the excess demand for all commodities equal the excess supply of money,

$$(XD \text{ for commodities}) = -(XD \text{ for money}).$$

In the present case of the single commodity, we can write, where $y*$ is the fixed (full employment) supply of output/income and $y(d)$ the notional demand,

$$p\{y(d) - y*(s)\} = M(xd)$$

or,

$$py(d) - py*(s) = M(xd).$$

The quantity equation can also be manipulated to produce an equation for the excess demand for commodities and money,

$$vpy* - M* = M(d) - M*$$

or,

$$pvy* - M* = M(xd).$$

Close inspection shows that both expressions for the excess demand for money cannot hold simultaneously. In the case of the first expression (from Walras' Law), $p\{y(d) - y*(s)\}$, a change in the price level yields an equal proportionate change in the excess demand for money (both terms are multiplied by p). In the second relationship, $pvy* - M*$, price enters against only the first term, so the excess demand for money increases more than proportionately with increases in the price level. Not even in theory are variables allowed to simultaneously increase by two different rates. One of the excess demand equations must be abandoned.[10] The inconsistency arises because Walras' Law is formulated on the basis of the homogeneity postulate, so the excess demand for commodities measured in physical units is unaffected by changes in the price level; i.e., the excess demand for money is directly proportional to the price level. In the Quantity Equation, on the other hand, homogeneity of any degree is ruled out by the assumption of a given money supply.

This contradiction does not invalidate neoclassical analysis of money exchange; nor does it undermine the principle of neutrality of money whereby a change in the money supply alone leaves all real variables unchanged (in full employment equilibrium). However, to render the model consistent, it is necessary to re-specify the demand for commodities. Patinkin's solution to the inconsistency, which has been generally accepted as valid after some resistance,[11] was to introduce the *Real Balance Effect*.

The Real Balance Effect inserts another 'real' variable into the demand equations, namely the nominal quantity of money divided by the price level – 'real balances', $M*/p$. This variable is introduced into the investment and consumption functions, so we must rewrite the previous specifications. The impact of $M*/p$ on consumption and investment is presumed to be positive – a rise in the purchasing power of money increases the demand for the single commodity. With the money supply given, the price level is negatively related to the demand for the single commodity.

$$(3a) \quad c = c(y, r, M*/p), \quad s = s(y, r, M*/p)$$
$$(3b) \quad i = i(y, r, M*/p)$$

Furthermore, the demand for money may also be a function of real balances, where the terms inside the brackets below denote a functional relationship, not a multiplicative manipulation.

$$(11) \quad M(d) = p[M(d)\{y, M*/p\}]$$

The excess demand for money now has a different form, namely,

$$M(xd) = p[M(d)\{y, M*/p\}] - M*.$$

The homogeneity postulate no longer holds. A rise in the price level results in a fall in real balances, which provokes in a decline in the demand for the single commodity both as an article of consumption and as an item of investment. Further, a change in the price level enters directly into the consumption and investment functions. The market for the single commodity and the money market are now integrated in a consistent way. Assume all markets are initially in equilibrium and the price level doubles. The logical result is to create an excess demand for money, for existing money balances have fallen in purchasing power. Simultaneously, the excess demand for money is balanced by an excess supply of the only commodity, and this is the result of the real balance effect depressing demand (depreciated money makes existing money holdings inadequate and existing commodity demand excessive). Walras' Law holds. Following the rules of Walrasian markets, excess commodity supply will cause a fall in the commodity's price, restoring equilibrium there. At the same time, the falling price will reduce the excess demand for money to zero. Everything returns to its original state of equilibrium; the doubling of the price level cancels itself out.

Further, money is neutral in the re-specified, consistent model. Should the initial equilibrium be disturbed by the monetary authorities increasing the nominal supply of money (from $M*$ to $2M*$, for example), an excess demand for the commodity will result (via $M*/p$), exactly balanced by an excess supply of money (again via $M*/p$). The excess demand for the commodity will force price up in a Walrasian world, which eliminates both the excess demand for commodities and excess supply of money. The original 'real' equilibrium is regained at a doubled price of the commodity. The neutrality of money and the equilibrium mechanics in a model incorporating the real balance effect are explained in more detail in Chapter 6. As shall be shown there, the neutrality of money breaks down when the real balance effect is generalised to include forms of wealth other than money (e.g. bonds).

In a widely-used textbook there is an interesting analogy to illustrate the demand for real balances. The author asks the question, what would happen to the behaviour of economic agents if everyone awoke one morning to discover that the national currency had been re-denominated so, for example, one new dollar replaced ten old dollars?[12]

Is there any reason for you to change your demand for money? No. All prices, incomes, and wealth values would have changed proportionately, reduced to 1/10 their former values. Nothing real has changed.

But this is the same as if the price level just changed overnight by the same amount!

The message is that changes in the price level are inconsequential events, arbitrary occurrences that are treated by economic agents as water off a duck's back. To the extent that the analogy holds, it is a direct result of the model in which the analogy is posed, and the relationship to any actual economic process is not obvious. It is to be recalled that the model presumes an autonomous money supply over which the monetary authorities have strict and absolute control. On the basis of this assumption, changing the denomination of the currency and changing the money supply are more than formally equivalent; they are the same thing.

Further, it must be remembered that the 'thought experiments' in neoclassical analysis that involve changes in the money supply are usually in the context of a one commodity model. As a consequence, the only 'real' decision that an economic agent has to make is whether to buy the commodity or not to buy it (in which case money is held). Any lags between expenditure and production, production and payment of receipts, and receipts and expenditure, have been eliminated through the general equilibrium method. When the price level is the price of a single commodity and price changes translate directly and instantaneously ('overnight') into money income changes, it is small wonder that nothing else changes. Indeed, what is surprising is that neoclassical theory has found it so difficult and complicated to prove this, requiring Walras' Law, the real balance effect, and an autonomous money supply. This and other apparently simple propositions in the neoclassical analysis of money prove esoterically complicated as a result of the theoretical inadequacy of valueless money.

To summarise this section, we have seen that transposing the real solution to the neoclassical model into nominal variables via the quantity equation is not possible, as tempting as its apparent simplicity may be. Rather, an additional variable, $M*/p$, real balances, must be introduced. This leaves open to question what relevance the solution to the barter model has to the model that includes money. The issue of relevance is pursued in the next section. Notwithstanding the crucial theoretical importance of the real balance effect to the consistency of one version of the neoclassical model, it has been judged by some to be of no empirical consequence.[13] In general, our purpose in this book is to explore the logic of the neoclassical model, rather than to seek its inadequacies with respect to the actual phenomena it wishes to explain. However, when a theory must be rescued by a mechanism that many judge to be of no practical importance, the question is raised whether the theory has been rendered more robust by the inclusion of a heretofore overlooked element of strategic importance, or salvaged by a fortuitous discovery of an *ad hoc* method of exit from a blind corner. As we shall see below, the real balance effect exhibits a sufficiently jerry-rigged character that many neoclassical economists play it down in favour of the same mechanism in a more general form (the *Pigou effect*).

Finally, it should be stressed that neoclassical logic suggests on *theoretical* grounds that the real balance effect may be miniscule, even zero. These arguments involve the controversy over 'inside' and 'outside' money. For the real balance effect to operate, $M*$ must represent a *net asset* in the model. This means that what serves as money cannot be an asset for one group of economic agents and a liability to another set. If it were the case that assets and liabilities cancelled each other out, the net effect of a rise in the price level would be to reduce the real value of assets while off-setting this by an equal change in the real value of liabilities. Therefore, demand deposits or bank-reated money cannot enter into the operation of the real balance effect, for some of these are both an asset (for the depositor) and a liability (for the bank). That part of demand deposits which is equivalent to the loans banks create is not a net asset. Money which is not net wealth is called 'inside' money'.[4]

What, then, is outside money? Over this issue there is great controversy. Suffice to say, the extent to which the controversy is unresolved is indicated by encountering in the neoclassical literature the two extreme positions – there is no such thing as outside money,[15] and all money is outside money.[16] It is quite extraordinary that neoclassical theory, for which the analysis of monetary phenomena is so central, cannot sort out its definitions of money and wealth.

However, pursuing the debate over outside and inside money is beyond the scope of this book. The importance of the debate for our current discussion is that *it indicates that one inconsistency (Walras' Law and the Quantity Equation) has been resolved only by creating another which is equally serious (establishing the existence of outside money).*[17] The reproduction of essentially the same inconsistency in altered form is characteristic of neoclassical theory and the consequence of the theoretical inadequacy of the initial concepts – in this case valueless money.

4.5 THE MONEY SUPPLY FURTHER CONSIDERED

Before treating the general equilibrium solution to the neoclassical model with a money market, further consideration of the concept of an autonomous money supply is required. The entire theory of valueless money collapses if the supply of money is not independent of the demand for it. This independence is the necessary (though not sufficient condition) for the existence of monetary authorities who somehow determine changes in the money supply. Were there no other theoretical difficulties, failure to establish the theoretical existence of a determinate, autonomous money supply would render the neoclassical model invalid in its analysis of a money economy.

The theoretical role of a fixed money supply is not merely a question of sorting out the price level in the model. While one can reach a general equilibrium solution to the 'real' system (see Chapter 2), because of the inconsistency between Walras' Law and the quantity theory this solution cannot be transposed, as it were, to the system of nominal values. The general equilibrium solution of system with money is not and cannot be the real system with all relevant variables multiplied by p. With the necessary presence of the real balance effect in the consumption function and demand for money functions, the price level must be determined *simultaneously* with the values of the real variables. In other words, the system with money has its own particular equilibrium adjustment process, determined in part by $M*$ and p. While it is true that the real variables will be invariant with respect to changes in p and $M*$ in full employment equilibrium, this is a property of the solution to the monetary system itself, not a relationship between a dichotomised real solution and its monetary analogue. The neutrality of money, which holds in the model we have been discussing, *does not imply the relevance of a real solution to its monetary analogue*. By 'monetary analogue' we mean a system characterised by all the same behavioural relationships (parameters), differing from the real system only by the presence of the money market.

The solution to the system of monetary variables requires that any $M*$ imply a unique p. If a valid argument cannot be made for a money supply independent of the demand for money, then $M*$ does not imply a unique price level. If the price level is not unique, then the real variables are not unique. In effect, the presumption of an autonomous $M*$ 'closes' the neoclassical system, making it determinate. The fact that a model of barter exchange as presented in Chapter 2 has a determinate general equilibrium solution is irrelevant to the solution of a model with money, though the two models be identical in every other respect.

The stakes riding on the autonomous money supply are high indeed. As mentioned above, there is considerable controversy over whether or not it can be established theoretically that the supply of money is independent of the demand. One of the most perceptive critics of the neoclassical treatment of money plays down this theoretical controversy, arguing that the definition of money need not be resolved at the level of abstract theory, but is rather a 'practical matter'.[18] For an empirical investigation referring to a specific context, the judgement is valid. However, at the level of abstract theory, the elements of a model must conform to the rules set by the model itself, and the synthesis model has quite clear rules which govern the analysis. In order that the model be valid, it must be determinate – with no 'loose ends' requiring *ad hoc* resolution at the last moment when one discovers that all has not emerged from the logic as it should. At the level of abstract logic, the rules of analysis require that the concepts employed be unambiguous and possess the properties sufficient unto their theoretical role. We saw this in the case of the real balance effect, which is theoretically key to one version of the synthesis model, though empirically trivial in the opinion of many economists.

The definition of money must be particularly equal to its theoretical task, for the presumption of its autonomy is central to the 'thought experiments' of neoclassical theory, Typically the adjustment dynamics of the neoclassical model are investigated by presuming a change in some parameter or autonomous variable. Perhaps the most common of these to select for arbitrary manipulation is the money supply – to presume its change in response to action by the monetary authorities, then pursue the logical consequences. Such a thought experiment cannot legitimately be initiated unless it has been established *theoretically* that the money supply is independent of the demand for money.

4.6 NEOCLASSICAL MONEY AND REALISM OF MODELS

Those readers who were distressed in the first two chapters by the divergence of the 'real' system from any semblance of an actual economy may have looked forward hopefully to the inclusion of money as a vehicle to draw the synthesis model closer to reality. If one had such hopes disappointment must now reign. The introduction of money if anything renders the model more abstract and ideal. One can imagine the economics professor saying to his student, 'let us be more realistic by considering money'. But money is introduced in a manner no less ideal than the character of the 'real' system itself.

Indeed, money appears on the stage in a manner arbitrary and counter-factual unique to itself. Instead of approaching, reality recedes further into the mist of assumptions. A new layer of counter-intuitive masonry is constructed upon the previous, with the theorist isolated inside. These layers of ideal isolation render the theorist increasingly immune to any infection from the concrete world (to mix a metaphor). The theorist, like the medieval priest, is safely sequestered in a world of his or her own making, a world of ideas which is treated as a world of real existence. And like the world of the medieval priest, the neoclassical model is not without its purpose. It stands as an ideological construction to guide the thoughts and actions of those who move in the reality outside of it. In the next chapter we begin to consider in detail the mechanics of this ideal neoclassical world.

5 The Classical False Dichotomy Model

5.1 INTRODUCTION

The previous chapters set out the basic elements of the neoclassical macroeconomic model. In this chapter, the equilibrium solutions to the simplest version of the model will be treated in detail. The purpose is not merely to reproduce what can be found in standard textbooks on macroeconomics. The intention of this and the next two chapters is to substantiate a previous assertion.

It was asserted that holding to strict logic, the model cannot produce a solution in which there is an unqualified automatic tendency to full employment equilibrium and in which money is neutral. To sustain this assertion, the presentation begins with a simple formulation of the model which is flawed by the 'false dichotomy'. This flaw is rectified in the next chapter by the introduction of Patinkin's real balance effect. As will be seen, the Patinkin model does ensure a full employment equilibrium and the neutrality of money, but for reasons explained below it is not satisfactory to leave matters on this basis. Also, in Chapter 6 an alternative solution to the false dichotomy is given, one more 'Keynesian' in character, in which the demand for money is assumed to be interest-elastic. In this case money plays a neutral role, but full employment is not guaranteed for all possible parameters of the model. In Chapter 7 the logical extension of the real balance effect, the wealth or Pigou effect, is introduced. Invoking the Pigou effect provides for full employment equilibrium, but money is non-neutral (Section 4.1). In all of these models the solution is presented graphically and by use of simple algebra.

5.2 A FALSE DICHOTOMY MODEL

The first step in the investigation of the equilibrium mechanics of the neoclassical system with money is to present a model in which the real variables are directly converted to nominal values by the application of the quantity theory of money. In this case there is a strict dichotomy between the real and monetary sectors of the model and money is neutral. As explained in the previous chapter the model is inconsistent, for it incorporates two contradictory relationships for the excess demand for money. Particularly in older textbooks, models very similar to that developed below are presented as a summary of the pre-Keynesian ('classical') treatment of macroeconomic relationships, without noting its internal inconsistency.[1] The purpose of beginning with an invalid model is purely pedagogical. The simplicity of the model provides a useful introduction to graphical and algebraic manipulation, both of which will become quite complicated as the analysis proceeds. In addition, false though the model may be, it offers a clear indication of the basic result that neoclassical analysis wishes to achieve, but can do so only in more complicated renditions, if at all.

The analysis begins with the labour market. For mathematical simplicity, it is assumed that the supply of labour is fixed, $l(s) = l_*$. To obtain the demand for labour, an explicit form of the single commodity output/value added function is required. The simplest functional form is that called the Cobb–Douglas function, which takes the algebraic form, $y = k^a l^{[1-a]}$. This function incorporates the property of diminishing returns to the variable factor, as well as being extremely easy to manipulate mathematically.[2] By making appropriate assumptions, this output/value added function can yield an expression for the demand for labour. By definition, the net revenue of a firm is sales minus cost. *If* it were the case that all of the firm's output could be sold at the prevailing market price (the case of a 'price taker'),[3] and *if* it were the case that there were no inputs other than labour and capital (using the neoclassical definition of these), then one could write,

$$y = k^a l^{[1-a]} \quad \text{(output/value added function)} \quad (5.1.1)$$
$$NR = py - [pwl + rpk] \quad \text{(net revenue)} \quad (5.1.2)$$

If it is not necessary to reduce price to sell more, then sales revenue is simply py. The two terms within parentheses remind one that he or she is in the one commodity world, in which the real wage (w) and the capital stock (k) are same product, not only measured in units of the single commodity, but comprised of this commodity. As a consequence, pw is the money value of what is paid to workers, the nominal or money wage, W. Similarly, pk is the money value of the capital stock, K. On the assumption that the firm in question can sell as much as it produces at the prevailing market price, the only discretionary variable for the firm is the level of output. That is, price, the interest rate and the money wage are given in perfectly competitive markets, and the capital stock is fixed in the short-run model. Usually in neoclassical microeconomic analysis it is presumed that the level of output is selected to minimise losses or maximise net revenue (profits) in the short run. This presumption is called 'optimising behaviour'. Since the level of output is determined by the level of employment given the output/value added function, the employment decision is the optimising decision. Optimisation is achieved mathematically by taking the first derivative of net revenue with respect to the labour input and setting it equal to zero. When expression (5.1.1) is substituted into (5.1.2), one gets the following.

$$p\{[1 - a]k^a l^{-a}\} - W = 0 \tag{5.1.3}$$

If one substitutes, $y/l = k^a l^{-a}$, $l^{-a} = y/k^a l$

$$W = p[1 - a]y/l$$
$$l(d) = [1 - a]y[p/W] \qquad \text{(demand for labour)} \tag{5.2}$$

In (5.1.3) the first term is called the value of the marginal product of labour, which is marginal product of labour times the price of output. Under perfectly competitive conditions, the value of the marginal product measures the sales revenue resulting from hiring an additional infinitesimally small unit of labour. Optimisation is achieved by equating this to the money wage. In the case of the Cobb–Douglas function, the marginal product of any factor is proportional to its average product, making matters very simple. When the symbol for the labour input is moved to the left of the equality, one obtains the demand for labour schedule, expression (5.2). Combined with the labour supply assumption, $ls = l_*$, one can set the equilibrium condition for the labour market. Assuming a fixed demand for labour has avoided the problem of a quadradic expression for labour market equilibrium.

$$l_* = \frac{[1 - a]p}{W} \qquad \text{(labour market equilibrium)} \tag{5.3}$$

In terms of mathematical solution, this relationship stands on its own, for both y and p/W are direct functions of l_* under the assumptions of perfect competition and optimisation. However, elsewhere in the model the nominal values p and W must be determined, consistent with the optimisation condition that $W/p = [1 - a]y/l_*$. But first we turn to the other real variables in the system, consumption and investment. Again, simple relationships are assumed. Terms with stars represent constants, or intercepts when the functions are plotted on graphs. The symbol b is the marginal propensity to consume and d is the rate of change of investment with respect to the interest rate, both constants.

$$c = c* + by \quad \text{(consumption function)} \qquad 5.4$$
$$i = i* - dr \quad \text{(investment function)} \qquad 5.5$$

By definition,

$$s = y - [c* + by].$$

With these equations, one can simplify the graphical analysis by using a relationship called the IS (saving = investment) schedule, which is defined as a locus of points for which savings and investment are equal. Along the IS schedule, the market for the single commodity is in equilibrium. The IS curve is derived in Figure 5.1, according to the following conditions.

$$y = c + i \quad \text{(aggregate expenditure)}$$
$$y = c + s \quad \text{(aggregate income)}$$
$$c + i = c + s \quad \text{(commodity market equilibrium)}$$
$$i* - dr = y - [c* + by]$$

$$y = \frac{[i* + c*]}{[1 - b]} - \frac{dr}{1 - b} \quad \text{(IS curve)} \qquad (5.6)$$

In Figure 5.1(a), saving is shown as a function of income, and in (b) investment is drawn as a function of the interest rate. Assume that the interest rate is fixed at $r(o)$. If income were above $y(o)$, saving would exceed investment, implying that all of the single commodity would not be sold. As a result, income would fall, reducing saving until $s(o) = i(o)$ at $y(o)$. The point $e(o)$ in quadrant (c) marks such an equality. The point $e(1)$ is associated with interest rate $r(1)$ and so on. Quadrant (d) merely transfers income from one axis to another. In terms of mechanics, the IS curve allows one to reduce two diagrams into one (Figure 5.1(a) into (c).

Keynesians see in the IS curve a procedure considerably more pernicious than analytical simplification (Chick (1983), p. 4). As mentioned in the second chapter, the neoclassical model makes no distinction between consumption and investment on the supply side, and in this it is faithful to Keynes himself. With the introduction of the IS curve, any difference between the two on the demand side is

Figure 5.1   Graphical construction of the IS curve

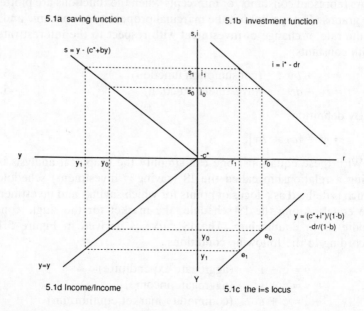

5.1a saving function   5.1b investment function

$s = y - (c^* + by)$

$i = i^* - dr$

$y = (c^* + i^*)/(1-b)$
$-dr/(1-b)$

$y = y$

5.1d Income/Income   5.1c the i=s locus

also eliminated. Now aggregate demand in general is an undifferentiated function of income and the interest rate. If one believes that investment is considerably more volatile than consumption – a belief for which there is considerable empirical evidence – then combining the two into a single expression is rather like adding oranges and apples. Further, the two are put together in an equilibrium condition, so that disequilibrium in the commodity market is obscured.

In a sense, submerging consumption and investment into one behavioural relationship is the logical extension of the single commodity model. It indicates that commodities as such play no role in the analysis. In effect, the IS curve does not connect points of commodity market equilibrium, but is the equilibrium between nonspending in the current period and spending out of current income in future periods. In Section 2.2 it was pointed out that investment in the neoclassical macro model, because its capacity-expanding aspect is ignored and consumption and investment involve the same commodity, is treated implicitly as deferred consumption. Thus, when one traces back the definition of terms, the so-called 'goods market' equilibrium condition ('commodity market' here) states that deferred consumption in terms of income (saving) must be equal to deferred consumption in terms of the single commodity (investment). There is a strong hint of tautology in such a condition. Finally, and of immediate import, it should be noted that use of the *IS* curve shifts all attention to the labour market for adjustment mechanics, particularly since the money market will also be formulated in terms of an equilibrium condition.

With regard to the money market in this False Dichotomy model, the demand is that implied by the simple quantity theory of money, along with a fixed supply.

$$M(d) = vpy \qquad \text{(demand for money)} \qquad (5.7)$$
$$M(s) = M* \qquad \text{(supply of money)} \qquad (5.8)$$
$$M* = vpy \qquad \text{(money market equilibrium)} \qquad (5.9)$$

These equations complete the specification of the False Dichotomy model, and the analysis can move on to the equilibrium solution.

5.3 FALSE DICHOTOMY GENERAL EQUILIBRIUM

With the necessary relationships defined, we can turn to Figure 5.2, where general equilibrium is derived graphically. First, it is useful for pedagogical purposes to solve this general equilibrium algebraically. Full employment equilibrium in the labour market requires that $ld = l*$, which with a fixed capital stock yields directly the full employment level of output/income as $y(e) = k*^a l*^{[1-a]}$. To keep notation simple, the full employment level of y will be written simply as $y(e)$. Saving and investment are then,

$$s(e) = i(e) = y(e) - [c* + by(e)]$$
$$= [1 - b]y(e) - c*$$

The other real variable to determine is the interest rate, done by substituting the last expression, which is equal to full employment investment, into (5.5).

$$r(e) = \frac{\{[i* + c*] - [1 - b]y(e)\}}{d}$$

It only remains to determine the nominal wage and the price of the single commodity. From (5.9) one obtains the value of p,

$$p = M*/vy$$
$$p = M*/vy(e)$$

Since the money wage is pw, price times the commodity ('real')
wage, this variable's full employment value is given by the following
expression.

$$W = \left[\frac{M_*}{vy(e)} \right] \left[\frac{(1-a)y(e)}{l_*} \right]$$

Which simplifies to the following.

$$W = \frac{[1-a]M_*}{vl_*}$$

The nominal values of consumption, investment, and income are
similarly obtained, by multiplying each by the price which has been
derived above. It is to be noted, and this is the heart of the 'classical'
version of the model, that all real variables are independent of the
price level and the money supply. In this false dichotomy model
money is strictly neutral. Ignoring the problem of the inconsistency
between Walras' law and the quantity theory with regard to the
excess demand for money, a doubling of the money supply leaves all
real variables unchanged, while p and W double. This is the result
that the more sophisticated versions of the synthesis model seek to
maintain.

The graphical solution is given in Figure 5.2, presented in six parts.
First, as in Chapter 2, there is the labour market, which determines
the level of output, and the IS curve. The saving and investment
schedules are not shown. The money market is introduced by the
horizontal line in Figure 5.2(e), $y = M_*/vp$. Values marked (e)
indicate the global equilibrium for which both the money market and
the commodity market are simultaneously cleared. Figure 5.2(d) and
(e) explicitly show the relationship between commodity output and
nominal output and between nominal output and the price level.
Finally, Figure 5.2(f) gives the real wage as a ratio of W and p.

The result of an increase in the exogenous money supply is simply
demonstrated. Should M_* rise to $2M_*$, the quantity equation yields
$y = 2M_*/vp$. With y determined by equilibrium in the labour market
and v a constant, only p can change. This is shown in Figure 5.2 (d)
by a rotation clockwise of the price line, implying an increase in
nominal income and movement along the line $1/v$ in Figure 5.2(e).
The rise in the price level is associated with an equal proportionate
rise in the nominal wage, consistent with labour market equilibrium.
This simple model can be used to demonstrate the synthesis view of

Figure 5.2   General equilibrium in a false dichotomy model

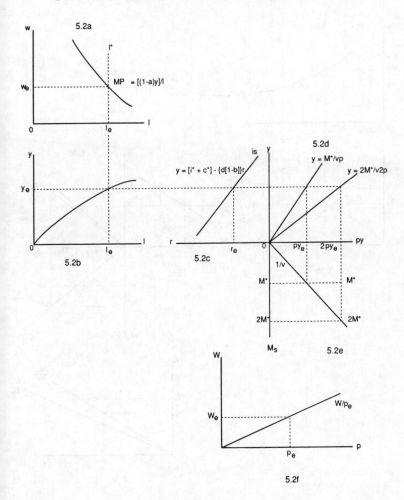

unemployment. In Figure 5.3 the previous set of diagrams is reproduced, with the additional assumption that the money wage is fixed at
$W(o) = W_*$ (see Figure 5.3(f)). When called upon to relate the
assumption of fixed money wages to the observed world, economists
frequently justify it by the alleged power of trade unions and state
minimum wage regulation. Once a fixed money wage is assumed, the
level of employment cannot be deduced from the labour market

Figure 5.3   False dichotomy model with rigid money wage

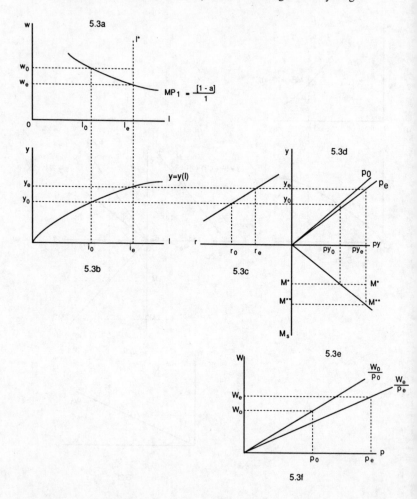

alone (Figure 5.3(a)), since that market is defined in terms of the real wage. However, one knows,

$$l(d) = \frac{p[1 - a]y}{W_*}$$

Since the money wage is above the full employment level, the level of labour input in the output/income function will be determined by

$l(d)$, the demand for labour. This level of employment will be indicated in Figure 5.3 as $l(o)$. Due to the form that has been chosen for the output/income function, the demand for labour can be solved immediately. Substituting $y = M*/vp$, one gets,

$$l(d) = [1 - a]\left[\frac{M*}{vp}\right]\left[\frac{p}{W*}\right]$$

$$l(d) = \frac{[1 - a]M*}{vW*}$$

The demand for labour, given a fixed nominal wage, is determined by the money supply, the velocity of money and the output/income function parameter $[1 - a]$.[4] With the level of employment determined, it follows that the output of the single commodity is determined.

$$y(o) = k*^a\left[[1 - a]\frac{M*}{vW*}\right]^{[1 - a]}$$

The other real variables in the solution derive directly from $y(o)$.

$$c(o) = c* + by(o)$$
$$s(o) = y(o) - c(o)$$
$$i(o) = s(o) \qquad \text{(commodity market equilibrium)}$$
$$r(o) = [i* - i(o)]/d$$

It only remains to solve for the price of the single commodity,

$$p(o) = \frac{M*}{vy(o)}$$

The real or commodity wage, at which the demand for labour is less than the supply, completes the solution. It can be expressed in two ways.

$$w = \frac{W*vy(o)}{M*} = \frac{[1 - a]y(o)}{l(o)}$$

The first expression is the commodity wage in terms of nominal influences (M and W), and the second is the marginal product of labour.

The set of values associated with the nominal wage $W*$ is shown in Figure 5.3. A few purely technical points are in order. It is to be noted that when the rigid wage equilibrium indicated by (o) is compared with the full employment equilibrium (e), employment has fallen more than the output of the single commodity. This follows from the principle of diminishing returns, and is another way of saying that the commodity wage has risen (w). Second, the money value of the output of the single commodity has not changed. This follows from the quantity equation. Since equilibrium in the money market requires $M* = vpy$, if $M*$ and v are constant, py must be constant. Therefore, price must rise by the same proportion in which y falls, or $p(o)/p(e) = y(e)/y(o)$. However, this proportionate increase in price is less than the proportion by which the fixed money wage exceeds the full employment equilibrium money wage, $W*/W(e)$; that is, the real wage has risen, as explained above.

Two results of this analysis, which will be found in subsequent versions as well, stand out as counter to one's commonsense. First, the model implies that a fall in production and sales is associated with a *higher* price level; and, second, that a fall in employment is accompanied by (caused by) a *rise* in real earnings for employed workers. Yet one commonly observes the opposite in both cases: real earnings rise when labour is in short supply, and prices rise when output and sales are expanding. And certainly most people would not associate higher *money* wages with an excess supply of labour, as this model does. It could be argued that these conclusions are the result of static analysis; that we do not observe these basic relationships because in the real world there are many simultaneous changes which hide the true relationships between wages and employment and prices and output. By this argument, one concludes that the simple model and its more sophisticated versions reveal what the complexities of reality conceal. If it is the case that an increase in employment must be bought at lower wages (contrary to what one observes), then the model is powerful indeed.

Paul Samuelson has offered an analogy to justify such counter-intuitive conclusions. In physics we learn that an object dropped from any height within the earth's gravitation pull accelerates at 32 feet per second. This, however, refers to conditions in a perfect vacuum. Any actual falling body will accelerate slower, due to air resistance. The conclusion with regard to real earnings and employment is allegedly similar. The argument goes that were economists able to isolate social phenomena as physicists do natural phenomena, the conclusions of the synthesis model would be verified.

The analogy would be more convincing if unsupported bodies

occasionally rose instead of falling (lighter-than-air balloons might be considered an example). Ignoring this quibble, it is not the case that the two counter-intuitive conclusions reached above are the result of a static analysis which abstracts from extraneous complexities. The first conclusion, that price and output are negatively related, is purely the result of the assumption of an exogenous money supply and a constant velocity. If the money supply is endogenous, or has a significant endogenous component, then price and output are not necessarily inversely related even in a static model. Similarly, the second conclusion, that a drop in employment is associated with a rise real earnings,[5] is not inherent in static analysis. This conclusion results from specifying production in terms of a single commodity output/income function. The inverse relationship between employment and real earnings (the commodity wage) is a logically consistent argument if and only if the model involves one and only one commodity.[6] Perfect vacuums can be approximated in laboratory conditions and in inter-planetary space. One commodity economies cannot be approximated in any experiment outside the mind of the theorist.

In this model, as in all neoclassical models, unemployment is the fault of workers themselves, either because they demand a money wage 'too high' or support political intervention in the labour market to establish legal minimum wages. It is common to read in this context that organised labour benefits at the expense of unorganised labour. Higher wages for the employed are only achieved at the expense of unemployment for workers who are so unfortunate as not to be in strong unions or protected by minimum wage legislation. This seems a powerful critique of the alleged monopoly power of organised labour and has passed into the folklore of conventional wisdom. As shown, there is nothing immutable about this conclusion. It follows from the arbitrary treatment of the economy as a one commodity system.

It should be pointed out that the model as constructed presents a simple solution to the problem of unemployment. Given the quantity equation, an increase in the autonomous money supply will call forth an immediate increase in the price of the single commodity. Given $W*$, a rise in price will result in a fall in the commodity wage, $W*/p$. A fall in the commodity wage will induce a higher level of employment and output/income. Unemployment can always be eliminated by a sufficient increase in the money supply in this model.[7] This is shown in Figure 5.3 by a shift in $M*$ to $M**$. Given this new level of the money supply, the money value of output rises to $py**$, consistent with all of the full employment levels of the real variables, noted by (*e*).

Neoclassical economists have traditionally taken a jaundiced view of this remedy for unemployment in their model. The judgement is commonly encountered that monetary expansion involves 'endorsing inflation' – what increasing the money supply achieves would also result from a fall in the money wage. Workers should be indifferent between the two paths to full employment, since both result in the same real wage. Many economists prefer the real wage adjustment on the grounds that it involves the automatic working of the market, while monetary expansion requires government action.

5.4   THE ARBITRARINESS OF THE FULL EMPLOYMENT SOLUTION

Even ignoring the false dichotomy inconsistency, the full employment solution to this model is unsatisfactory. A look back at Figure 5.2 shows that the investment and saving schedules were drawn such that they yielded $i = s$ at a positive interest rate for the full employment level of output/income. As one of his three famous exceptions to automatic full employment, Keynes suggested that the saving and investment schedules might be of the form in Figure 5.4.[8] In this case, there is no point on the IS curve that corresponds to full employment. This is sometimes referred to as an 'inconsistency' between saving and investment.[9] For all positive interest rates, the clearing of the commodity market implies excess supply for labour. As the model stands, disequilibrium in the labour market cannot be corrected. If money wages are flexible their fall will not induce more employment, for any output in excess of $y(o)$ (assuming r cannot fall below zero) cannot be sold. If falling money wages result in falling prices, then the model experiences continuous deflation with no tendency to full employment. In the next chapter the inclusion of the real balance effect eliminates this problem.

Before proceeding to more complex models, it is useful to summarise the results obtained so far. In the case in which none of the variables of the model is constrained (e.g. flexible money wages) and the functional relationships in each market are constructed to be consistent with full employment (e.g. $i = s$ for $y\{e\}$), all real variables are independent of the exogenous money supply when they have achieved their full employment values. Money is strictly neut-

Figure 5.4   An 'inconsistency' between saving and investment

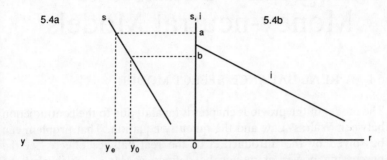

ral, determining only the price of the single commodity and the money wage, which stand in the same proportion no matter what value is arbitrarily assigned to $M*$. If the money wage is fixed above the equilibrium level, then all variables, real and nominal, move with changes in the money supply. However, any change that might be brought about by an increase in the exogenous money supply would also be achieved by a fall in money wages. The essence of the model is incorporated in two arbitrary assumptions – that the money supply is exogenous and that there is only one commodity.

6 Logically Consistent Money-neutral Models

6.1 A REAL BALANCE EFFECT MODEL

The model of the previous chapter is invalid, due to the contradiction between Walras' Law and the quantity equation. That problem can be solved by the introduction of the real balance effect. Let the purchasing power of money be defined as $M*/p$, which shall be referred to as *real balances*. In this section we shall assume that money is the only form in which people can accumulate and hold wealth. A more general treatment of wealth-holding will be presented in Chapter 7.

For each individual consumer it is reasonable to assume that his or her consumption expenditure will be affected by the value of real balances – a rise in the price level reduces the wealth of holders of money, while a fall in the price level increases their real wealth. On the presumption that people have in mind some desired level of real balances (real wealth), it is reasonable to conclude that a rise in the price level, by reducing real wealth, will stimulate a lower level of expenditure, and the opposite for a fall in the price level.

What seems reasonable with regard to the behaviour of people taken individually is not necessarily true for all people taken together. If all money is *inside money* (see Section 4.3) then in the aggregate the real balance effect is zero, for the gains (losses) of asset holders are exactly off-set by the losses (gains) of holders of liabilities. In the model presented in this section it is arbitrarily assumed that all money is a net asset ('outside'). To keep matters simple, it is assumed that the real balance effect influences consumption but not investment. However, the purchasing power of money must logically affect the demand for real balances. If a person is holding a certain amount of money and is content with this amount, a rise in the price level will reduce the real value of that amount of money and leave the person with an excess demand for real balances (and nominal balances, since one must acquire nominal wealth in order to increase real wealth). Except for the consumption function and the demand for money functions, all schedules remain as in Chapter 5. The new explicit consumption function takes the following form.

80

$$c = c* + by + g[M*/p]$$

The demand for money now has two parts, the transactions demand as such and the demand for real balances.

$$M(td) = vpy$$
$$M(bd)/p = f[M*/p]$$
$$M(d) = vpy + fM*$$

These new functional relationships should make sense in terms of the distinction between real and nominal variables. Consumption demand in real terms (in units of the single commodity) is a function of real variables only, real income and real wealth (real balances). Were one to multiply the consumption function by p, the result would be a function in which the money expenditure on consumption was determined by money income and nominal wealth. If the price level and the money supply were both to double, money expenditure on consumption would double, but consumption measured in units of the single commodity would be unchanged. Using the new consumption function, the IS curve is,

$$y = \frac{[c* + i*]}{[1 - b]} - \frac{dr}{[1 - b]} + \frac{g}{[1 - b]}\left[\frac{M*}{p}\right]$$

Clearing of the money market requires $M* = M(td) + M(bd)$. Again, behaviour has been re-specified in terms of real balances. The demand for money function being used shows that agents in the aggregate hold a proportion f of the money supply as idle balances, independently of the price level. This simple assumption indicates that their desire is to maintain a certain level of real wealth, rather than seeking to maintain some specific level of nominal balances. Were agents to set their goal in nominal terms, the result in neoclassical language would be called 'money illusion'.[1] The equilibrium condition is,

$$M* = vpy + fM*$$
$$M* = vpy/[1 - f]$$

Before considering the equilibrium of this model, it should be verified for internal consistency. It was explained previously that the excess demand equations for money implied by the simple quantity equation and Walras' Law contradicted each other.[2] This inconsistency has now been eliminated.[3] From a position of full employment equilibrium, should the price level double, the real balance effect in the demand for money equation creates an excess demand for cash balances; operating in the consumption function, it simultaneously generates excess supply of the single commodity. In other words, a rise in the price level induces people to hold more money and to buy fewer commodities. Excess supply in the commodity market results in a fall in price, which eliminates the disequilibrium in both markets.

As before, the general equilibrium solution is first worked out algebraically. The labour market functions are the same in this model as in the previous, so the commodity wage at full employment is as before,

$$w(e) = \frac{[1 - a]y(e)}{l_*},$$

where

$$y(e) = k_*{}^a l_*{}^{[1 - a]}$$

In the previous model it was possible at this point to move to the *IS* curve and determine $i(e)$, $s(e)$, and $r(e)$. Now, however, the *IS* relationship includes the real balance effect, so one must first derive $p(e)$ in order to set the equilibrium value of M_*/p. From the condition for money market equilibrium one can write $p = [1 - f]M_*/vy$; therefore,

$$p(e) = \frac{[1 - f]M_*}{vy(e)}$$

The money wage is pw, and when the substitutions are made, one gets the following.

$$W(e) = \frac{[1 - a][1 - f]M_*}{vl_*}$$

Now it is possible to return to the IS curve.

$$y(e) = \frac{[c_* + i_*]}{[1 - b]} - \frac{d}{[1 - b]r} + \left[\frac{g}{1 - b}\right]\frac{M_*}{p(e)}$$

This can be simplified to eliminate $p(e)$, so y is a function of r only.

$$y(e) = \left[\frac{\{[c_* + i_*]\}}{\{[1 - b][1 - f] - gv\}}\right] + \left[\frac{d[1 - f]}{\{[1 - b][1 - f] - gv\}}\right]r$$

Since $y(e)$ has been determined, the equilibrium interest rate, $r(e)$, can be found, as well as $c(e)$, $i(e)$, and $s(e)$. Money is neutral in this model. If one looks back over the solution to the full employment equilibrium, neither the money supply nor the price level can be found to enter the equation for any real variable. By introducing the real balance effect, Patinkin pulled off an extremely clever conjuring trick. Superficially, money appears to play a more central role in this model than in the Classical false dichotomy case. But the ultimate effect of making the demand for money more complex is to achieve the Classical goal of neutrality while resolving the excess demand for money dilemma upon which the Classical model floundered. The trick has been achieved by introducing another 'real' variable $M*/p$, which, it develops, is merely a fractional part of real output/income itself, $v/[1 - f])$. Further, the introduction of y in disguised from has a profound consequence – the possibility of a full employment solution being blocked by the inconsistency between saving and investment has been eliminated (see below). For thirty years no one has been able to improve upon the simplicity of Patinkin's rescue of the Classical system from its internal inconsistencies.

The full employment solution to the model with the real balance effect can now be presented graphically. This is done in Figure 6.1, where again the analysis begins with the labour market. By this point in the presentation it should be clear that the full employment equilibrium solution in itself is of relatively little interest. One considers it to establish that it indeed exists and that there are no conditions which would render it a special case. In the previous model, one saw that full employment was a special case even if wages and prices were flexible, for there was no guarantee that saving and investment could be equated at the full employment level of output/income. Now that problem can be eliminated. Consider the possibility that the investment schedule is $i*$(bd), completely interest inelastic and below the full employment level of saving for saving schedule s'. At point a (part 6.1c), $i = s$, and no positive values of r are consistent with full employment. With saving schedule s', investment would have to be $i(1)$ for full employment. For $i*$ aggregate demand is always less than aggregate supply (supply in the commodity market).

Let us designate the initial price level as $p(1)$. The excess supply of commodities in a Walrasian world induces a fall in price. The fall in price results in a rise in $M*/p$, which brings the real balance effect into operation. With real wealth increasing, there is a movement to the right along the savings schedule in Figure 6.1(f) (where s is a function

Figure 6.1   General equilibrium in a 'classical' model with a real balance
effect

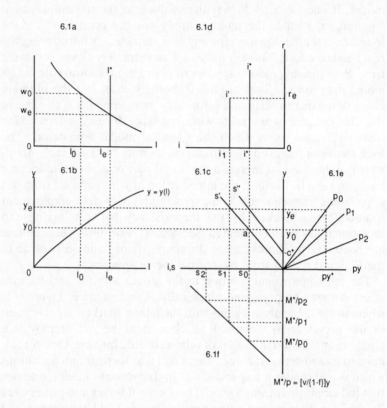

of $M*/p$), which implies a shift to the right of the saving schedule in
Figure 6.1(c) (where s is a function of y). A falling price shifts the
saving-income function such that less is saved at each level of income.
When the saving-income function has shifted down enough (so that
schedule s'' prevails), the full employment level of output/income is
achieved such that $i = s$.

This logical sequence allows one to see the extent to which the
entire solution to full employment is derivative from the labour
market. At first inspection it appears that the consumption function
(and, therefore, the saving function) was independent of other functions in the system, though sharing some of the same variables. Now
one sees that the position of the saving function in Figure 6.1(c) is
dictated by the labour market. Given equilibrium in the labour

market, $M*/p$ is determined: the money supply is exogenous and only one price level is consistent with full employment. Two components of the solution, $y(e)$ and $M*/p(e)$ determine everything. This can be seen in Figure 6.1 by again referring to investment schedule $i*$ and saving function s'. Investment $i*$ implies a level of saving of $s(o)$ Figure 6.1(c). Moving left to 6.1(b), one sees that this level of saving implies income level $y(o)$ and level of employment $l(o)$. Figure 6.1(a) reveals that the labour market is in excess supply and that the real wage is above its equilibrium level. Thus, income level cannot be an equilibrium.

However, momentary unemployment in this case is not the result of the real wage being too high. This is an extremely important point to understand and will loom large in the next chapter. The excess supply of labour is the result of the position of the investment function; that the real wage is above its equilibrium level is merely a necessary symptom or manifestation of a problem arising in the commodity market (where s and i cannot be equated at the full employment level of income). Keynes sought to establish precisely such a conclusion: if the real wage is above its equilibrium level this is the consequence not the cause of unemployment.[4] But the real balance effect brings the blame for unemployment back to roost in the labour market. Were there no mechanism to shift the saving schedule (with a view to eliminating the 'inconsistency' between i and s), then unemployment would unambiguously be 'involuntary' in the model. Idleness would be thrust upon workers by circumstances over which they had no control. Thus, the real balance effect plays an important ideological role by removing the prefix 'in-' from 'involuntary unemployment'.

Now return to Figure 6.1(c). If one moves to the right, it is discovered that the less-than-full-employment level of single commodity income, $y(o)$, implies a level of money income the same as at full employment, $py*$, just as in the false dichotomy model. The money value of income does not change because nominal balances are a constant portion of the money supply, so the money left over for transactions balances does not change. Because money income is invariant to changes in the level of output, the notation $py*$ rather than $p(e)y(e)$ is used in Figure 6.1(e). If money income is not changed while production of the single commodity is lower $(y(o) < y(e))$, then the price of the commodity must have risen. This is made explicit in Figure 6.1(e), where the price line rotates in a clockwise direction. The rise in price $(p[1]$ to $p[2])$, however, renders the less than full employment solution inconsistent. A higher price results in a fall in $M*/p$, which increases saving and increases the excess supply in the commodity market. Back in the labour market this inconsistency is being resolved, for $(l(d) < l*$ results in falling money wages, as all workers re-contract under the gavel of the auctioneer (see section 2.3). In a perfectly competitive world, falling money wages prompts a falling price. While this cannot directly equilibrate the labour market, it results in a reversal of the fall in $M*/p$. As $M*/p$ begins to rise, there is a moment along the saving schedule in Figure 6.1(f), which dictates a shift downwards in the saving-as-a-function-of-income schedule in Figure 6.1(c). This continues until the latter schedule finds its intercept at point $(-c*)$ on the income axis in Figure 6.1(c). No other intercept for the saving function is consistent with the functions in the model.[5] Not only is full employment achieved, but $r(e)$ is unique.

The docile movement of the saving function to serve the needs of equilibration in the labour market indicates how far the neoclassical model has moved from Keynes's analysis in *The General Theory*. Keynes's general conclusion was that the level of employment in a capitalist economy was dictated by conditions in the commodity market – effective demand. The real balance effect returns one to a Classical world in which the clearing of all markets is derivative from the instantaneous, Walrasian adjustment of wages and prices. In the next section we turn to a more Keynesian neoclassical model in which the commodity market can under limited circumstances achieve the importance Keynes assigned to it. Its moment in the spotlight is brief, however, for in Chapter 7 the real balance effect is re-introduced in general form and the commodity market again plays at best a supporting role.

6.2 INTEREST-ELASTIC MONEY MARKET MODEL

In this section we present what was once commonly called 'the Keynesian model' or the 'complete Keynesian system'.[6] It characteristically omits the wealth effect, though writers frequently make *ad hoc* reference to it when discussing exceptions to full employment equilibrium. What allegedly makes the model 'Keynesian' (in addition to treating consumption as a function of income, which we have done throughout our presentation) is the introduction of the interest rate into the function for the demand for money.

Unsynthesised Keynesians as well as pure neoclassicals agree that the demand for money should be modelled as interest-elastic, but controversy has waxed and waned as to the theoretical justification. In *The General Theory* the interest elasticity of the demand for money is closely related to Keynes's treatment of uncertainty and expectations of capitalists derivative from uncertainty. It was the view of Keynes that a capitalist economy creates an environment of inherent uncertainty. He argued that to a great extent economic fluctuations are a result of uncertainty and the behaviour of capitalists in response to uncertainty. Central to Keynes's treatment of uncertainty and expectations was the presumption that the future is both unknown and unknowable. That is to say, no amount of information about the past and present can do more than indicate what will occur in the future. Further, predictions based upon full knowledge of the past and present may well be contradicted by what actually occurs in the future.

With regard to the demand for money, Keynes argued that capitalists tend to hold cash for speculative purposes. In Keynes's treatment of the issue, speculation is an activity which exists because the future cannot be accurately predicted. The role of speculation in the demand for money can be shown by assuming the simple case in which wealth can be held in only two forms, money itself and interest-yielding bonds. For the moment we ignore the transactions demand for money. In this simple example of money and bonds, assume that one knew without doubt that the prevailing interest rate would persist for the foreseeable future. On the basis of such knowledge there would be no reason to hold money, for with each passing moment the holder of money forgoes potential interest income. If, however, one has suspicions that the interest rate might rise or fall (but is not certain), the situation is different. A fall in the interest rate would have the result of increasing the market value of bonds, while a rise would decrease the value of bonds.[7] It seems reasonable to presume that holders of wealth will keep a large portion of their wealth in money form if they anticipate a rise in the interest rate and in bonds if they anticipate a fall in the interest rate. However, were all wealth holders to have the same anticipation of what the interest rate would do at any moment, it would be the case that they all would either want to hold money only (anticipating a rise in the interest rate) or to hold bonds only (anticipating a fall).

Because it seemed to him self-evident that the future could not be accurately predicted, Keynes presumed that everyone would not have the same guess about what coming events would bring. Thus, at any prevailing interest rate some wealth holders anticipate a rise in r, while others anticipate a fall (and some think it will not change). As a result of these mixed anticipations, some hold money and others hold bonds. If one goes on to presume that the higher is the interest rate the fewer are those who think it will go still higher (and *vice versa*), one obtains a demand for speculative balances which is inversely related to the interest rate. It might be said that Keynes viewed the bond and money markets analogously to a horse race. A horse race may have a predicted winner (the 'favourite', which has the lowest payoff). But, all parties do not bet on the favourite, because the favourite does not always win. People bet on different horses because the outcome of a horse race is inherently uncertain; one can have possession of all possible knowledge and still select a losing horse. Most people would say that the bond market and other asset markets are similar with regard to predictability.

This view of of the material world, that it is dynamic and subject to changes which at best one can only vaguely anticipate, has been rejected by the neoclassical synthesis. This is most explicit and unabashed by the rational expectations–New Classical Economics school, treated in later chapters. Not only do these latter-day pre-Keynesians model a world of predictable outcomes, they also assert that the actual world is no different. This is indeed a case of 'nature imitating art'. Here we note that the synthesis, even in its pre-rational expectations days, was never at home with Keynes's treatment of uncertainty. His explanation for an interest-elastic demand for money was rejected in the literature in favour of explanations that yield similar functional forms consistent with a world of certain outcomes.[8]

Modern monetary theory has reformulated the interest-elastic demand for money in terms of opportunity cost – interest income lost as a result of holding money. To the extent that Keynes's speculative motive has been retained it bears little resemblance to the original concept in which the non-predictability of the future and the volatility of expectations played such a central role. Indeed, an interest-elastic demand for money can be inferred from the transactions demand alone. The idea is quite simple. An agent has a certain chronological sequence of income receipts and a certain sequence of payments to make. In general these two sequences do not coincide. Assuming there to be some cost in shifting funds from bonds (and other forms of wealth that bear a return) to cash (which by definition has a zero return), the agent will hold some cash idle even if the income sequence and the payment sequence are known with perfect certainty. In other words, a wealth holder will not send a sell order to his broker every time he buys an ounce of caviar. However, other things equal (such as the brokerage cost of a transaction on bonds), the higher the rate of interest the less attractive it will be to keep on hand a given amount of cash to meet payments.[9] This line of argument implies that the transactions demand for money is a function of the value of exchanges to be made and the interest rate.

As in the previous model, the demand for money is specified in terms of real balances. In general form, this can be written as $M(d)/p = L(y, r)$, with the letter L indicating that this is the liquidity preference function. As before, the exchange-motivated demand for money is vpy. To this we add an interest rate element, and obtain the following.[10]

$$\frac{M(d)}{p} = vy + [h - jr]$$

The notation for the demand for money is indicated simply by the letter 'd' in parentheses, indicating that the reader can attribute its interest elasticity to a number of motivations (transactional, precautionary, and speculative) and obtain the same function. Equilibrium in the money market requires that supply equal demand, or $M*/p = M(d)/p$. This yields the LM curve, which shows all possible points of equilibrium for the supply and demand for money. As with the IS curve above, it can be solved for y in terms of r.

$$y = \frac{[M*/p - h]}{v} + \left[\frac{j}{v}\right] r$$

With regard to money market equilibrium, income is a positive function of the interest rate. Prior to receiving an explanation of this, the reader can note that it is a quite satisfactory result. Since in the commodity market equilibrium income is negative function of the interest rate, one now has two functions in y and r, which if they intersect at all in the positive quadrant must yield a stable equilibrium.[11] The LM curve has a positive slope because a higher interest rate results in a fall in holdings of cash. This represents a shift of cash from idle to active balances, which means that this money is available for and seeking commodity transactions. If price is assumed constant, equilibrium can be maintained only by an increase in output/income.

Put in other terms, a rise in the interest rate creates an excess supply of idle balances and an excess demand for commodities. If price is assumed fixed, the excess demand for commodities calls forth a greater supply to satisfy it.

If the post-Keynesians are discontented with the neoclassical treatment of consumption and investment (combining them in the IS curve), they should be hardly more pleased with the LM curve. In both cases all distinction between more and less volatile economic behaviour has been obliterated. Treating investment and consumption as equally stable functions of two variables, income and the interest rate, eliminates what Keynes and other economists considered as the main source of fluctuations on the demand side. In particular, the IS treatment implies a virtual abandonment of what in the thirty years after *The General Theory* was called 'business cycle theory', an attempt to explain why developed capitalist economies exhibit systematic fluctuations in the level of aggregate economic activity. If one presumes the investment function to be stable and analytically indistinguishable from the consumption function, then stability and equilibrium are the subject of theory, not fluctuations.

As in the case of investment and consumption, Keynes distinguished between the income-related demand for money and the rate of interest-related demand precisely in order to focus upon the relative stability of the former and the relative instability of the latter. His point was that the interest-elastic demand for money was an inherently unstable function, and, therefore, a central cause of the cyclical volatility of capitalist economies. This, in turn, was part of his argument that money economies are inherently unstable if left unregulated.[12] If the demand for money is volatile – agents quickly and unexpectedly change their targets for idle balances – then all markets are rendered unstable. The commodity market is upset by sudden shifts in demand, which are passed on to the labour market. The money market is affected directly, undermining the role of the rate of interest in equilibrating saving and investment.

With the introduction of the LM curve, the demand for money has been discarded as a possible source of instability. The model has indeed become complete. First, the labour market was specified in terms of the commodity wage and the notional demand for labour which presumes that there is no sales constraint upon firms. This was followed by formulating the commodity market to eliminate the distinction between consumption and investment (and, therefore, any distinction between saving and investment). Now the money market has been modelled to ensure stability there. It only remains to solve the complete model for equilibrium.

Prior to solving the model, it should be investigated whether it is consistent with Walras' Law. The situation is now complicated by the introduction of another market. It is to be recalled that this model has an additional vendible article, 'bonds'. With the introduction of bonds, the excess demand for money is no longer identically equal to the excess supply of the commodity, but equal to the *sum of the excess demands for the commodity and bonds*. Looking at the excess demand for money implied by the liquidity preference function, one sees that it is determined by the interest rate, the commodity price, and the level of income (which is held constant for this exercise). The same is the case for the excess demand for the commodity and bonds. A rise in the price level increases the excess demand for money and decreases the excess demand for the single commodity. A rise in the interest rate increases the excess demand for bonds and decreases the excess demand for money. The two excess demand equations for money are consistent.[13]

We move to the full employment general equilibrium solution. The steps follow as before, beginning with the labour market, where the same functions are employed as in the first two models.

$$y(e) = k_*{}^a l_*{}^{[1-a]}$$
$$w(e) = [1-a]y(e)/l_*$$
$$c(e) = c_* + by(e)$$
$$s(e) = [1-b]y(e) - c_*$$
$$i(e) = s(e)$$
$$i(e) = i_* - dr(e)$$

Not until this point does one encounter anything different from before. Unlike in the previous model, here the interest rate must work to clear the money and bond markets as well as to equate investment to saving. But be that as it may, the equilibrium interest rate must satisfy the commodity market. Following convention, we solve for the r which satisfies the IS curve, then use that r elsewhere as needed. Such a procedure is valid only if one knows in advance that all functional relationships are consistent with full employment, since the solution is a simultaneous one in which r must satisfy more than one equation. As in the false dichotomy model, solving for $r(e)$ yields the following.

$$r(e) = \frac{[c* + i*]}{d} - \frac{[1 - b]y(e)}{d}$$

With the interest rate determined, one moves on to the demand for money, $M(d)$.

$$M(d) = p(e)[vy(e) + h - jr(e)]$$

This expression contains a variable yet to be determined, the equilibrium price, $p(e)$. The value of this nominal variable can be found from the equilibrium condition for the money market, the LM curve.

$$M* = p(e)[vy(e) + h - jr(e)]$$

From which it follows,

$$p(e) = \frac{M*}{[vy(e) + h - jr(e)]}$$

It only remains to determine the money wage, $W(e)$.

$$W(e) = \frac{\{[1 - a]y(e)p(e)\}}{l*}$$

Money is neutral in this model. Looking at the equation for $p(e)$, one sees that both y and r have been determined elsewhere (by the equilibrium condition $i = s$) and can, therefore, be taken as given. Should the money supply, $M*$, double, the price level will double with no change in any real variable. Since a doubling of $M*$ implies a doubling of p, the implicit real variable $M*/p$ (and $M[d]/p$) is also unchanged.

The full employment general equilibrium solution is perhaps more easily grasped diagrammatically. In Figure 6.2 the analysis begins with the labour market. In order to make the equilibrium conditions explicit, IS and LM curves have not been used, but rather the functional relationships which underline them. By now the sequence of logical events should be familiar. In Figure 6.2(a) we have the notional demand curve for labour and the notional supply (assumed fixed at $l*$). One should remember that the demand for labour presumes that firms act as if they have no sales constraint; i.e. it presumes a Walrasian process in which there is no False Trading. Here output/income is determined, unless somewhere else in the model one encounters conditions that contradict full employment. Below, in Figure 6.2(b), full employment output/income is shown

Figure 6.2   General equilibrium in the 'complete Keynesian system'

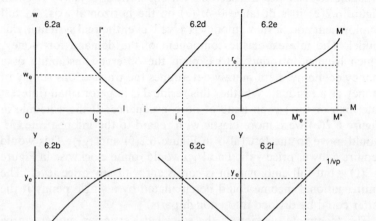

explicitly as $y(e)$. To the right is the saving function in Figure 6.2(c), and above that in Figure 6.2(d) is the investment function, which shows that the interest rate adjusts to equate investment and saving. All of this differs in no way from the False Dichotomy model, and can be said to establish the values of the 'real' system, with the exception of $M*/p$.

What is new in this model appears in Figure 6.2(e), where the interest rate, already determined, acts to divide the money supply between idle and active balances. At this point it is convenient to define a new term, M', which is that portion of the money supply which is not held as idle balances. Thus,

$$M' = M* - p[h - jr]$$
$$= M* - M(b).$$

As defined, M' is the portion of the money supply which is available to facilitate transactions (in equilibrium equal to vpy). In Figure 6.2(e) it is distance $0-M'(e)$ on the horizontal axis. At full employment equilibrium, money is a 'veil' over the real system in this model. The interest-elastic component of the demand for money, which Keynes introduced to explain the observed instability of a money economy, here merely determines the transactions supply of money as a residual. Whether this residual is large or small (interest rate high or low) is an issue of no consequence. If the schedule in Figure 6.2(e) were more elastic with regard to the interest rate, M' would move to the left (also in Figure 6.2(f) and (g)). This would require a lower price – the line $1/vp$ would rotate clockwise in Figure 6.2(f) – but full employment is consistent with any price level. The entire national income could be circulated by a single penny if the latter could be divided into enough parts.

This 'complete' version of the so-called Keynesian model can be reconstructed to generate unemployment by assuming a fixed money wage. The result is hardly different from invoking the same assumption in the false dichotomy model. This is shown in Figure 6.3, which should be compared with Figure 5.3. Let $W = W*$, with $W*$ above the full employment equilibrium level. Now it is considerably more complicated to solve the system for the values of the variables than was the case in the same model with unconstrained full employment. The complication arises because the level of employment is determined by the commodity wage, but the commodity wage cannot clear the labour market because the *money wage* is above its only possible full employment value. In this case the commodity wage, $w(o)$ is derivative from the level of employment, not *vice versa*. Employment is set by the level of aggregate demand, which ultimately reflects the two arbitrary parameters $M*$ and $W*$.[14]

Understanding in this case is facilitated by dispensing with the algebra and going directly to Figure 6.3. As we know, only one money wage is consistent with the commodity wage $w(e)$. Since by assumption $W*$ is above $W(e)$, the model cannot be at full employment. If some labour is unemployed, this requires that the commodity wage associated with $W*$ be above the full employment commodity wage, $w(e)$. When employment falls below $l(e)$, to $l(o)$, output/income falls to $y(o)$. Since saving is a function of income, saving falls, to $s(o)$. This lower level of saving must be equated to a lower level of investment in order that the commodity market clear. With investment greater than saving, the interest rate must rise to

Figure 6.3   Rigid money wage in the 'complete Keynesian system'

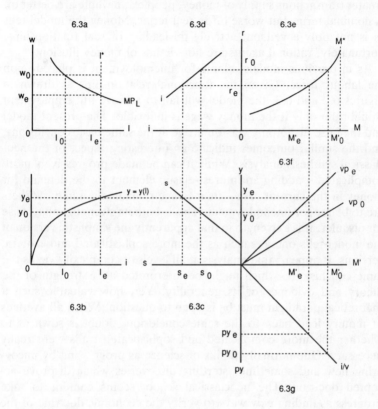

clear the commodity market. A higher interest rate creates an excess demand for bonds and an excess supply of money, which increases the money available for transactions, M'.[15] The price level rises, because the level of output/income is lower and the quantity of money chasing commodities has risen.

This last sequence, the release of more money for transactions, results in yet another of those strikingly counter-intuitive conclusions of neoclassical theory. As we saw before in simpler models, falls in employment and output/income were predicted to be accompanied by a rising commodity wage, money wage, and price level. Now a fourth unexpected relationship is introduced. With the inclusion of an interest-elastic demand for money, less than full employment equilibrium is associated with a level of *money* output/income higher than at full employment. Because a higher interest rate implies a greater transactions supply of money, people as a whole are better off in nominal terms but worse off in real terms. Money the model tells us is not only a veil but actively misleading of real relationships. Fortunately, rational agents are not victims of money illusion.

As in previous models, blame for unemployment is placed upon the labour force. Given the functional relationships as drawn in Figures 6.2 and 6.3, the model will fail to achieve full employment equilibrium only if the money wage is inflexible. The present model and the false dichotomy version arrive at the same basic conclusions, and the similar outcomes indicate an interesting aspect of the neoclassical synthesis analysis. While it can be made progressively more complicated – adding an interest-elastic element to the demand for money in the current case – its message remains the same: workers are to blame for unemployment. This is both its strength and a cause for disquiet. It is a strength in that apparently the simplistic version of the model tells one as much as the more sophisticated and esoteric versions. It appears that analysis at all levels of complexity yields the same conclusions, which might be interpreted as a strength of the theory and evidence of its generality. Yet, how valuable such a theoretical paradigm must be is open to question. When all avenues of inquiry lead back to the same conclusion, doubt is sown as to whether the more complicated and sophisticated trails were really necessary. One normally thinks of science as progressing by uncovering new and sometimes startling discoveries which disprove accepted doctrine. The neoclassical school seems content to take progress as finding new ways to verify the economic doctrine of the early twentieth century.

6.3 THE 'LIQUIDITY TRAP'

The full employment solution in this last version of the synthesis model is in serious need of the Wealth Effect. The inconsistency between saving and investment, pointed out in Section 6.1, is equally appropriate here. Its impact upon this model is exactly the same as before, so there is no need to labour it. However, the introduction of the interest-elastic demand for money creates the possibility of another logical barrier to full employment, the 'liquidity trap'. The liquidity trap refers to the possibility that at some low rate of interest the demand for idle balances may become infinitely elastic.[16] One explanation for the existence of the liquidity trap is that the interest rate might at some moments be so low that all wealth holders would anticipate it to rise in the near future. This would imply a fall in the price of bonds and, therefore, induce wealth holders to have a strong preference for money to avoid a capital loss. Alternatively, wealth holders might wish to hold only money because the rate of interest is so low as not to justify the default risk involved in holding bonds.[17] Whichever the case, liquidity trap behaviour need not necessarily present a problem for the logic of full employment equilibrium. Difficulty would arise if the interest rate required to equate saving to investment at full employment were *below* the interest rate at which the demand for idle balances becomes infinitely elastic.

The logical consequence of the liquidity trap is demonstrated in Figure 6.4, where only the commodity and money markets are shown. First, the mechanism by which the interest rate changes in this model needs to be made explicit. Changes in the interest rate are the result of disequilibrium in the portfolios of wealth holders. If there is an excess demand for money, wealth holders sell bonds, which drives down the bond prices and pushes up the rate of interest. If there is an excess supply of money, the resultant purchase of bonds drives the interest rate down. Therefore, if at any moment the interest rate is above the full employment level, what is required is an excess supply of money which will induce bond purchases by wealth holders. That is, an increase in the demand for bonds increases the price of bonds, which by definition implies a fall in the interest rate. In the case of Figure 6.2, an excess supply of money could be brought about by the commodity price falling according to Walrasian rules. Were price to fall, the transactions need for cash would decline, creating an excess supply of money and an excess demand for bonds. The situation is different in Figure 6.4. As before, disequilibrium in the commodity market logically causes price to fall, and a decline in p releases money from transactions needs. But in Figure 6.4 a decline in price cannot rectify the situation, because wealth holders are content to absorb any amount of money into their portfolios as idle balances. The situation depicted is indeterminate. With an instantaneously adjusting money wage and price the model implies continuous deflation with no remedy in logic.

If one wished to relate the diagram to some real world process (where presumably wages and prices do not fall without limit), it would be sufficient to presume that the demand for money were extremely elastic with respect to the interest rate, rather than in-

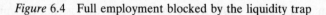

Figure 6.4   Full employment blocked by the liquidity trap

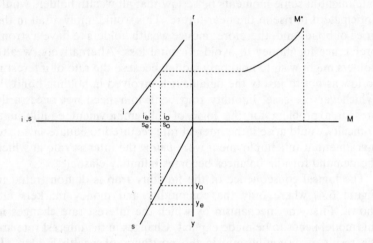

finitely so. Then one could say that, while in theory a full employment equilibrium exists, the price decline necessary to achieve it would be so massive as to be catastrophic to the economy. This is the judgement traditionally taken by Keynesians. Their remedy for a near-liquidity trap situation would be to increase aggregate demand through state expenditure (or reducing taxes). Graphically, fiscal intervention could be represented by a parallel shift to the left of the investment schedule, so it becomes $(i + a)$, with a standing for real state expenditure.

There has been considerable debate over the empirical importance of the liquidity trap. Some economists deny its existence altogether or assert that at most it would occur only in a severe depression. However, empirical arguments are irrelevant in the context of the synthesis model. Were one to start requiring empirical credentials for concepts, the liquidity trap would fare quite respectably alongside the wealth effect, the interest-elasticity of the investment schedule, and the aggregate production function – not to mention the assumption of a single commodity world and the instantaneous equilibrating of markets. The model is a logical one, and to seek to defend it by singling out awkward aspects for the acid-test of empirical evidence while exempting others from the same test is inconsistent. The issue is a logical one: can the synthesis model be formulated in such a way as to preclude theoretically the possibility of the liquidity trap blocking the full employment solution? The answer is 'yes'. The rescue is achieved by introducing the wealth effect, not as an aside to be placed in a footnote, but as an integral part of the model. This approach is pursued in the next chapter.

7 The 'Complete' Model with a Wealth Effect

7.1 INSIDE AND OUTSIDE WEALTH

The final version of the synthesis model which we consider introduces the wealth effect. It differs from the real balance effect model in Section 6.1 in an important respect. In that model the only form in which wealth could be held was money. Once the demand for money is interest elastic, the former treatment is no longer sufficient, for the model includes bonds. It is important to stress that the inclusion of bonds as part of wealth is not arbitrary, but logically necessary. If the demand for money is interest elastic, then there are bonds in the system and these bonds are part of wealth; if the demand for money is not interest elastic, then one is back to the naïve 'classical' model of Chapter 5.

Before considering the wealth effect, it is necessary to refer back to the discussion in Chapter 4 of 'inside' and 'outside'. Money is 'inside' if it does not represent a net asset (for each unit of money there is a debtor and a creditor). Outside money in contrast refers to money for which there is no cancelling liability. Debate has raged over whether the money supply in abstract models and actual economies should be treated as primarily inside or outside. A similar debate has raged over bonds. Bonds issued by corporations are obviously not net wealth by the neoclassical test – the debt of the issuing institution cancels the credit of the bond holder. The controversy arises over bonds issued by the state. This controversy need not distract us, though it is of central importance to neoclassical monetary theory.[1] In this chapter it will be assumed that the bonds in the model are outside (represent net wealth). If there are no outside bonds, then one is back to the complete Keynesian model of the previous chapter, in which money is neutral but there may be no full employment solution.

The argument over inside and outside wealth indicates the extent to which economic agents in capitalist societies are controlled by property relations. Private bonds (and other private securities) presumably represent productive assets – buildings, machines, vehicles, etc. These productive assets are by any commonsense judgement society's true wealth, the source of its material well-being. For example, in a non-exchange society, no one would argue that land and the means of producing on land were not net wealth. The debate over inside and outside money and bonds involves what Marx called 'commodity fetishism', in which the fundamental character of wealth is obscured because of its role as a commodity. By passing through a moment in which they are exchanged, productive assets assume a money form, though their essential character is that of material wealth. The method of neoclassical theory is to focus upon the exchange of assets and discard their role as real wealth. Emphasis upon *individual exchange* completes the process by which the material nature of assets is lost, for in every exchange there is a buyer and a seller. In the case of bonds, the buyer purchases the credit aspect of the bond and the seller receives the debit aspect. Though this is true by definition, it in no way changes the fact that the exchange may have involved a net accumulation of wealth for society as a whole.

7.2 SPECIFYING THE WEALTH EFFECT

In this section it is arbitrarily assumed that the bonds in the following model are 'outside'. With regard to notation, $B*$ will stand for the aggregate interest yield on bonds. That is, bonds are assumed to be issued with a fixed contractual interest yield in pounds, dollars, etc. The total interest yield is given at any moment, since the number of bonds in circulation is given. If the market rate of interest is r, then the aggregate market value of bonds is $B*/r$; e.g., if the interest yield on bonds is ten billion dollars and the market rate of interest is 10 per cent, then the aggregate value of bonds is one hundred billion dollars. If all bonds and all money are outside, then aggregate wealth, Q, is $[M* + B*/r]$, and real aggregate wealth is

$$q = \frac{M* + B*/r}{p}$$

The impact of q upon the various variables in the model is the wealth effect, or Pigou effect. This new variable, q, must now be introduced into all of the relevant function relationships – saving, investment, the demand for money and the demand for bonds. Further, the interest rate is now included as a determinant of saving.

To keep notation simple, the functional relationships will be written in implicit form, breaking with the practice of the previous two chapters.

$$s = s(y, r, q\{r, p\})$$
$$i = i(r, q\{r, p\})$$
$$\frac{M(d)}{p} = m(p, y, r, q\{r, p\})$$
$$\frac{B(d)}{p} = b(p, y, r, q\{r, p\})$$

The discussion of adjustment to general equilibrium will prove quite complex, so a clear understanding of each behavioural relationship is necessary. The *saving function* is familiar, but now more complex. As before, increases in income call forth more saving. However, the interest rate has both a direct effect and an indirect effect via its impact on wealth. An increase in r directly induces more saving by raising the opportunity cost of current consumption, and *also* induces more saving since it reduces the real value of bonds. The decline in the value of bonds reduces total wealth, provoking people to save more to restore the desired real wealth position. Finally, a rise in the price level also stimulates saving by reducing real wealth.

The interest rate also plays a dual role in the *investment function*. The direct result of an increase in r is to reduce investment expenditure. Working through real wealth, q, the increased interest rate also depresses investment by reducing the real value of bonds (and thus total real wealth). This relationship, that decreases in real wealth reduce investment (and *vice versa*), is based upon a portfolio-adjustment argument. Presuming that a firm's portfolio composition is the desired one, a decrease in the value of financial assets (e.g. due to r increasing) would provoke a reduction in investment in productive assets to restore the original portfolio balance. Similarly, a *ceteris paribus* rise in price depresses investment by reducing real wealth (both for money and bonds in this case).

Interactions become more complicated for the *nominal demand for money function*. The impact of output/income is straightforwardly positive as before, but price and the interest rate both have dual effects. For the interest rate the direct and indirect effects are in the same direction: directly an increase in the interest rate raises the opportunity cost of idle balances. Working through q it reduces the value of bonds, and with less total real wealth agents desire to hold less money in real terms. The impact of price is ambiguous, however. An increase in price raises the nominal value of exchanges, inducing larger nominal holdings of money for transactions; but by reducing real wealth (both for bonds and money) it reduces desired real money holdings.

The impact of variables on the *real demand* for bonds is analogous to the impact on the commodity. Increases in income raise the demand for bonds, and an increase in price decreases it (operating to reduce real wealth). Here it is the interest rate which plays an ambiguous role. By reducing the real value (price) of bonds, a rise in the interest rate stimulates demand, but by simultaneously reducing real wealth via those same bond prices, an increased interest rate also depresses the demand for bonds. However, the net effect of the interest rate on the demand for bonds is positive.

7.3 MECHANICS OF THE WEALTH EFFECT

With all of the above considerations to complicate matters, analytical simplicity is sought by assuming throughout the discussion the model is at full employment, so the level of output/income is given.[2] This assumption has already been justified. In the classical real balance effect model, we saw how the limited version of the wealth effect eliminated any problem of an inconsistency between saving and investment, and a more inclusive definition of wealth strengthens the logic of that argument. The wealth effect also takes the wind out of the sails of the liquidity trap. The liquidity trap involved an across-the-board decision by wealth holders to absorb any available money into cash balances. Now, however, the demand for money is determined in part by the real wealth of agents. If a liquidity trap situation prevails, the logical result is deflation, as argued in the previous section. Deflation (falling p) increases the real value of wealth which shifts both the consumption function and the investment function upwards, raising aggregate demand. At some point price will fall sufficiently that the downward shift of the saving function and the upward shift of the investment function equate full employment saving and investment at the 'trapped' interest rate.[3] We can proceed confident that nothing but rigid money wages will prevent an instantaneous move to full employment.

The analysis now limits itself to the markets for the commodity,

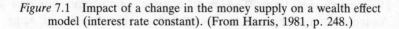

Figure 7.1   Impact of a change in the money supply on a wealth effect model (interest rate constant). (From Harris, 1981, p. 248.)

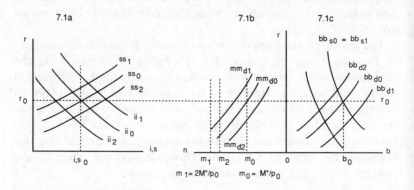

money and bonds. The mechanics of these markets under present assumptions are shown in two diagrams, Figures 7.1 and 7.2. These diagrams show two stages in the equilibrium-adjustment process, divided in order to minimise confusion. It is to be recalled, however, that this division is purely heuristic. In logic all the adjustments occur instantaneously and there are no steps or stages. With income given, each market can be drawn as a function of the interest rate, and shifts in any schedules are the result of changes in the wealth variable alone or the price of the single commodity. In each market the relationship between r and the variable in question refers to the direct impact only. The indirect impact of r (embodied in B_*/rp) is part of the shift-parameter, $q = [M_*/p + B_*/rp]$.

The exercise in the two diagrams is to investigate the impact of a change in the money supply upon the real variables in the system. It shall be demonstrated that money is not neutral in this version of the neoclassical model, the most complete so far. Since this is not a detective story with suspense until the end, the source of non-neutrality can be betrayed at the outset. As shown above, wealth is the sum of money and bonds, both of which are exogenously given. When the money supply doubles, for example, and the supply of bonds remains unchanged, neither nominal nor real wealth can double. Therefore, a change in the money supply necessarily results in a change in at least one real variable, q.

In Figures 7.1 and 7.2 specific values of variables are noted with

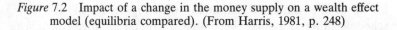

Figure 7.2   Impact of a change in the money supply on a wealth effect
model (equilibria compared). (From Harris, 1981, p. 248)

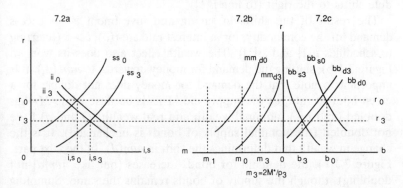

single letters (e.g., $i[o]$ is the equilibrium value of investment for
interest rate $r[o]$), and schedules are assigned double letters (e.g. $ii[o]$
is investment demand for all interest rates given q and y). All
variables are price-deflated, not only the already-familiar i and s, but
also $b = B/p$ and $m = M/p$. The analysis begins with the schedules
marked (o), and the reader is reminded that the labour market is
permanently in full employment equilibrium. Looking at the two
diagrams, one might be initially confused to see that in Figures 7.1(b)
and 7.2(b) the price-divided money supply is drawn as a vertical line,
while the price-divided bond supply has a negative slope in Figures
7.1(c) and 7.2(c), though the nominal supplies of both are fixed. This
is explained by the logic that, given the price level, the value of the
money supply is invariant with respect to the interest rate, while the
value of bonds decreases as the interest rate increases. Other things
equal, a fall in the interest rate is equivalent to the issuance of more
bonds had the interest rate remained the same. This is a rare case in
neoclassical theory in which a demand curve is upward sloping and a
supply curve downward sloping with respect to a price variable.

   With these preliminaries, consideration of the diagrams may begin.
From the equilibrium marked (o), let the nominal money supply
double, from $M*$ to $2M*$. Prior to any other change, the impact effect
of this is to shift the vertical line in Figure 7.1(b) (representing the
real money supply) to point $m(1)$, where $[0 - m(1)] = 2[0 - m(o)]$.
However, the increase in the nominal supply of money sets off shifts

for all of the schedules. Beginning with Figure 7.1(a), the saving schedule shifts to the left (becoming $ss[1]$) and the investment schedule shifts to the right (to line $ii[1]$).

The result of the shifts in saving and investment is an excess demand for the commodity, for at interest rate are $r(o)$, $i > s$ (referring to schedules $ii[1]$ and $ss[1]$). The wealth effect also does its work in Figure 7.1(b), shifting the demand for money upwards, to mm (d_1). It is important to note that the demand for money does not double for a given interest rate, as the supply did. This is because while $M*$ has doubled (and $m*$), nominal wealth and real wealth (Q and q) have not doubled (the nominal supply of bonds is unchanged). It is the change in wealth that determines the shift in $mm(d)$. In the next part, Figure 7.1(c), the demand for bonds increases (but like $mm[d]$ not doubling), though the supply of bonds remains the same. Summing up the situation for the shifts from (o) to (1), we are left with an excess demand for the commodity ($i > s$), an excess supply of money, and an excess demand for bonds at interest rate $r(o)$.

If the rules of Walrasian markets are invoked, the excess demand for the commodity results in a rise in price, and the excess demand for bonds provokes a fall in the interest rate (bond prices rise). Now all schedules must shift in response to the price change. The real money supply and the real supply of bonds move toward their respective vertical axes (decline), saving increases for any interest rate, and the investment schedule falls. All of these shifts again represent the work of the wealth effect, generated in this second phase by a rise in p, as opposed to an increase in $M*$ in the previous phase. The second wave of shifts is noted as (2).

Now the neutrality hypothesis can be tested. If money is neutral, then the increase, $M*$ to $2M*$, should imply an increase of price, from $p(o)$ to $2p(o)$, with no alteration in any real variable. Let the schedules marked (2) be associated with $2p(o)$. They cannot logically be associated with the same equilibrium interest rate that began the exercise ($r[0]$). Consider saving and investment. The schedule $ss(o)$ was implied by $y(o)$, $p(o)$, and $q(o)$, when the latter was the following,

$$q(o) = \frac{M*}{p(o)} + \frac{B*}{r(o)p(o)}$$

However, $ss(2)$ is set by an altered wealth effect. We know by assumption that schedules noted by (2) are associated with price level $2p(o)$. Since neutrality cannot be counted on, the interest rate associated with price level $2p(o)$ is unknown at this point. Let this unknown interest rate be designated as $r(?)$.

$$q(2) = \frac{2m*}{2p(o)} + \frac{B*}{r(?)2p(o)}$$

In order that no real variables be changed, it is necessary that $r(?) = r(o)$ *and* that $q(o) = q(2)$, since both of these are real variables. If one sets $q(o) = q(2)$, and attempts to solve for r, one discovers that real wealth is unchanged only if the interest rate falls. If the interest rate falls, other real variables must also change. Money is not neutral and the reason should be clear – the nominal supply of money has doubled, but nominal wealth has not ($B*$ is unchanged). No shifting of the schedules can bring one back to equilibrium at the initial interest rate after a change in the money supply.

Pursuing further the position associated with a doubled price level, one should note that it would involve a shift in the real money supply back to its original position, $m(o) = M*/p(o) = 2M*/2p(o)$. However, the doubling of the money supply and the price level does not leave q unchanged, for $B*/2rp(o)$ is less than $B*/rp(o)$. With real wealth lower than before, the demand for money falls compared with the initial situation. Over in the bond market real supply has fallen, cut in half by the doubled price level. Thus, if the price level were to double, the result would be an excess supply of the commodity and money, and an excess demand for bonds.

If the reader finds this sequence confusing, the situation can be summarised more simply: from an initial position of general equilibrium, the nominal money supply and the price level double. By definition the real supply of bonds must be cut in half, but the real demand for bonds declines by less than this due to the wealth effect. Thus, the impact of a change in the money supply on the bond market alone requires a fall in the interest rate, for supply has decreased relatively to demand (recall that the demand for bonds is *negatively* related to the interest rate).

The final equilibrium position is shown in Figure 7.2, with the relevant schedules noted by (3). An increase in the nominal supply of money has provoked a wave of once-and-for-all changes. While involving full employment, the new equilibrium bears little similarity to the initial position. The rate of interest is lower, as are the market-clearing quantities of m and b. In this model the wealth effect ensures that money cannot be neutral. Each equilibrium is set by the

nominal values of money and bonds. In the next chapter the implication of lost neutrality is explored. Here one can note that, among
other things, it is no longer true that a change in the nominal money
supply results in an equi-proportionate change in the price level. The
quantity theory parable does not hold, in the short, long or any run.

Thus betrayed in the financial markets by the mechanism invoked
to save the model from Keynes's inconsistency between saving and
investment and the liquidity trap, some neoclassical economists have
sought a solution that could salvage neutrality. One such is to suggest
that bonds be 'indexed'. That is, let us assume that bonds (or equities
in their place) are issued such that their real value is independent of
the price level (price of the single commodity, to be precise). This is
not a serious hypothesis, for it amounts to nothing more than invoking an arbitrary institutional assumption to extract oneself from the
undesired results of one's own logic. But even if one allows this
convenient assumption, it must be accompanied by further assumptions even more arbitrary. In order that indexed bonds serve their
purpose of rendering q impervious to changes in p, the nominal stock
of bonds $B*$ must be independent of the nominal stock of money. To
assume this to be the case contradicts both the theory and practice of
monetary policy. In advanced capitalist countries the typical instrument used by the state to affect the money supply is the buying and
selling of state bonds. A sale of bonds by the monetary authorities
allegedly has the affect of reducing the money supply by taking
money out of the hands of people and banks,[4] while the purchase of
bonds has the opposite effect.[5] An apparently simple parable –
increase the money supply and the price level increases proportionately – has proved impossible to sustain in a model in which Walrasian market-clearing full employment equilibrium is guaranteed.

7.4 NON-NEUTRALITY AND THE WEALTH EFFECT

It is worthwhile to labour the last point of the previous section, for
one can come across statements in the neoclassical literature suggesting that neutrality is an inherent property of money, directly deriv-
able from first principles or common sense. For example, Harry G.
Johnson, one of the most distinguished monetary theorists of his
generation, summed up the neutrality issue as follows:

Money's property of being desired for its ability to purchase other things results in the property of homogeneity whereby an equal proportionate change in the nominal quantity of money and prices results in no change in behavior. (Johnson, 1972, p. 55)

Despite its distinguished source, this statement is false. It suggests that the assumption of valueless money is sufficient unto itself to make money neutral. Or put more explicitly, it asserts that if a model is constructed faithful to the property that money is 'desired for its ability to purchase other things', money will be neutral in that model. Yet the model of the previous section was constructed faithful to that property and money most certainly is not neutral in it. Neutrality is not an inherent property of valueless money, no matter what presumptions are made about the motivation for desiring it. Neutrality cannot be deduced from first principles. Rather, neutrality or non-neutrality emerge from the interaction of the variables in a model. One or the other results as the end-product of general equilibrium solution, and the theorist is proceeding invalidly if he or she assumes neutrality at the outset. Neutrality cannot be assumed. This last point will loom large in the discussion below of the New Classical Economics.

As a final point, a warning needs to be issued with regard to the wealth effect. While the wealth effect ensures that there can be a full employment solution to the neoclassical macro model as presented here, it cannot be taken as a definitive refutation of the liquidity trap and the inconsistency between saving and investment. The models dealt with in this chapter have an extremely important characteristic, namely that no creditor ever loses the value of a loan; i.e., debtors do not go bankrupt. It is to be recalled that the models have treated private assets as 'inside' – for each credit there is a debit. If the possibility of bankruptcy is allowed, private assets are no longer 'inside' wealth; or, to be more precise, they are at some moments (when no bankruptcies occur) and not at others. Bankruptcies represent a potentially powerful effect which renders inappropriate the assumption that changes in the price level result in no distributional shifts between debtors and creditors.[6] Further, one would expect that the distributional effects of bankruptcies in general would be to reduce the real wealth of agents. If this is accepted as a reasonable working hypothesis, then the wealth effect is seriously undermined. It is precisely the process which activates the wealth effect – falling prices – which is closely associated with waves of bankruptcies in the real world. The wealth effect, like the real balance effect, might be thought of as a convenient logical solution to nagging problems in an abstract model rather than a mechanism of practical significance. However, this book focuses upon the logic of the neoclassical model, and in subsequent discussion the wealth effect will be taken at face value.

Part II

A Critique of Self-adjusting Full Employment

8 Neutrality and Full Employment

8.1 LOGIC OF THE MODELS SUMMARISED

In the previous three chapters four versions of the neoclassical macro model were presented, along with a running critique. In this chapter a synthesis of the various critiques is provided by focusing upon the neutrality of money and full employment. The discussion is more easily followed by first providing a concise summary of the central features of the various models previously considered, found in Table 8.1.

The differences among the four models can be briefly stated. Only in the first is there a strict dichotomy between real and monetary variables. The dichotomy is a false one due to the clash of Walras' Law and the quantity theory of money over the excess demand for money when the model is not in general equilibrium. In the second model this inconsistency is eliminated, but the introduction of the real balance effect results in no real solution as such. Money is strictly neutral, so the values of real variables are not altered in full employment equilibrium by a change in the nominal money supply alone. However, unlike in the False Dichotomy variant, the nominal money supply enters directly to determine the value of each real variable. Real and nominal variables cannot be partitioned. Further, the model is of heuristic interest only. Central to its operation is the wealth-holding of agents, but no interest-bearing assets are included.

The third model solves the problem of the inconsistency between Walras' Law and the Quantity theory in a different way. Here interest-yielding bonds are introduced, so the demand for money is interest-elastic. Again there is no separation between real and monetary variables, though money is strictly neutral for full employment equilibria. Due to the possibility of an inconsistency between saving and investment and the liquidity trap, full employment is a special case in this model. In the final model the logical barriers to full employment are eliminated, but the introduction of the wealth effect renders money non-neutral. There is no real solution.

In Table 8.2 the summary of the neoclassical models is continued, with selected theoretical predictions listed down the left-hand side,

Table 8.1　Summary of the characteristics of the neoclassical model

Category/ model	(1) False Dichotomy	(2) 'Classical with RBE'	(3) Complete Keynesian'	(4) Keynesian with WE
Commodity market	$c = c(y)$ $i = i(r)$	$c = c(y, M*/p)$ $i = i(r)$	$c = c(y)$ $i = i(r)$	$c = c(y, q)$ $i = i(y, q)$
Money market	$M(s) = M*$ $M(d) = vpy$	$M(s) = M*$ $M(d) = vpy$ $+ fM*$	$M(s) = M*$ $M(d) = vpy$ $+ [h - jr]$	$M(s) = M*$ $M(d) = vpy$ $+ M(r, q)$
Automatic full employment?	**No** inconsistency i, s	**Yes** RBE acts on c	**No** inconsistency i, s; Liq. Trap	**Yes** q acts on c, i and $M(d)$
Neutrality of money?	**Yes**	**Yes**	**Yes**	**No**
Comment	Logically invalid, WL and QT clash	Heuristic value only, no bonds, requires 'outside' $M*$	Not to be confused with the model of *The GT*	Requires 'outside' $M*$ and $B*$

Notation

QT　　– Quantity theory of money
RBE　– Real balance effect
GT　　– *The General Theory of Employment, Interest and Money*
WE　　– Wealth effect
WL　　– Walras' Law
c　　– consumption in units of the single commodity
i　　– investment in units of the single commodity
y　　– income in units of the single commodity
r　　– the interest rate
p　　– price of the single commodity
M　　– money, $M(s)$, money supply; $M(d)$, demand for money; $M*$, level of money supply
B　　– nominal interest yield on bonds
q　　– real wealth, $[M* + B*/r]/p$

followed in subsequent columns by analytical commentary. The predictions refer to the relationship between variables when displaced by clearing of the labour market from an initial position of less than full employment. In other words, the predictions indicate what happens to various variables according to the logic of the model when one moves from a lower to a higher level of employment. The

Table 8.2   Theoretical predictions of the neoclassical model (from an initial position of less than full employment)

The model predicts	Necessary conditions	Casual empiricism
1. Real wages fall when employment rises	Diminishing returns with a one product production function (see note below)	Real wages rise when employment rises
2. Money wages fall when employment rises	As above, and exogenously given money supply, $M(s)$	Money wages rise or remain constant when employment rises
3. Price level falls when output rises (nominal value of output can *fall* in models 3 and 4)	Diminishing returns, one product, exogenous $M(s)$	Price level rises or constant when employment rises
4. Interest rate falls when output rises	Interest-elastic investment, exogenous $M(s)$ (r-elastic $M(d)$ in models 3 and 4)	Interest rate rises or is constant when output rises

Note: Diminishing returns requires single product aggregate production function for reasons given in Section 2.1 and also implied by the Capital Controversy, presented in Chapter 10.

predictions refer to an 'other things equal' situation; i.e., the parameters of all functions remain the same and exogenous variables ($M*$ and $B*$) do not change. As pointed out before, the neoclassical model predicts than an increase in employment is associated with lower real wages, lower money wages, a lower price level, and a lower interest rate. These predictions are contingent upon the assumptions of a single commodity production function (ensuring diminishing returns) and an exogenous money supply.

Casual empiricism suggests that these predictions are rarely realised in practice (final column of the table). One's experience and an inspection of short-run economic statistics published by governments suggest that when employment rises, real wages, money wages, the price level, and the interest rate all tend to rise also, not to fall.[1] Keynes made much of these empirical relationships when counselling against money wage cuts as a solution to unemployment in the 1930s.[2] That one's casual or even systematic observations do not correspond to the predictions of a theory does not in itself represent a refutation of that theory. As Marx said, were it possible to deduce correction explanations from observation alone, economic and social theory would be unnecessary.

However, the divergence of economic relations as they appear from economic relations as they are predicted to occur is troublesome for neoclassical analysis for two reasons. First, with regard to competing economic paradigms neoclassical writers are quick to apply the test of empiricism. For example, in histories of economic thought by neoclassical writers one finds the assertion that Marx's theory can be judged false because it predicts a falling standard of living for the working class as capitalism develops and this has not occurred; that it predicts the profit rate to decline secularly and this also has not occurred; that labour cannot be the sole source of value because this would imply that labour-intensive industries would be more profitable than capital-intensive ones, which is not systematically the case; and so on. It would be equally valid for a critic of neoclassical theory to assert that IS–LM analysis is wrong, because in general expansions of employment are associated with upward pressure on prices, while the theory predicts the opposite.

Second, the test of empiricism has a particular sting to it for neoclassical theory because the very concepts which the theory employs are so counter-empirical, bearing little relation to observed economic categories. Two of these, homogeneous output and the money supply, have been dealt with at length. Neoclassical practitioners would no doubt argue that as abstract and ideal as their concepts are, these are constantly subjected to empirical test. The mainstream journals are full of empirical studies, not to mention hundreds of books and monographs published every year. However, the method of these empirical studies is to first formulate a model incorporating neoclassical concepts, then to see if the subsequent statistical results sustain the predictions of the model. This procedure is not a test of the validity of the model, but only an exercise to see if there exists a formulation of the model which certain empirical evidence will not refute. To take an analogy, the Ptolemaic model of a geocentric planetary system was rendered by its adherents to be consistent with the observed movement of the planets, moon, and sun in the sky. This was possible because the Ptolemaic system can be treated as a mathematical analogue of a heliocentric system. Notwithstanding its 'empirical validity', the geocentric model of the solar system is wrong.

While all theories must have an empirical analogue, this analogue does not establish their validity. Key to establishing validity is nature and adequacy of the concepts the theory employs and the logical consistency of the conclusions reached from those concepts. In the preceding chapters the basic neoclassical concepts were challenged on grounds of internal consistency. Below we take the process further and consider the two key conclusions based upon those concepts.

8.2   THE SIGNIFICANCE OF NEUTRALITY

After considerable treatment of standard neclassical models, it has been established that the clearing of markets (instantaneously flexible price, wage, and interest rate) results in a full employment equilibrium if the model includes a wealth effect. However, inclusion of a wealth effect renders money non-neutral. Only in a model with no financial assets other than money can neutrality be consistent with full employment with no qualifications. One might at this point legitimately say, 'so what?'. Presumably the central issue is whether a capitalist economy tends automatically to full employment. If this can be demonstrated, surely the neutrality question is icing-on-the-cake; a bit more than a curiosity, but not much more.

However, one is dealing here with considerably more than a minor point. While certainly the major issue is whether a capitalist economy has a natural tendency to full employment, this is inseparably linked with the issue of the neutrality of money. Within the debate over neutrality, arcane and esoteric as it may seem, lurks a powerful ideological message. With regard to the fundamental question of whether state intervention in a capitalist economy is justified, the issue of the neutrality of money has importance equal to that of the hypothesis that there is an automatic tendency to full employment.

That money is neutral with respect to real variables is the keystone of what might be called the 'naturalistic' view of capitalist society. Always implicit and frequently explicit in neoclassical theory is the assertion that economic life is governed by laws which have the status and inexorability of the laws of physics and chemistry. These laws are timeless and objective; i.e., they exist independently of whether one perceives and understands them. Central to this naturalistic view of economic phenomena is the dichotomy between real and monetary variables, and, therefore, the relationship between a barter economy and a money economy.

To develop the argument, let us assume for the moment that the real world of economic relations is characterised by (1) an automatic tendency towards full employment through market clearing, with no exceptions; and (2) that money is neutral. If this is the case, then there exists a combination of real variables at full employment which is unique.[3] Being unique, it is the *only* set of real variables for which output/income and employment will be at a maximum. All other sets of real variables will result in lower output/income and employment. Ignoring distributional effects and presuming more output/income to be desired compared with less, the full employment solution is not only unique, but desirable (optimal) above all others. Now, if one goes a step further and presumes that there is a tendency for 'unregulated'[4] markets to bring about this unique and most desirable set of real variables automatically, then there is no place for state intervention. At best, the state can only attempt to do what the process of market clearing would bring about automatically. At worst – and considerably more likely by this line of argument – intervention by the state will prevent market clearing from generating the optimal result.

In this conception of a unique and optimal full employment solution, state intervention is characteristically referred to as creating 'distortions'; i.e., creating arbitrary conditions that 'distort' the economy from its natural, optimal equilibrium. These distortions may take many forms. Excessive state borrowing will create 'crowding' in money markets, transferring credit from the private sector to the state. State expenditures will also redistribute resources from private hands to the state. Only if the state can limit its action to the minimum, and at the same time have a purely neutral impact on private decision making, will its behaviour not reduce the general welfare.

An absolutely necessary (though not sufficient) condition for this anti-interventionist argument to hold *is that money be neutral*. If money is not neutral, then the full employment solution is not unique. In the second model of the previous chapter $y(e)$ and $l(e)$, full employment output/income and employment itself, are unique (i.e., there is no other level of employment for which the labour market is cleared),[5] but these values are consistent with an infinitive variation in the other real variables. Put another way, *there is no real solution (or system) as such*. By changing the money supply, 'the monetary authorities' (i.e. the state) can produce an infinite variation upon the full employment theme, none of which can be singled out as preferable to others without explicit value judgements. The free market does not produce the most desired result; indeed, without state action it produces no result at all since the state determines the money supply.

For example, the state might wish to achieve a higher rate of economic growth, and could do this by increasing the money supply, which would drive down the rate of interest and increase investment absolutely and relatively to consumption.[6] Alternatively, the state might seek to change the functional distribution of income between wages and profits (the latter not distinguished from interest in the neoclassical model). This could be done again by acting upon the interest rate and the money wage via the money supply.[7] More fundamental than these examples is the point that when money is not neutral, all full employment equilibria are arbitrary. Each is unique only with respect to a given money supply and a given supply of bonds. *State intervention (via M* and B*) is one of the defining characteristics of every equilibrium.* Non-neutrality of money renders the debate over the desirability of state intervention moot. The relevant issue becomes, what form of intervention and to what extent?

Fundamentally, the argument that the natural forces of the free market generate an optimal solution which governments distort at the cost of the general welfare rests upon a presumption of the neutrality of money. Neutrality is indeed a thin thread by which to hang such an ideologically powerful message. Granting all assumptions, neutrality could not be justified in the simple classical model because of the inconsistency between Walras' Law and the quantity theory (see Chapter 4). Once the money market includes the interest rate, the theorist is forced to chose between a guaranteed employment solution and neutrality, the one excluding the other.

In this context one might recall that Patinkin claimed that the real balance effect was the *sine qua non* of all monetary theory. Neoclassical economists have tended to reject this as a grandiose assertion.[8] Yet there is a sense in which Patinkin was correct, for the narrowly-defined real balance effect (referring to money only) produces the only model in which neutrality and full employment can be unambiguously combined. This is an excellent example of the cliché, 'the exception that proves the rule'. A model with no bonds is too restrictive to be taken as more than a heuristic exercise, even among neoclassical theorists.

8.3   FULL EMPLOYMENT FURTHER INVESTIGATED

While the hallmarks of the standard textbook version of the neoclassical model are the neutrality of money and an automatic tendency to full employment in the absence of 'arbitrary' constraints (inflexible money wages), it has been demonstrated that the two are not in general compatible. This incompatibility was demonstrated in the previous chapter, where most attention was focused upon states of full employment equilibria. At this point a critical eye is turned to the concept of full employment itself; or rather, that concept as it manifests itself in neoclassical analysis. It was shown that with the introduction of the wealth effect, it is possible within the synthesis paradigm to reach a value judgement that unemployment of a portion of the labour force must always be 'voluntary', in the sense that unemployment of labour can only occur in logic if money wages do not fall to clear the labour market. Since employers might reasonably be assumed not to oppose lower wages in the simplest case, the cause for wages being too high must come from the implicit or explicit actions of workers, individually or collectively. In a word, workers must accept the 'blame' for unemployment.

While the logic of the neoclassical model seems to grind inexorably to this conclusion, the issue is not as cut-and-dried as it may seem. In the first instance, it is open to question whether the neoclassical model can assert any conclusions about unemployment at all. The difficulty which arises might be called 'the case of the missing excess demand'. If one looks back to the 'complete Keynesian model' with rigid money wages (Chapter 6), one notes that less than full employment equilibrium is associated with equilibrium in the commodity market and the money market: saving equalled investment and the demand for money equalled the supply, with the bond market implicitly in equilibrium. Therefore, rigid money wages yielded a solution in which the labour market was characterised by excess supply, but the excess supplies and demands in all other markets were zero (not only in sum, but individually). Such a situation is inconsistent with Walras' Law, which requires that the sum of excess demands and excess supplies be zero for the system as a whole. It would appear that even 'voluntary' unemployment – employment resulting from rigid money wages – is logically inconsistent with the neoclassical market-clearing mechanism (Walras' Law) which is so central to the entire theory. This logical difficulty has preoccupied some neoclassical economists, provoking a search for the missing excess demand to match the excess supply of labour.[9] While *ad hoc* solutions to this difficulty can be produced,[10] the result has a decidedly jerry-rigged appearance.

The basic difficulty is that the model presupposes full employment. This presupposition arises from the nature of Walras' Law, which should now be briefly reviewed. At one level Walras' Law is the salvation of the neoclassical model by ensuring that the clearing of individual markets is consistent with global market-clearing. The elimination of excess demand and excess supply in one market does not in-and-of-itself move the neoclassical model toward general equilibrium; on the contrary, the clearing of one market can make full employment impossible to achieve (see discussion of false trading in Section 3.4). Walras' Law avoids this difficulty. As counter-factual as its mythical auctioneer may be, no systematic tendency to full employment is logically possible without the Law, no matter what other assumptions are made.

On another level, Walras' Law is a curse upon the neoclassical model, for it cannot be applied to any stable equilibrium except one of full employment. If the labour market is not cleared (due to rigid money wages), then the Law requires that some other market also not be cleared. *But only in the labour market is non-clearing consistent with a stable solution.* Should it be the commodity market which is nominated to balance the excess supply in the labour market with an excess demand, then the situation is logically inconsistent: an excess demand for the single commodity, provoking a rise in price and output/income, implies that the money wage is *too low* (a labour shortage), contradicting the initial situation of excess labour supply and rendering the downward inflexibility of the money wage irrelevant. The commodity market must be rejected, for the only possibility there consistent with unemployment is excess supply which makes the logical difficulty worse (two unanswered excess supplies instead of one).

The only other candidate is the money market, but disequilibrium there would seem inconsistent with equilibrium in the commodity market. If the commodity market is in equilibrium (on the IS curve), then both output/income and the interest rate are in equilibrium unless disturbed elsewhere. Since the nominal supplies of money and bonds are exogenous and the demands for money and bonds are set by precisely the variables rendered stable in the commodity market (the interest rate and level of income/output), the 'elsewhere' referred to above cannot be the the the financial markets.

The fundamental sources of the difficulties reflected in the logical problem of Walras' Law at less than full employment are two. First, in the neoclassical model the labour market is only formally linked to the other markets. As long as the demand for and supply of labour are specified in terms of the commodity ('real') wage, the positions of these schedules must always be independent of what happens in all other markets. This first source of difficulty arises from carrying forward a labour market analysis appropriate to a barter economy into models in which 'real' solutions either are no longer relevant or do not exist at all.

The second source of difficulty arises from the treatment of the commodity which workers sell. Formally, the commodity workers sell is no different from the other commodities in the model. However, only in the labour market can an arbitrary limitation upon the value of the price variable prevent market clearing. Consider the consequences of rigidity of the other two price variables in the model, the price of the single commodity and the interest rate. If price is inflexible downward, the commodity market will clear (saving will be equated to investment) by a change in the level of output/income, which will also imply a change in the interest rate (movement along the IS curve). The money market will be cleared in the same manner. If the interest rate is inflexible, income will again equilibrate the commodity and money markets. While an inflexible price or inflexible interest rate will produce excess supply or excess demand in the labour market, neither can result in a stable situation in which there is excess supply or demand in the commodity or financial markets.

While the discussion so far has been somewhat complex, the fundamental difficulty can be stated clearly. In a system governed by Walras' Law, equilibrium is achieved by the adjustment of price variables to notional (full employment) supplies and demands. No points on demand and supply schedules except those of full employment are ever achieved *even in theory* (false trading prohibited). In contrast to this, a less than full employment equilibrium, even reached according to strict neoclassical rules, is a non-Walrasian position, for it is by definition a position of false trading. It is invalid to conclude from the neoclassical model that unemployment is 'voluntary', or to assign blame to workers for demanding excessive money wages. These judgements are invalid because the neoclassical model, firmly grounded in Walras' Law, has no analysis of unemployment at all, be it voluntary or involuntary.[11]

The basic problem can be traced back to the nature of Walras' Law itself. It is singularly inappropriate for the purpose assigned to it in the neoclassical model, though absolutely necessary. Walras formulated his law for a market situation during which no production occurred; i.e., commodity supplies are given throughout the trading period. By contrast, the neoclassical macro model purports to analyse a situation in which the output of the single commodity is a decision variable. In the original Walrasian system agents were precluded from manifesting their disappointment by varying the quantity of commodities they brought to the market. In the neoclassical macro model firms come to the market with nothing, for all would agree that labourers must be hired and set to work before there is anything to sell.

The Walrasian model of Walras never pretended to consider the question of what portion of the population might be gainfully employed. Walras sought a solution to the relative prices of commodities in a many-commodity system in which the supplies of these commodities was given. By the criterion of logic, Walras can be judged to have provided a determinate answer to the question he posed, though it is difficult to conjure up an actual situation which corresponds to his solution. Neoclassical theorists assign a quite different task to the hypothetical Walrasian market day and to Walras' Law. Ignoring the central issue posed by Walras (relative commodity prices) by presuming a one commodity world, they attempt to apply Walrasian analysis to a situation in which the quantity of the single commodity is variable. It is hardly surprising that Walras' principles prove inconsistent in all cases save when the supply of the single commodity is in effect fixed (i.e. at a unique point of full employment equilibrium).

Having said all of this, does it not remain the case, with or without Walras' Law, that an excessive level of money wages will result in unemployment? A commonsense argument would seem to serve as well as the esoterica of Walrasian general equilibrium: if money wages are high, labour costs to firms are high, and this induces firms to hire less labour than they would were money wages lower. But once one abandons a Walrasian world, it is not at all obvious that lower wages would increase employment. Causality as it appears to the individual capitalist may not be valid for all capitalists taken together. Lower wages reduce the demand for commodities, and if all markets do not clear simultaneously the level of employment could fall. In the absence of the strict discipline of the Walrasian auctioneer, the impact of lower wages on employment is an empirical question, about which no general theoretical conclusion can be drawn. While neoclassical analysis can produce a formally elegant model of full employment, it has no theory of unemployment. This conclusion seems startling for an analysis which offers such definitive prescriptions for economic policy; none the less it is true. The absence of a theory of unemployment is why neoclassical theory, like its 'classical' forerunner, is a special case, and why Keynes by dealing with situations of less than full employment contended that his was the general theory of employment, interest and money.

8.4   THE 'UNEMPLOYMENT' OF CAPITAL?

Even should we ignore the logical difficulties associated with Walras' Law, the synthesis treatment of unemployment presents a troubling anomaly. As shown in Chapter 2, neoclassical theory treats output/income as the result of the combination of capital and labour. These two inputs into the production (value added) function are treated as being strictly analogous. In contemporary literature the analytical similarity of the two is emphasised by use of the terms 'capital services' and 'labour services', each of which is seen as flowing from assets (physical and human capital). But in the neoclassical macroeconomic model the strict similarity between capital and labour as inputs seems to breakdown in a dramatic way – in the short run model labour can be unemployed but capital apparently cannot. Investigation of this apparent anomaly provides insights into the synthesis model, as well as anticipating the post-Keynesian critique of the neoclassical model which follows in Chapters 10 and 11.

Before proceeding further with the consideration of the possibility of capital being unemployed, it must be stressed that we do not refer to under-utilisation of capacity, which is a non-neoclassical concept. Capacity utilisation refers to a situation in which part of plant and machinery lie idle because of insufficient demand for the commodity which that plant and equipment produce. Because of the assumption of substitution between capital and labour, demand conditions cannot induce an individual maximising capitalist to use less than all of the available capital stock in a neoclassical world. In the short run, capital costs are fixed, so for any level of anticipated output unit costs will be minimised by minimising variable (labour) costs, which with a given wage rate implies hiring as few workers as possible. Competition among firms, requiring each to sell at lowest achievable unit cost (and all neoclassical firms are assumed identical), ensures that the entire capital stock will be utilised by whatever labour is hired.

Let us attempt to treat labour and capital strictly analogously, a manner of treatment characteristic of the neoclassical model in general. In doing so one would expect that if a real wage above the full employment equilibrium rate results in the unemployment of labour, then a rate of return on capital above the equilibrium level would result in unemployment of capital. Consider the possibility illustrated in Figure 8.1. In part 8.1(a) are drawn the production isoquants, showing contour lines, each representing a constant level of output in the two-dimensional capital–labour space. The capital stock is fixed at $k*$ and the labour supply at $l*$, and if the labour market clears, equilibrium full employment output is $e*$. The top left-hand quadrant shows the 'demand curve for capital', with the marginal product of capital equated to the rate of return, r,[12] since maximising behaviour implies $MP(k) = r$, just as it implies $MP(l) = w$. Figure 8.1(d) shows the labour market, which is familiar to us. Finally, in Figure 8.1(c) we give the ratio of the commodity wage to the rate of return, or the 'factor price ratio'. Equilibrium with full employment of labour *and of capital* is associated with $r(e)$ and $w(e)$. The first point to note is the sense in which capital is fixed and labour is variable. Because it has been assumed that the labour supply is invariant with respect to its only determining influence, the commodity wage, both factors are fixed in the sense that their potentially available quantities are given. In what sense, then, is capital fixed and labour variable (being the manner in which neoclassical theory treats the two in the short run)?

This question can be answered by proceeding in the attempt to treat capital and labour in a strictly analogous manner in Figure 8.1. Assume that the equilibrium money wage is some $W(e)$ and workers as a whole refuse to sell their services for less than $W(o)$, which is greater than $W(e)$. As we saw in the previous chapter, given the money supply, $W(o)$ will imply a commodity wage, $w(o) = W(o)/p(o)$, which is higher than the full employment equilibrium commodity wage, $w(e)$. These two commodity wage levels are shown in Figure 8.1(d). With employment lower at $l(o)$, the marginal product of capital schedule shifts inwards, and the rate of return falls. All of the values noted by (o) indicate the situation when rigid money wages result in the unemployment of labour while capital remains fully used.

Now, let the situation be reversed, indicated by values (1). In this

Figure 8.1 'Unemployment' of capital in the short run

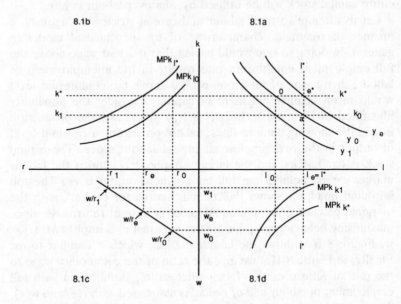

case, capitalists demand a certain rate of return, $r(1)$, the consequence of which is to leave part of the capital stock 'unemployed', $k* - k(1)$. With the employment of capital at level $k(1)$, the marginal product of labour shifts towards the origin, and full employment of labour is achieved at a lower commodity wage than before, $w(1)$. As said, this particular 'thought experiment' in which capital is not completely used is not treated in neoclassical theory. In this case, neoclassical theorists are quite correct, for the 'experiment' is nonsensical. In attempting to treat labour and capital as strictly analogous and parallel factors of production, one reaches a nonsensical result because the two factors are not analogous and parallel.

It is worth repeating that the logical sense of unemployed labour in the short run, on the one hand, and the logical nonsense of capital being unemployed in the short run, on the other, has nothing to do with the available quantity of one factor being fixed and the other being variable. In the model being analysed, the supplies of both factors are exogenously given. This is the same treatment as in the previous chapter, where there was no difficulty producing conditions under which part of the fixed labour supply was unemployed[13] (no difficulty ignoring the nagging problem of Walras' Law being violated out of full employment). Analysing labour as partially unemployed makes sense, but doing the same for capital does not because the nature of competition among workers is different from the competition among capitalists. If capitalists combine to administer a fixed market price, for example, individual capitalists who are initially a party to this agreement can gain by violating it. By under-selling the fixed price, the maverick can expand his or her market share and gain a larger profit than operating within the agreement. This fact of competition among capitalists tends to make coalitions unstable. However, a worker who is an employed member of a trade union that has negotiated a fixed wage can only lose by under-selling: he or she sells the capacity to work, not what he or she produces. This difference between competition among capitalists and among workers reflects capitalist *relations of ownership*.

Neoclassical theory reaches a profound truth when it ignores the possibility of unemployed capital, though for the wrong reason. As said, the neoclassical reason for treating capital as fully employed is that in the short run rational capitalist behaviour will dictate utilising the existing capital stock with whatever labour is available. The basic truth of this assertion arises from the fact that no exchange need occur for capital to be employed, while employment of labour requires a successful sale and purchase.

Here one must move from the world of imaginary models to the actual world of economic and social relations. The machinery and equipment available for use at any moment is the property of capitalists. It has already been exchanged and is in place, hence it is called the capital *stock*. The output resulting from the capital stock must eventually be sold profitably to justify continued use of machinery and equipment. However, the 'services' of capital associated with a given output are not for the most part exchanged, except implicitly as cost entries on a ledger.[14] Labour 'services' by contrast must be repeatedly exchanged, and unemployment results from the fact that workers do not own the means by which production is carried out and, therefore, must sell their working capacity in order to participate in the production process. Their motivation for this participation is that they lack the means to produce: they cannot directly provide themselves and their families with food, clothing, etc. In other words, workers can be unemployed because they must work for others (non-workers), and they must work for others because they lack the means which would enable them to work for themselves.

The relevance of this discussion to the neoclassical macro model is that it indicates the fundamental cause of unemployment: workers do not have direct access to the means by which production is carried out. Workers must first sell before they can work. The property relations of a capitalist economy are the fundamental cause of the phenomenon of the idleness of part of society's human resources. The use of the term 'capital services' tends to obscure this basic cause of unemployment by suggesting that labour and capital are strictly analogous in production and exchange, which they are not.

The property relations of a capitalist economy imply that the labour market is fundamentally different from the other markets in a capitalist economy. In every developed capitalist country the history of the labour movement has been the struggle to reduce competition among workers. By contrast, commodity and money markets are inherently competitive. Here we can note that neoclassical economists, particularly the more conservative, have always taken a sceptical view of arguments alleging systematic price-fixing through collusion by capitalists. Their argument is that such arrangements tend to break down under the pressure of competition from disgruntled sellers already in the market or potential competitors outside the market who are eager to enter when profits are high (as argued above). This argument has considerable empirical support as well as a sound basis in Ricardian and Marxian theory (see Weeks, 1982, ch. 6).

The asymmetry between capital and labour, which implicity manifests itself in the synthesis macro model in the manner indicated above, has not gone unnoticed by those who adhere to the general neoclassical paradigm. Leijonhufvud, whose critique of the neoclassical model is treated in Chapter 11, refers to the asymmetry as the 'transactions structure' of a money economy (Leijonhufvud, 1981 p. 90). His argument is that in a money economy characterised by self-employed craftsmen and farmers, unemployment would be impossible. Without employers there are no employed persons, thus no unemployed. The point is a profound one, rarely made explicit in mainstream economics.

9 Expectations and Full Employment

9.1 PERFECT, STATIC AND ADAPTIVE EXPECTATIONS

In recent years a new and according to some 'revolutionary' element has been added to the neoclassical macroeconomic model, the rational expectations hypothesis (REH). Closely associated with the REH is what has been called the new classical economics, which is our primary concern. While it was the members of the new classical economics school who were instrumental in introducing the REH into the economics profession, the REH is no longer theirs alone. It has been taken on board by many who call themselves Keynesians. In order to fully appreciate the implications of the REH, it is necessary to consider other neoclassical treatments of expectations which predated the REH.

Except in reference to Keynes's treatment of the demand for money, there was little explicit reference to expectations in the previous chapters. However, a particular treatment of expectations, 'perfect foresight', was present throughout under a different name. It should be recalled that the simultaneous clearing of all markets required a ban on false trading – all exchanges must be general equilibrium exchanges. The creation of an imaginary auctioneer to oversee trades served to enforce the prohibition against false trading. If the auctioneer is taken away, then market-clearing requires that each trader enforce upon herself or himself the discipline not to buy or sell at disequilibrium prices. A trader can only avoid 'false' prices by knowing the general equilibrium prices which will prevail when exchanges are made at the end of the day. In other words, traders must know without error what will happen in the future. Assuming an omniscient auctioneer is formally equivalent to presuming perfect foresight on the part of all traders. Implicitly or explicitly, pre-Keynesian general equilibrium analysis and much neoclassical analysis subsequent to Keynes assumed perfect foresight.

The objections to the perfect foresight hypothesis (PFH) are many. In the neoclassical literature one frequently finds the argument that the PFH is unsatisfactory because it is inconsistent with utility maximisation. In order to have perfect foresight, it is argued, one would have to amass more information than a rational agent would ever attempt. The gathering of information has a cost, and like any other commodity it will be 'purchased' (by money, time, or both) up to the point where its marginal benefit equals its marginal cost. This is not an intellectually serious argument, for it presupposes an impossibility; namely that with enough information one could obtain perfect foresight. The fundamental difference between the past and the future, upon which all can presumably agree, is that the past has occurred and the future has not. The only way to be absolutely sure about what will happen tomorrow is to wait for it to occur. Otherwise there would be no need for the word 'accident' as well as many others in a dictionary. On balance, assuming the existence of an omniscient auctioneer is preferable to assuming perfect foresight, since the former assumption incorporates no allusions to spurious realism. Perfect foresight is not a hypothesis at all in the strict sense, but an invoking of the impossible.

Alternatively, one can venture the static expectations hypothesis (SEH), in which it is assumed that agents act as if the future will be exactly like the present. This hypothesis at least meets the minimum test of credibility, and an example is the famous Cobweb solution to market clearing in comparative static analysis of a single market. Since it allows for False Trading, the SEH will not serve for general equilibrium models. A variation on the SEH is the adaptive expectations hypothesis (AEH), according to which agents determine their expectations of the future on the basis of experience of the past. Expectations in this case are 'adaptive' because as each period passes predictions of the future are adjusted in light of most recent experience. Past experience is not ignored, only discounted to some degree. The AEH results in less volatile models than the SEH for reasons that should be obvious. If a dramatic change occurs in the economy, an agent governed by the SEH will respond in an equally dramatic way, on the belief that the change will recur. An agent subject to the AEH will move more cautiously with behaviour partly governed by past trends and fluctuations. The AEH literally 'smoothes things out'. Perhaps the best known use of the AEH is by Friedman, in order to argue that monetary policy is ineffective in the long run.[1]

9.2   THE RATIONAL EXPECTATIONS HYPOTHESIS

The rational expectations hypothesis has swept away all before it. This is partly due to its fundamental difference from the other expectational hypotheses. In contrast to the other hypotheses which postulate stylised behaviour of economic agents within the context of formal, abstract models, the REH purports to specify the actual behaviour of agents with regard to real world influences. Specifically, it seeks to establish a relationship between agents' expectations and actual outcomes of the economic system. As a result of this differ-ence, the REH must be assessed against criteria different from those relevant for the other hypotheses. In the case of the first three, it is not valid to demand they satisfy the test of realism (though they should be credible), for they are purely logical exercises. In the case of the REH its own assumptions demand it to stand or fall on the test of realism.

The REH can be stated simply: (1) if economic and social relations are deterministic;[2] (2) if all aspects of these determinate relations are known (this complete knowledge of economic and social relations is referred to as the 'formal model' of the economy); (3) if economic agents form their predictions of the future upon this complete knowledge;[3] then (4) the predictions (expectations) formed in this manner will on average be correct and any divergence between anticipated and actual outcomes will be the result of purely random influences.

At the outset there are three serious difficulties with the REH. First, it presupposes a strict dichotomy between systematic and random influences which at best is a rather naïve and simplistic approach to causality. In effect, it asserts that what is known repre-sents the sum total of systematic influences and all other influences are by definition random events. This places an unbearable burden of identification upon theoretical analysis. Only if the theory has com-pletely and correctly specified all relevant behavioural relationships and estimated them correctly with unbiased data can the unexplained residual be considered purely random. To assert that this is possible even in principle shows considerable faith – arrogance, one might say – in one's knowledge of human affairs. It is the assertion that at some moment our knowledge of economic relations will be complete, which is considerably stronger than the assertion that it could be complete, itself a controversial scientific position.

But quite astounding is the REH assertion that a state of full and complete knowledge of the workings of the economy actually exists.[4] The view is that there exist 'the economic agent who fully under-stands how the economy actually operates' (Shaw, 1984, p. 52), having obtained this knowledge from the discoveries of economic science. This claim, that economics has revealed the true and complete operation of the capitalist economy, is of a type made by no other intellectual discipline, be it a social or a physical science. Indeed, the physical sciences, where new discoveries continuously challenge the existing body of accepted truth, are considerably more humble in their claims.[5] What is being alleged is the literal omniscience of neoclassical economic theory, that it has discovered all one needs to know about the economy at this moment in time. A cynic might say that the enthusiasm with which the profession has embraced the REH might in part be explained by the pleasing effect of the hypothesis upon the professional egos of economists. While the perfect foresight hypothesis postulated the impossibility of knowing events prior to their occurring, the REH posits the naïve incredibility of complete knowledge. It is also worth adding that if it is the case that economic science has in the 1980s reached the state of bliss in which it has correctly and completely modelled the capitalist economy, economists do not agree upon what that correct and complete model might be.[6] Relevant here is the old saying that if all the economists in the world were laid end-to-end, they would fail to reach a conclusion. Thus, on many grounds, scientific method,[7] state of knowledge, and the intense controversies within the economics profession, it simply is not credible to presume that a correct and complete model of the capitalist economy exists as a reference for economic agents.

Frequently when suggesting behaviour on the part of people which is *prima facie* incredible, neoclassical theory seeks to establish credibility through an 'as if . . .' statement. For example, in consumer theory it is argued that the analysis does not require that people know their utility functions and act to maximise them (subject to their budget constraint), but only behave 'as if they did'. A similar argument is advanced in the case of cost-minimising firms. The 'as if they did' treatment has been applied to the REH.[8] In the case of consumer theory, the 'as if' treatment can be justified on grounds that the assumption of utility maximisation is in any case tautological – any conceivable behaviour is consistent with utility maximisation, since one can always argue that the person in question would not have selected a particular action in the market had it not brought him or her the maximum marginal gain. In the case of the theory of the firm, one might argue that cost minimisation is forced upon capitalists by competition – those who do not behave in this manner are driven out of operation.

Neither of these justifications applies to the REH. Presuming people to have complete knowledge of the economy is not tautological, since the REH itself grants that even under the best of conditions some people will not behave as the REH predicts. Further, it is not correct to assume that mistakes in forecasting will necessarily lead people to close in on the correct model by trial and error, though some authors argue on this basis.[9] However, the argument that failing all else people can arrive at the correct model by trial and error is the last line of defence of the REH. This final defence assumes what it seeks to prove and is theoretically invalid.

First, let us consider the proposition that a rational agent could 'close in on' the correct model by noting discrepancies between his or her predictions and actual outcomes. To do this, first assume the world to be strictly deterministic and that the hypothetical agent *does* know the correct model. In such circumstances, the fact that each chronological event is unique (individual behaviour never repeats itself in precisely the same circumstances) would create no problem. A change in the tax rate on individuals, for example, would be correctly anticipated as having the same impact whether prices were rising or falling. If, however, one has the wrong model in mind, one cannot properly hold to the 'other things constant' assumption. One might sometimes generate the right prediction by accident or for the wrong reason. In any case one would be unable to distinguish between which forecasting errors were the result of wrong specification of the model and those which were the result of random influences displacing predictions made on the basis of a perfectly correct model. This problem with the 'trial and error' argument can be put another way. The REH itself implies that people's predictions will more often be off target than they will hit the bull's-eye; the hypothesis is that they will be correct on *average*. In order that a person reformulate his or her model on the basis of off-the-mark predictions, it must be known which deviations of predicted from actual outcomes are systematic modelling errors (in which case something must be done to the model to correct them), and which are only random deviations from the true mean (in which case nothing should be done to the model). Without this knowledge, the REH agent could well spend time reformulating a correct model or resting complacently in the belief that systematic errors were only random 'noise'.[10] One could successfully use trial and error as a method of establishing the correct model only if one knew the correct model in the first place.

Closely related to the above is the fact that *even in theory* each prediction made by the REH agents is a unique, 'one-off' exercise.

The REH agent is in effect operating with an econometric model estimated from historical data[11] (also incorporating some information about the future such as government policy changes). An elementary principle of econometrics is that the unbiased probability distributions of the estimated parameters of a model refer to *hypothetical* outcomes, for there is one and only one actual outcome, except in science fiction stories involving parallel worlds. No competent econometrician would argue that an econometric model could be arrived at through trial and error. On the contrary, the whole body of econometric theory denies such *ad hoc*-ery. We know in theory that there are no alternative outcomes for the rational agent to observe.[12] Yet it is such a theoretically invalid approach that is defended in the REH literature.

Using the REH in economic models involves what Coleridge called 'willing suspension of disbelief', which is a pleasant ingredient when reading fiction but of questionable appropriateness when constructing economic models. To give some spurious verisimilitude to the REH, its practitioners tend to employ extremely simplistic models – notwithstanding the initial assertion that agents are supposed to have complete and full knowledge of how the economy operates, and not merely some simple analogue. The policy implications of the REH, particularly those reached by the new classical economists, almost invariably follow from extremely simple and sometimes logically flawed False Dichotomy models.

9.3   THE NEW CLASSICAL ECONOMICS AND THE REH

The old (pre-Keynesian) classical economics was characterised by its faith that capitalist economies tended automatically to adjust to full employment equilibrium in some vaguely defined 'long-run' period with money strictly neutral. The new classical economics takes the same full employment-money neutral position, but argues that it applies to the short run. In other words, the new classicals argue that deviations from full employment equilibrium *in actual practice* will tend to be minor. The favourite situation considered within the REH hypothesis involves a presumption of aggregate money wage bargaining between capital and labour in a context in which the only change is that of an autonomous money supply.[13] The typical model has only three equations, an IS curve, an LM curve, and an aggregate supply of output curve.[14] The last of these is specified in terms of a single commodity.[15] The fact that most workers do not know the 'true' model is brushed aside by the contention that their trade union representatives have done the homework to arrive at full and complete knowledge.[16] On the other side of the table, capital is presumed to have knowledge of the same model linking the nominal variables in the economy to the real ones. Let us suspend disbelief (ignoring for example that economists cannot agree on how the economy operates) and inspect how this simplistic model is used in the hands of the new classical economists.

As said, assume an aggregate wage bargain in which both sides to the bargain possess the unique complete formal model of how the economy works. Further, assume that all prices are flexible, so that at the time of the wage bargain the commodity market and labour market are in equilibrium. The assumption of equilibrium involves the introduction of a concept central to the new classical economics, 'the natural rate of unemployment' (and its close companion, 'the natural rate of output'). The two concepts require some scrutiny. Here one has the naturalistic tendency of neoclassical economics in its most blatant manifestation. By whatever definition, unemployment is not 'natural' and use of the term is purely ideological. As argued in Chapter 8, the necessary condition for the existence of unemployment is that workers do not own the means by which production is carried out. If they did, they would have no need to offer their services for sale in the first instance. One may think that capitalism provides the best of all worlds, but workers without property is no more natural and ordained by nature than slavery was.

Second, by the definition used in the new classical economics unemployment certainly cannot be natural. In the abstract, the 'natural' rate is defined as the rate of unemployment which prevails when the labour market is in equilibrium. Since equilibrium is an ideal state which the actual economy only approximates, equilibrium unemployment is also an ideal concept. Michelangelo's David may be a beautiful representation of the human figure, but it is not a natural one. Third, the empirical manifestation of unemployment cannot be natural in the sense of having been generated by forces of nature – by some Smithian 'invisible hand' – outside the evolution of human beings. As an empirical category, the 'natural rate of unemployment' is supposed to refer to those people who voluntarily chose to be without employment. The 'natural rate' hypothesis explains such a choice by people on the basis of optimising behaviour.[17] For example, a person may chose not to work at the prevailing wage because the cost of relocating to take an available job may be too great, or the prevailing wage may lie below the worker's customary wage, making it rational to wait some period of time in hope of a better offer materialising. Such decisions are crucially influenced by the institutions of society, such as the level and duration of unemployment compensation, access to retraining programmes, and discrimination on the basis of sex, age and ethnicity. Indeed, the new classical economists point to unemployment compensation as being in part the cause of 'voluntary' unemployment. These factors can be changed by legislation and government decree. What sense does it make to call a rate of unemployment 'natural' when it can be altered by passing a law or winning a class action suit in a court?

It might be thought that much is being made out of a purely semantic issue. However, there is a fundamental theoretical issue here. The term, 'the natural rate of unemployment', as it is used by the new classical economists is nothing other than *full employment equilibrium*. To call it what it is, full employment equilibrium, is to identify it clearly as an ideal concept, a product of an abstract economic model which incorporates a number of extremely problematical concepts, such as the aggregate production function and an exogenous money supply. Full employment in the sense of there being no one who wishes to work at the going wage but cannot find employment may not exist outside of the arcane models of neoclassical economists. It is a *hypothesis*.[18] Invoking the word 'natural' reflects an attempt to repackage an extremely dubious concept to make it more acceptable. The repackaging has been a success. The term has gained wide respectability within the economics profession despite the objections of a number of prominent neoclassical theorists.[19]

But let us for the moment suspend disbelief, accept the 'natural rate of unemployment', and investigate the REH–new classical economics wage bargaining story. To avoid misrepresenting the story, we shall follow closely a standard presentation. Recall that the correct and complete model of the economy is assumed to be known by both capital and labour. The story goes as follows,

> [T]he equilibrium expected real wage at the date of the nominal wage bargain is made is assumed to be set in the expectation of clearing the labour market. . . . Thus I assume that nominal wages are set each period to produce an expected real wage which is

expected to generate unemployment at the Natural Rate . . . (Begg, 1982, p. 37)

From the quotation we see that the assumption of full employment is made from the outset. Before going further, it should be noted that the postulated situation bears no resemblance to what occurs in any actual economy. In the first place, in very few capitalist economies does anything like an aggregate wage bargain take place, and in most Western capitalist countries the majority of wage and salary earners are not even organised into trade unions. In the United States, for example, hardly more than a fifth of the workforce is covered by effective bargaining units. Second, the assumption is made that the parties to the wage bargain seek a nominal wage which will clear the labour market. This is a completely arbitrary assumption and a particularly strange one to be made by neoclassical economists. For decades neoclassical economists have argued that trade union leaders tend to be most influenced by their direct constituency, the dues-paying members, and show little concern for the non-union employed, much less the unemployed. It is unclear what prompts the new classical economics to attribute such selfless motives to trade union leaders throughout the capitalist world. The assumption that a wage is set to clear the labour market is nothing but the Walrasian auctioneer disguised in a blue collar and cloth cap.

Third, the assumption is implicitly made that there is no conflict of any significance between capital and labour, since both parties to the bargain seek the wage which will clear the labour market. What is being described in fact involves no bargaining at all. Since by the REH both capital and labour know with certainty the true model of the economy and both seek to establish the full employment real wage, it would be a waste of time for them to meet. The trade union leaders could confidently leave wage-setting to the capitalists (and *vice versa*), since both parties have the same information and seek the same result. Completely ignored is that the wage bargain in part involves a struggle over the distribution between wages and profits.

While the story has more superficial realism than the general equilibrium parables in previous chapters, in fact it is no closer to reality. It is that same general equilibrium thought experiment disguised as a real world process, and the REH is incidental to the story. It must be stressed that this story is not merely an exercise in abstract model building, but has pretensions to explain actual events. In its attempt to do so, it begins by assuming that the labour market is in equilibrium. This assumption requires that all markets have cleared according to Walrasian rules. Walrasian market clearing requires the assumption of perfect foresight (to avoid False Trading), either in the form of the PFH itself or that same assumption embodied in a mythical auctioneer. Rather than replacing the PFH, the REH is introduced *in addition* to the presumption of perfect foresight. The assumption of perfect foresight is required to ensure the market clearing that establishes full employment each market period,[20] and the REH merely provides a spurious link between one market period and the next.

The implicit necessity for the PFH can be demonstrated via a thought experiment. Again, recall that here we deal with an analysis alleging to refer to actual real world outcomes, not merely theoretical possibilities in the abstract. Assume that at the outset of a market period agents establish their predictions upon the basis of a complete and correct model. If able to do so a large number of times, they will on average predict the general equilibrium outcome. However, in any particular case, random influences will result in the actual outcome differing from general equilibrium, and false trading will occur. Further, each prediction exercise is a unique event which can never be repeated in practice. Hypothetically there exists an average of many outcomes equal to the general equilibrium outcome. But each market period is unique, so the theoretical existence of a zero mean in deviations from general equilibrium is of no help in avoiding false trading, for now the argument refers not to an abstract model but to the real world.[21]

Even were it the case that the REH yielded general equilibrium for one-off events, the approach is unsatisfactory. As shown in previous chapters, full employment general equilibrium is a theoretically fragile concept, requiring a number of problematical assumptions and concepts. At least pre-REH neoclassical theorists for the most part felt it incumbent upon themselves to demonstrate the existence, uniqueness, and stability of general equilibrium. The new classical economics takes full employment equilibrium as its starting point.

9.4   THE NEW CLASSICAL ECONOMICS AND POLICY

With these critical comments in mind, we can turn to what are considered the 'remarkable' policy conclusions of the REH–new classical economics story. Perhaps the most remarkable aspect of these policy conclusions is that they have been taken seriously and had such influence. Recall that the wage bargain has been struck in the context of full employment with both parties seeking a money wage which will preserve that full employment in the next time period. To continue the story,[22]

> Under Rational Expectations, the remarkable implication . . . is that, no matter how we define the rest of the model and no matter which systematic parts of the [government economic] policy rule are altered, the effect on the path of real output will be nil.

The story apparently has the following moral: if agents act according to the REH rules, no matter what the characteristics of the formal model of the economy, no systematic government economic policy will have any effect upon real output (and therefore employment) during the life of the wage contract. This statement is false. To understand why it is false, first we investigate the conditions under which it would be true. Assume that the state plans to increase the money supply during the period when the wage agreement applies. If the increase is based upon some reasonable and systematic policy guidelines, then it will be anticipated by the parties to the aggregate wage bargain (or so the story goes). In anticipation of the implementation of the policy rule, the bargainers will agree on a nominal wage which clears the labour market with the specific policy in mind. For example, if the state plans to increase the money supply by 10 per cent, the bargainers will set a market-clearing nominal wage consistent with this change in the money supply. On the assumption that the wage bargainers do this, under what circumstances will there be a nil effect upon real output? *This will result if and only if money is strictly neutral.*[23] In other words, application of the REH tells one nothing that economists have not known for at least two generations: if the economy is at full employment equilibrium and money is neutral, a change in the money supply will leave all real variables unchanged. The 'remarkable' REH conclusion is the neutrality condition and nothing more. It differs from the same story told in traditional Walrasian market theory only in that the all-knowing auctioneer has been replaced by all-knowing wage bargainers. The economic policy nihilism of the new clasical economics is a repackaging of the economics of Pigou, Keynes's famous theoretical adversary.

The quotation is wrong in the first instance because there are many specifications of how the economy operates in which money is not neutral. If one were allowed non-neoclassical specifications, there are the models of the neo-Ricardians, neo-Keynesians and Marxists. But even if respectability is granted to neoclassical models alone, it was shown in Chapter 7 that introduction to the wealth effect can render money non-neutral.[24] If money is non-neutral, then the hypothetical 10 per cent increase in the money supply will alter the rate of interest, as well as directly affecting real investment and consumption. If the supply of labour is sensitive to the interest rate, then the market-clearing level of employment will change.

Second, even on the assumption that money is neutral, it is not true that changing systematic policy rules will have no effect upon real output, for there exist fiscal policy rules which even if unchanged would affect real output. If the tax structure is progressive, then a rise in nominal wages and prices will increase tax revenue more than proportionately to the money income rise. In a neoclassical world a higher average tax rate for the economy would affect the work–leisure trade-off and shift the supply of labour schedule (Hahn, 1980, p. 2).

The old classical (pre-Keynesian) economics was forced to retreat before the attack of Keynes, and remained largely an undercurrent during the heyday of the neoclassical synthesis. Its two central messages, the neutrality of money and automatic full employment equilibrium, were treated with considerable scepticism by policy-oriented economists. The new classical economics has changed this situation, and now the believers in full employment and neutrality have seized the high ground of economic theory on the basis of the REH. Upon inspection one finds that the REH resolves none of the theoretical problems which plagued both the old classicals and the neoclassicals; rather, it adds additional logical problems of its own. Its popularity in the profession is largely a political phenomenon. With the election of right-wing governments in the United States and the United Kingdom, the new classical economics was a doctrine whose time had come, its theoretical failings notwithstanding.

9.5 EVALUATING THE NEW CLASSICAL ECONOMICS

Having been quite critical of the new classical economics and its rational expectations patent medicine, we must give it its due. While many liberal and progressively minded neoclassical economists are appalled at the right-wing policy nihilism of the new classical economics,[25] the latter can with some justification claim to be the true standard bearer of the synthesis tradition. For at least thirty years after the end of the Second World War there existed a strong consensus among mainstream economists with regard to macroeconomics. In the realm of high theory, a successful counter-attack was launched against *The General Theory*. It was accepted in the profession that Keynes had done little more than to demonstrate that rigid money wages would prevent full employment from being automatically achieved in a capitalist economy.[26] However, this theoretical victory of the pre-Keynesian paradigm appeared singularly hollow, for the other part of the consensus was that money wages were rigid in practice. So while those who held to the pre-Keynesian paradigm were left to pursue their interest in the analysis of full employment equilibria if they wished, practitioners of economic policy and macroeconomic empirical studies devoted themselves to situations of less than full employment and developing rules for interventionist policies of governments. With the exception of a few graduate schools, young economists-in-training were required to learn the intricacies of full employment solutions as something to get behind them in order to go on to the serious work of analysing situations involving unemployment and what could be done about it. Walrasian general equilibrium theory was frequently ostracised to no more than a topic within advanced courses in microeconomics (which, one can note, is where Walras himself had located it).

The decline in influence of what Keynes had called classical economic theory reflected the political environment of the post-war period, which was moulded in the developed capitalist countries by two traumatic events – the Great Depression of the 1930s and the Second World War. It had been the most developed capitalist country (the United States) which had suffered the greatest economic decline during 1929–1933, and another developed capitalist country (Germany) which had unleashed organised barbarism on a historically unprecedented scale both with regard to its own population and its neighbours. One did not have to be a communist or even a social democrat to believe that modern capitalism required state intervention to control its more flagrant economic and political abuses.

However, the pragmatists of less-than-full employment had few theoretical differences with the general equilibrium idealists (particularly in the United States). Further, the so-called 'frontier' of macroeconomic theory was dominated by Walrasian methodology. Mainstream macroeconomics for thirty years was characterised by a split personality – it swore theoretical allegiance to Walras, but unceremoniously abandoned him when treating concrete problems of economic policy. Economists such as Joan Robinson on the Left and Milton Friedman on the Right pointed out the discipline's contradictions between its theory and practice, but made little headway in obtaining a consensus for rendering the two consistent. Perhaps like the Catholic Church, the profession flourished on the basis of rigid doctrine in the Vatican and heterodoxy among the clergy.[27]

In the name of reaching a concordance between microeconomics and macroeconomics, the economics of Walrasian full employment achieved complete *theoretical* ascendancy over the economics of effective demand, involuntary unemployment, and systemic instability. Certainly by the mid-1950s, the theoretical core of economics was again general equilibrium. What the new classical economics has done is to unite theory and practice. After all, if theory tells one that the natural working of the market mechanism will produce full employment and the state is at best a burden upon the economy, and if that theory is accepted as the collective wisdom of the profession, should not one treat the world accordingly?[28] In the new classical economics neoclassical theory finds its purest expression and, perhaps, has run its course to its logical and practical conclusion.

10 Full Employment and Multi-commodity Production

10.1 INTRODUCTION

At a number of points in previous chapters we referred to critiques of the neoclassical model which involve the use of an aggregate supply of output function. We now consider that issue in some detail, particularly those objections that come from writers who feel that the neoclassical synthesis is a serious distortion, even a perversion, of Keynes's contribution to economic theory. The purpose is not to cover all critiques arising from writers who consider themselves as correct interpreters of Keynes, but rather to restrict the discussion to those who address certain broad and fundamental issues of theory.

Keynes explicitly accepted marginal productivity theory,[1] but at a number of points in *The General Theory* he makes arguments and comments that contradict the concept of a neoclassical production function,[2] either aggregate or at the firm level. One group which sees itself in the tradition of Keynes judges his acceptance of marginal productivity theory to be a fatal theoretical and tactical compromise. Central to their critique of the neoclassical synthesis is their attack upon the aggregate production function. This group of writers, within which the late Joan Robinson is the most distinguished, we shall refer to as the 'neo-Keynesians'.[3] A brief word on varieties of Keynesians is necessary, for there is a second group critical of the neoclassical model, some of whose members share the scepticism about the aggregate production function. However, this second group centres its critique of the synthesis model on the general equilibrium analysis of Walras' Law. Here major writers are Clower and Leijonhufvud. Their approach we call 'disequilibrium-Keynesian' and is treated in the next chapter.[4] By current usage in the profession, both groups are often referred to as 'post-Keynesian', a catch-all category which we shall avoid.

At the risk of over-simplification, the theoretical position of the neo-Keynesians can be summarised as follows. They seek to reconstruct the analysis of *The General Theory* in terms of a macro analysis which discards the concept of an aggregate production function. In this approach, the neoclassical treatment of capital–labour relations as a harmonious one determined by purely technical influences (the production function and factors supplies) is rejected in favour of placing the distributional struggle between capital and labour at the centre of the theory.[5]

10.2   SWITCHING TECHNIQUES AND THE FACTOR PRICE FRONTIER

A basic tenet of neoclassical theory is that holding other things equal, more employment can only be achieved at a lower real wage. This is a powerful ideological message, for it implies that attempts by workers to improve their conditions of pay if successful will be self-defeating by generating unemployment.[6] If the labour market is left to operate freely without interference, full employment will result. Intervention can only result in the employed gaining at the expense of an increased number of the unemployed. Further, society as a whole loses, because unemployment implies that total output is below its maximum level. This argument, that there is a trade-off between the level of the real wage and the level of employment, derives directly from the concept of the aggregate production function.

In order to be clear as to what is at stake in the debate over the aggregate production function, a detailed investigation of how the real wage-employment trade-off is supposed to occur is called for. On the supply side of the macro model, neoclassical theory begins by assuming that the total production of the economy can be treated as a single product. It then postulates that at any moment there exists a known range of techniques that can be used to produce this single commodity. This known range of techniques is usually referred to as 'the state of technology'. All of these techniques are part of the same production set, and differ from each other by the ratio in which capital is combined with labour. Each technique is economically efficient in that at some ratio of the wage to the rate of return on capital each will produce the single commodity at the lowest cost. Therefore, the aggregate production function represents a locus of many techniques, all of the possible capital–labour combinations which are economically efficient. Further, the capital–labour substitution always involves the full use of the capital stock, since it is always rational for capitalists to engage their entire capital, whatever might be the labour input (see Chapter 8).

As one moves along a production function, as in the stories told in Chapters 5 to 7, one is not simply substituting labour for capital (or *vice versa*), but *switching techniques*. That is to say, no one seriously argues that a given production process allows a wide range of capital–labour ratios. It may be that some production processes do, but this is an empirical issue and cannot be the theoretical basis of capital–labour substitution. The theory of capital–labour substitution asserts that there exists a book of blueprints of many possible production alternatives, and when the factor price ratio changes, optimising capitalists are prompted to switch to a different technique.

The above discussion is illustrated in Figure 10.1, which shows the aggregate production function in three manifestations. The map for four techniques available for the production of the single commodity, with a given capital stock of $k*$ is represented in Figure 10.1(a). Each of these techniques, A, B, C, and D, is characterised by fixed coefficients; that is, when using technique A, capital and labour can be combined only in the ratio $0_{k*}/0l(a)$. Additional input of labour (adding amount $0l(a) - 0l(b)$, for example) has no impact on the level of output. The straight lines from the origin in Figure 10.1(a) are called activity vectors. As drawn, equal increments out from the origin along any activity vector yield equal increases in output (constant returns to scale). When points of equal output on different vectors are joined, the result is an isoquant (only the one for level of output $y[a]$ is shown). The isoquants in this diagram differ from those in Figure 8.1 in that here they are made up of straight-line segments. Were we to include more activity vectors (techniques) in between the existing ones, the isoquants would progressively begin to approximate smooth curves. Even were we to do this, it must be kept in mind that the curves would be constructed on the basis of discrete techniques, each characterised by fixed coefficients of production. Figure 10.1(b) shows the production function in the output–labour space, again involving a series of straight lines whose slopes diminish with regard to the level of employment. Finally, Figure 10.1(c) presents the implied marginal product of labour schedule, measured in units of the single commodity, though on a smaller vertical scale (y/n, where n is an appropriate scalar).[7] The marginal product schedule now takes the form of a step-function, with the operative portions of each techniques shown as solid lines. The purpose of this diagram is

Figure 10.1   The aggregate production function as a range of techniques

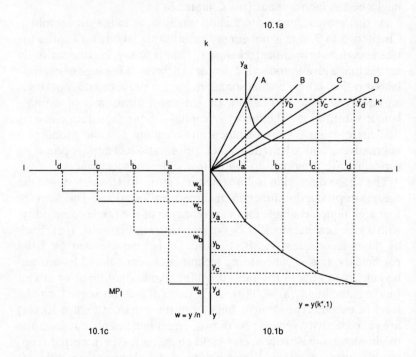

to demonstrate that the theoretical process by which labour is added to a given capital stock (or, more generally, labour substituted for capital) involves a switch from a fixed coefficient technique with a higher capital–labour ratio to one with a lower capital–labour ratio.

The next diagram, Figure 10.2, is a variation on the one before, in which the *factor price frontier* is derived using all four quadrants. In Figure 10.2(a) the isoquants are presented as before, with four fixed coefficient techniques. In the quadrant below (Figure 10.2(b)), the marginal product of labour schedule is derived. In this part of the diagram, one can find the real wage associated with each technique, measured on the vertical axis in units of the single commodity. In Figure 10.2(c), the relationship between the capital stock and the rate of return is shown, with *r* rising as techniques are chosen for which the capital–labour ratio falls. Here there is only one marginal product schedule (as a series of straight lines), because the capital stock is held fixed. In Figure 10.2(c) one has a series of shifting vertical

Figure 10.2   Derivation of the factor price frontier

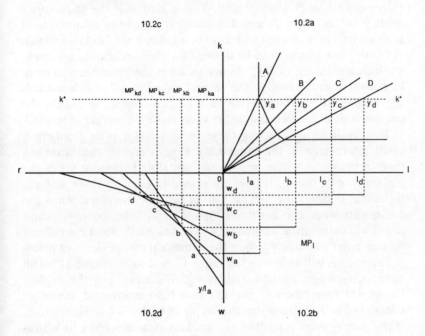

marginal product of capital schedules, because labour is varying while capital remains constant.

The shape of the curve in Figure 10.2(d) is explained by use of algebra. Since output is equal to wages plus profits, one can write for any of the four techniques, $y(i) = wl(i) + rk*$. Using technique A as an example,

$$y(a) = wl(a) + rk*$$
$$w = \frac{y(a)}{l(a)} - r\frac{k*}{l(a)} \quad (10.1)$$

and

$$r = \frac{y(a) - wl(a)}{k*}$$

In this equation, only w and r can vary, since there is only one ratio in which capital and labour can be productively used, namely $k*/l(a)$.

Further, the average product of labour, $y(a)/l(a)$, is unique when the entire capital stock is employed. This equation is the *factor price frontier* for technique A and it is linear. It shows the unique rate of return which is associated with any commodity wage (and *vice versa*). A factor price frontier can be derived for each technique, and these are shown in Figure 10.2(d). As one switches to techniques with more labour relatively to capital, the vertical intercept, y/l, crawls towards the origin, so each successive factor price frontier intersects the previous one at a lower commodity wage and a higher rate of return.[8]

The result of constructing these various factor price frontiers is easily interpreted. If the commodity wage is greater than level w_b, then technique A will be chosen by capitalists because it yields the highest rate of return. Between commodity wage levels w_b and w_c, technique B offers the highest rate of return. Therefore, when the commodity wage declines lower than level w_b (but above w_c), capitalists will switch from technique A to technique B. Point *b* is called a 'switch point'. Similarly, when the commodity wage declines below w_c, capitalists will switch to technique C, and to technique D for all commodity wage levels less than w_d. We now have the explicit theoretical foundation of the less-than-full-employment stories of Chapters 5 to 7. Assume that the supply of labour is l_c in Figure 10.2. If the money wage is flexible and markets clear according to Walrasian rules, then nominal variables will adjust so that commodity wage in the region between w_c and w_d prevails and labour is fully employed with technique C. If, however, workers combine to hold the money wage above the market clearing level, the commodity wage would rise, say to a level in excess of w_c. In this case, technique B would be the most profitable. When the total capital stock is converted to technique B, the maximum level of employment would be l_b, resulting in unemployment.

The moral of the story told from Figures 10.1 and 10.2 is neat, compact, and powerfully political. However, one must remember that it is a moral based upon a world created by the story-teller; it is not a tale of any actual economy. The entire logical argument presumes a one commodity system, in which the output of the production process is identical to the input which serves as the capital stock. This story of aggregate capital–labour substitution in response to a change in the economy-wide ratio of the commodity wage to the rate of return is strictly speaking only a parable – '[a] narrative setting forth something in terms of something else, fictitious story told to point a moral . . . [an] allegory.'[9] The narrative told in Figures 10.1

and 10.2 is fictitious: economies are not one product systems, no matter how convenient it may be to presume that they are. It is certainly setting forth something in terms of something else, for the actual capital stock of any economy is not homogeneous, nor is it identical to the output it generates. The fact that economies have more than one product, and particularly that capital inputs and consumption outputs are not the same thing, does not in and of itself invalidate the parable. However, the allegorical nature of the aggregate production function requires that its users demonstrate that the conclusions derived from it are not contradicted when one considers a system with more than one commodity. If it can be demonstrated that the capital–labour substitution story survives the minimal theoretical test of a multi-commodity model, then its judgement on wages and employment can be taken seriously. To be explicit, the demand is not that the aggregate production function stand the test of realism or even casual empiricism, *but only that it survive in a model no different from the general synthesis model with the exception that there are two products rather than one*. The Neo-Keynesian critique demonstrates that the aggregate production function cannot survive this test.

10.3   THE NEO-KEYNESIAN CRITIQUE[10]

Before proceeding with a presentation of the Neo-Keynesian critique of the aggregate production function, a brief digression is required. Readers familiar with what has been called the 'Cambridge Controversy'[11] might be surprised to find it in a treatment of macroeconomics, especially a treatment of macroeconomics which is restricted to short-run models. As it has developed, the debate over the logical consistency and generality of the neoclassical aggregate production function has focused almost entirely upon issues of distribution (determination of wages and profits) and choice of technique in response to changes in factor price ratios. The critics used their attack upon the aggregate production function primarily as a vehicle to discredit the neoclassical theory of distribution and marginal productivity analysis *inter alia*. The ability of the critique to achieve these formidable tasks is open to question. What is not open to question is the relevance of the critique to short-run adjustment mechanics in the neoclassical macro model. As Hahn points out,[12] it is strange that the critics have not pursued more vigorously the powerful short-run implications of their attack upon the aggregate production function.

The analysis begins with a very simple two commodity system in which there is one output, one input, and the input is completely used up each period (i.e. capital has a life of one period). Further, it shall be assumed that the system keeps to the same level of production each period, so an amount of the input is produced that is just sufficient to produce the output. Keeping to the approach used in the one commodity parable, it is assumed that there exists a range of fixed coefficient techniques for capitalists to chose among. Unlike before, each technique now involves two products, the input and the output. First, a typical technique (A) will be defined for one unit of output. The output is designated by the number 1, and the input by 2.

$$p(2)k(a_1) + p(a_1)wl(a_1) + (\text{profit}) \, (a_1) = p(a_1)$$

$$p(2)k(a_2) + p(a_1)wl(a_2) + (\text{profit}) \, (a_2) = p(a_2)$$

where $p(j)$ is the price of each commodity, $l(aj)$ is the labour input required to produce one unit of each commodity, $k(aj)$ is the amount of input (capital) required to produce one unit of each commodity, and w is the wage measured in units of the output.

It is assumed that competition results in the same wage and rate of return in the production of each commodity. The rate of return is defined as $r = rk/k$. In this simple case in which capital has a life of only one production period, the rate of return can be written as price minus cost divided by the input cost. Using the output, for example, the rate of return is

$$r(a_1) = \frac{[p(a_1) - p(a_1)w_1(a_1) - p(a_2)k(a_2)]}{[p(a_2)k(a_2)]} \qquad (10.1)$$

or, more generally,

$$r = \frac{\text{price} - \text{total cost}}{\text{input cost}}$$

As a further step in simplification, the technique will be defined for relative ('normalised') prices, so $p(a) = p(a2)/p(a1)$ (the price of the input), and the price of the output is unity. Since we shall only consider the case of a constant level of production, it is convenient to define one unit of the input to be that which is produced and used up in a time period, or $[k(a1) + k(a2)] = 1$. Finally, as long as we are dealing with only one technique in our example, the notation 'a' is superfluous. With these assumptions made, the summary of the technique can be rewritten in the usual form that one encounters it in the literature.

$$pk(1) + wl(1) + rpk(1) = 1$$
$$pk(2) + wl(2) + rpk(2) = p$$
(10.2)

or

$$[1 + r]pk(1) + wl(1) = 1$$
$$[1 + r]pk(2) + wl(2) = p$$
(10.3)

The 'factor intensity' of the input and the output is defined as $k(j)/l(j)$. If $[k(2)/l(2)] > [k(1)/l(1)]$, then the input is more 'capital-intensive' than the output. As will be shown below, comparing the factor intensities of different techniques is less straightforward than comparing the factor intensities of the two products within one technique.

The relevance of the above expressions (10.2 and 10.3) for the neoclassical macro model may not be obvious. They can, however, easily be converted into the familiar income/value added aggregates. If production of the output is constant, corresponding to IS–LM equilibrium in the neoclassical model, then the production of the input is completely exhausted in the current period by its use as an input to produce the input and as an input to produce the output. Recalling that equations (10.2) and (10.3) are defined for one unit of output, this implies the following.

$$p = pk(1) + pk(2)$$

If one subtracts from this the price equation for the input, $p = pk(2) + wl(2) + rpk(2)$, one obtains

$$pk(1) = wl(2) + rpk(2).$$

In words, the input cost of the output equals the value added generated in the production of the input. Now one can substitute for $pk(1)$ in the equation for the output.

$$wl(1) + wl(2) + rpk(1) + rpk(2) = 1$$
$$w[l(1) + l(2)] + rp[k(1) + k(2)] = 1$$
(10.4)

Thus, total wages and profits equal the production of the output. On the assumption that this technique is characterised by constant returns to scale, expressions (10.4) can be expanded to the level of aggregate output/income (y), and are equivalent to the neoclassical circular flow statement (Section 1.2) that wages plus profits equal final output. Note that $[l(1) + l(2)]$ is total labour utilised, $[k(1) + k(2)]$ the capital stock, and multiplying by p results in measuring the capital stock in units of the output. If we designate the capital stock in units of the output as K and y as the level of output, then equations (10.4) can be written simply as

$$y = wl + rK$$

and (10.5)

$$r = \frac{y - wl}{K}$$

The discussion below treats techniques at a unit level of output and is strictly equivalent to considering aggregate production (assuming constant returns to scale for each technique). This is appropriate, for the purpose of the exercise is to investigate whether techniques involving an input which is different from the output will produce a parable about wages and employment that is the same as in the one commodity macro model.[13] To investigate this, one must derive the factor price frontier, as was done before in the one commodity case. We seek the factor price frontier for the technique as a whole, since the two parts of it, the input and the output, form a single indivisible system of production. To obtain this relationship, each element of the technique is solved for p, the price of the input. Then the price of the input is eliminated by setting the two equations equal to each other.

$$p = \frac{[1 - wl(1)]}{[\{1 + r\}k(1)]}$$

$$p = \frac{wl(2)}{[1 - \{1 + r\}k(2)]}$$

The price term is eliminated by substitution.

$$\frac{1 - wl(1)}{[1 + r]k(1)} = \frac{wl(2)}{1 - [1 + r]k(2)}$$

This expression can be solved for r and w, the only variables. After some manipulation, one obtains the factor price frontier in the following form.

$$r = \frac{1 - wl(1)}{k(2) + w[k(2)l(1) - k(1)l(2)]}$$ (10.6)

This equation for the factor price frontier is considerably more complicated than the analogous expressions (10.1) and (10.5). In general it is not linear. The factor price expression (10.6) can be rendered equivalent to the case in which there is only one commodity. If the expression in brackets in the denominator of (10.6) were zero, then $r = [1 - wl(1)]/k(2)$. The bracketed term will be zero if

$$k(2)l(1) = k(1)l(2)$$

or, (10.7)

$$\frac{k(1)}{l(1)} = \frac{k(2)}{k(2)}$$

This condition (10.7) can be interpreted as meaning that the two commodity case reduces to the one commodity case if both products of the technique are characterised by the same capital-labour ratio. This is hardly surprising, since two products with the same factor intensity are but one product with respect to production. One can conclude that the two product technique will have a straight-line factor price frontier if and only if the two products are in fact only one. In the general case in which the capital–labour ratios of the input and the output are not the same, the factor price frontier will be non-linear. If the input is less capital-intensive than the output, then the factor price frontier will be bowed in towards the origin, and bulge outwards in the opposite case. These two general forms are shown in Figure 10.3, along with the one product factor price frontier. Some writers refer to the linear frontier as a special case of the two product economy, but this is incorrect. Linearity is the case of a one product system and of no other.

Figure 10.4 presents a two product economy with two available techniques, A and B. For technique A, the output has a higher capital–labour ratio than the input, and for B the input has a higher capital–labour ratio than the output. First, it will be investigated which *technique* is the more capital-intensive, on the basis of the capital–labour ratio. To do this it is necessary to derive a measure of the capital–labour ratio for a technique as a whole, considering both the output and the input used to produce the output. On the basis of equation (10.5), we can solve for the capital–labour ratio for each technique.

$$\frac{K(a)}{l(a)} = \frac{y(a)/l(a) - w}{r} \qquad (10.8a)$$

Figure 10.3   Factor price frontiers for a two commodity economy

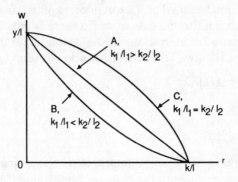

Figure 10.4   A two commodity economy with two available techniques.

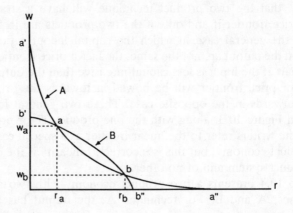

$$\frac{K(b)}{l(b)} = \frac{y(b)/l(b) - w}{r} \qquad (10.8b)$$

In words, the ratio of the capital stock to the labour employed can be measured as the average product of labour minus the wage (this numerator being equal to capitalists' profit per worker employed), divided by the rate of return. Using this method of calculation, it is easy to see in Figure 10.4 which technique is the more capital intensive. At points *a* and *b* the two techniques enjoy the same wage and rate of return, differing in terms of expression (10.8) only by the value of the average product of labour (y/l). In the diagram the vertical intercept of each technique marks the value of y/l, so one can conclude that technique A is the more capital intensive, for $0a' > 0b'$. This is the result one would expect from neoclassical production theory: the technique for which labour is more productive is the more capital intensive one.

We have employed the basic definition of factor intensity, namely the capital–labour ratio. It is to be expected according to neoclassical rules that the more capital intensive technique will be selected by capitalists when wages are high and the more labour intensive one when wages are low. Inspection of Figure 10.4 reveals that such is not the case. For a commodity wage above level w_a, technique A offers the higher profit rate, as suspected since A is the more capital-intensive. When the commodity wage drops below w_b, technique B is the more profitable and capitalists will switch techniques. All is well until the commodity wage edges below level w_b. Below w_b technique A, the more capital intensive, reappears as the more profitable. This reappearance is called 'reswitching' of techniques. Reswitching implies an unexpected conclusion. *Theory tells us that in general capitalists will not necessarily select more labour-intensive techniques when wages fall.*

This result is a potential disaster for the neoclassical macro model and its parable about real wages and employment. The generally accepted definition of factor intensity completely breaks down once one abandons a one commodity world. First, it is not the case that more capital-intensive techniques will always be chosen as the real wage rises. Second, and equally distressing for neoclassical analysis, the measured factor intensity of a technique is not determined by technology alone. Close inspection of Figure 10.4 demonstrates this. Consider technique A. Following equations (10.8), when the commodity wage is w_a, the measured capital intensity of technique A is double what it is at commodity wage w_b.[14]

This is a strange result indeed, for it means that changes in the wage and the profit rate alone, with no change in the technical coefficients of production, alter the factor intensity of a technique. This variability of the capital–labour ratio with respect to the distributional variables r and w throws into question a convention that we have employed throughout the first four chapters of this book. All of the discussion of the short-run macro model has been based on the presumption of a given capital stock; a fixed capital stock has been the defining characteristic of the short run. Now it is discovered that the capital stock is not fixed with respect to the distribution between wages and profits except in the case of a one commodity world. It should be noted that this has nothing to do with whether the capital stock treated as homogeneous (i.e. composed of a single type of machine). In the two commodity model represented in Figure 10.4, the capital stock is completely homogeneous. The 'perverseness' of the conclusion in the two commodity model is bizarre in the extreme: there is only one form of capital equipment and the thought experiment assumes that the total input of this homogeneous capital equipment is given: for example, at level $k(a1) + k(a2)$. Still, the measured capital stock varies with the wage and the profit rate!

How is it possible for a capital stock fixed in physical units to vary with the wage and the profit rate? The paradox arises from the need to render the production of the output equal to total value added for the technique as a whole. If one looks back at equations (10.4), one sees that the materials cost of the final output is replaced in the distributional expression by wages and profits generated in the production of the input. However, these wages and profits represent in their origin a certain amount of the input – a certain amount of a commodity other than the final output. In order to add these wages and profits arising from the input to the wages and profits of the final output, both sets of wages and profits must be measured in units of the final output. The denominating of the input in terms of the output was achieved by defining the two commodity system in terms of relative prices, $p = p(2)/p(1)$.

Now it is clear that 'dividing through' by $p(1)$ was not merely a step to simplify the mathematics of the solution to the factor price frontier, but necessary to aggregate value added for the technique as a whole. A side-effect of obtaining total value added was to measure the capital stock not as $[k(1) + k(2)]$, but as $p[k(1) + k(2)] = K$. While $[k(1) + k(2)]$ is invariant with respect to the wage and the profit rate, K is not. Because the factor intensities of the input and the output are different, p, relative prices, varies with the ratio w/r.[15] Knowing that the technical coefficients $k(ij)$ are invariant with regard to distribution is of no help in resolving the paradox of a variable factor intensity in a two product system. With regard to the factor price frontier and choice of the most profitable technique, there is no way to avoid measuring the capital stock as $K = p[ki1] + p[ki2]$.

10.4 FULL EMPLOYMENT AND RE-SWITCHING

The implications of the analysis for short-run employment determination can now be demonstrated. When the capital stock is measured in terms of the relative price of the output, factor price frontiers will cross more than once (as in Figure 10.4), and the parable about real wages and the level of employment breaks down. To pursue the implications of reswitching, let us return to the neoclassical analysis of the labour market. The Walrasian process of labour market clearing has a certain logical sequence. If there is excess supply in the labour market, the result is a fall in the money wage. This fall in the money wage results in a fall in the commodity wage, which induces capitalists to switch techniques (techniques, like everything else are undetermined at the beginning of the market day). The labour market will be cleared if the lower commodity wage stimulates the choice of a technique which requires more labour for the given capital stock. It is no longer sufficient to say, 'a more labour-intensive technique', because the analysis of the previous section has demonstrated that the very concept of 'factor intensity' is ambiguous except in a one commodity model. Figure 10.4 demonstrates that a fall in the commodity wage may provoke capitalists to chose a technique which employs *less* labour with the given capital stock.

The hypothetical adjustment process is clarified by Figure 10.5. Assume there to be three techniques, A, B, and C, as drawn. With the given capital stock fully utilised, technique A generates a demand for labour or level of employment of $l(da)$, technique B employment of $l(db)$, and technique C employment of $l(dc)$, where the letter 'd' indicates that these are the notional demands for labour associated with each fixed-coefficient process (shown in Figure 10.5(a)). The factor price frontiers are found in Figure 10.5(b), with one of them drawn as a straight line to keep the diagram as simple as possible. The supply of labour is assumed to be invariant (as in previous chapters) and to coincide with the demand for labour implied by technique C (when the short-run fixed capital stock is fully utilised). In the Walrasian general equilibrium parable, excess supply in the labour market results in a fall in the real wage, which provokes a slide down a smoothly-sloping, monotonic demand for labour schedule.

Now the story is quite different. Assume that the commodity wage is initially above w_a. The most profitable technique will be A, generating employment of l_a and leaving part of the labour force unemployed, l_c to l_a. Unemployment will cause the commodity wage to

Figure 10.5　Labour market adjustment in a two-commodity world
(capital stock fixed)

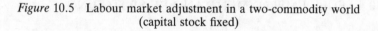
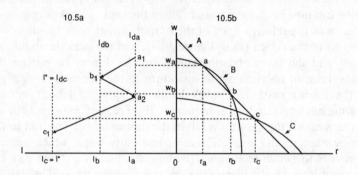

fall, and when it drops below w_a, capitalists will switch to technique B
and employment level l_b, following a path such as $a1$ to $b1$. However,
there is still unemployment, of $l_c - l_b$, so the commodity wage will
fall further. When it drops below w_b, 'reswitching' occurs, as technique A reappears as the most profitable. As a result, *employment
will fall*, back to level l_a (following a path shown by $b1$ to $a2$). Finally,
a drop in the commodity wage to below w_c will bring about full
employment with technique C. But with many techniques, the theoretical path by which full employment is reached involves a dizzy
Yo-Yo-ing from levels of higher to lower employment. Indeed, the
auctioneer would have to be on his or her toes to ensure that the
capitalists and workers did not become confused in such an erratic
process.

The adjustment to full employment equilibrium in a multi-
commodity world involves complications considerably more serious
than merely erratic jerks between higher and lower levels of employment, as Figure 10.6 demonstrates. Here only the relevant portions
of the factor price frontiers of two techniques are shown; i.e., only
those portions for which any particular technique is the most profitable. This curve, made up of the most profitable segments of the
curve for each technique, will be referred to as the economy-wide
factor price frontier.

In an n-commodity world, the economy-wide factor price frontier
is always downward sloping, but 'wiggly' rather than smooth.[16] Assume that the commodity wage, now a composite of a number of final

Figure 10.6   Labour market adjustment in a many-commodity world, economy-wide factor price frontier

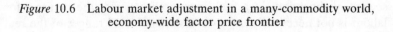
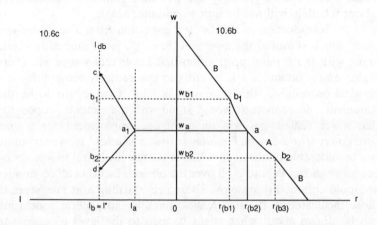

products, is initially at w_a, generating a level of employment of l_a when the fixed capital stock is fully utilised. At this wage and using technique A, there is an excess demand for labour of amount l_a to l_b. Since one knows that factor price frontiers cross in this multi-commodity world, assume that some technique B, the full employment technique, is most profitable at both $w(b1)$ and $w(b2)$. This last assumption is not arbitrary, for with reswitching there will always be techniques which appear as the most profitable at wage levels both above and below the prevailing wage. Figure 10.6 demonstrates that an adjustment of the commodity wage will indeed bring about full employment, *either via a fall or a rise in the wage!* A fall in the commodity wage results in full employment via the path a' to d, and a rise in the commodity wage has the same result along the path a' to c. One concludes that in a multi-commodity world, real wage increases are as likely to eliminate unemployment as real wage decreases.

We can now pass judgement upon the neoclassical wage-employment parable. There are two reasons why even in theory lower real wages are not the necessary condition to increase employment. First, and argued in the previous chapter, if money is not neutral, then the full employment equilibrium is not unique. Monetary policy alone can change the real wage at which full employment is secured (i.e. perhaps raising it; see Section 8.2). Now there is a second qualification: in a multi-commodity world, the demand for labour is not necessarily downward-sloping for all ranges of the real wage. On the contrary, theory tells us that in general the demand for labour schedule will not be unique and monotonic.

In the introduction to this book a quotation from *The Times* was cited, which ventured the assertion that '. . . few economists would argue with the general proposition that lower real wages will mean higher employment . . .' If it refers to theoretically competent neo-classical economists, this statement is false. Correct would be the statement, 'no economist would argue with the general proposition that lower real wages will mean higher employment *for a one-commodity world in which money is strictly neutral.*' However, there is a considerable doubt as to whether money is neutral in any actual economy and no debate at all over the obvious fact that all economies are multi-commodity systems. Therefore, startling as it may seem to those inculcated in the neoclassical parable, no general conclusion can be drawn about what might happen to the level of aggregate employment in response to a fall in the real wage.

Faced with this unpalatable theoretical result, some neoclassical economists have shrugged it off with the reply that reswitching of techniques is an 'empirical' question. The implication is that until someone demonstrates empirically that the demand for labour is not uniquely monotonic, the real wage-employment parable stands.[17] This line of defence gives the game away. That the relationship between the level of real wages and the level of employment is an empirical question, about which no theoretical generalisation can be made, is all that the critics of the neoclassical macro model need to establish. By conceding that the issue is an empirical one, the neo-classicals have posthumously accepted Keynes's argument that a falling money wage level is in general an unsound way of achieving full employment in a capitalist economy. In any case, the appeal to empiricism is a defence as empty as it is a surrender, for the wage-employment parable cannot be tested in a meaningful way.[18]

An economist no less distinguished than Paul Samuelson fervently defended the concept of the aggregate production function, invoking the laws of thermodynamics in its defence.[19] While no doubt considerations of the conservation of energy are relevant to the relationship between inputs and outputs in an economic system, they do not imply that in the aggregate the demand for labour is single-valued and downward-sloping with respect to the real wage in a multi-commodity model, much less in the real world. One can conclude that when referring to actual economic outcomes, there is no theoretical basis for the generalisation that lower real wages will stimulate more employment. The opposite conclusion has equal theoretical merit. The neoclassical parable, upon which so many policy prescriptions are based, is a false guide to real economies.

11 Full Employment and Disequilibrium

11.1 EFFECTIVE DEMAND AND THE MULTIPLIER

As shown in previous chapters, the effect of the synthesis of pre-Keynesian and Keynesian economics was to sanitise the Keynesian part of the logical possibility of involuntary unemployment. This was achieved (1) by the introduction a pre-Keynesian labour market (aggregate single commodity production function), (2) by rejecting the Keynesian view that expectations were inherently volatile, (3) by the inclusion of a wealth effect, and (4) by presupposing general equilibrium with Walrasian market clearing. From its beginning the synthesis version of macroeconomics left many theorists discontent.

Prominent among these theorists has been Clower, who over twenty years ago took issue with the manner in which Walrasian general equilibrium theory was used in the neoclassical model. Clower's objection did not involve a rejection of general equilibrium theory, but rather the argument that it was irrelevant to all situations except full employment.[1] As shown in Chapter 8, when the labour market is not cleared due to rigid money wages, Walras' Law appears to breakdown: all other markets can be in momentary equilibrium, leaving an excess supply (of labour) without a compensating excess demand. Clower's critique involves an attempt to reformulate adjustment dynamics along non-Walrasian lines. The key to this argument is the distinction between *notional* and *effective* demand (and supply), a distinction we have encountered previously. Notional demands are those in which the prices of commodities and services are the only variables considered by economic agents. In forming notional demands, agents take prices as given and consider only how much they desire to buy or sell at those given prices; *they need never concern themselves with the possibility that they might not be able to buy or sell the desired amounts*. Notional demands are unconstrained by demand or income, but only by price. The most important aspect of notional demand is the implication that income and, therefore, the amount of labour time offered for sale, is a decision variable.

Effective demand is the expenditure by agents based upon *actual* income.[2] Effective demand represents what is called 'the extra constraint' – in addition to prevailing prices, expenditure must conform to available or current income (in the case of a household) or to anticipated sales (in the case of a firm). The question then arises, under what circumstances will the additional constraint be binding? The answer is quite straightforward: in general, agent's decisions will be income- (or sales-) constrained if false trading occurs.

As briefly discussed in Chapter 3, trades at disequilibrium prices produce a result that can be interpreted as the operation of the familiar Keynesian multiplier process. Consider the case in which a firm sells its entire planned supply, but at a price below the Walrasian general equilibrium price. In this hypothetical example the market is cleared in that all output has been sold, but the revenue from the sale is inconsistent with full employment equilibrium. The firm in question will discover that the relationship between revenue and production cost does not justify maintaining the level of employment required to produce the planned (and sold) output, so employment will be adjusted downwards in the next period. A second consequence of the false trading is that the income paid out by the firm will prove insufficient to make its required contribution to the general equilibrium demands in other markets. In principle one act of false trading can result in a cumulative movement away from full employment general equilibrium.

11.2 GENERAL DISEQUILIBRIUM

An important implication of the Clower analysis is that unemployment can result *even if all wage bargains are struck at the general equilibrium money wage rate*. Leijonhufvud demonstrates this striking conclusion with a particularly instructive example, which he interprets as Keynes's diagnosis of the fundamental maladjustment that perpetuated the Great Depression. Leijonhufvud reads Keynes as saying that the Great Depression (and depressions in general) resulted from the long-term rate of interest standing at too high a level (asset prices too low). With the rate of interest on long-term assets too high, the rate of investment is too low to generate the aggregate demand necessary for full employment equilibrium.[3]

In this interpretation, false trading is occurring in the capital market. The false trading (at an interest rate above the general equilibrium rate) is explained by Keynes-as-interpreted-by-Leijonhufvud as the result of depressed state of long-run entrepreneurial expectations.[4] This emphasis upon a downwardly 'sticky' interest rate produces Leijonhufvud's striking conclusion, and it is worth quoting from him at some length (Leijonhufvud (1968), pp. 335–7).

> The essence of Keynes' diagnosis [of depressions] is this: the actual disequilibrium price vector initiating the contraction differs from the appropriate, hypothetical equilibrium vector in one major respect – the general level of long-term asset prices is lower than warranted . . . Observing unemployment, the 'Classical' economist . . . [e.g. Pigou] draws the conclusion that wages are too high and 'ought' to be reduced. In Keynes' theory, the maintenance of full employment depends upon the maintenance of a 'right' relation between . . . asset prices and the wage . . . Keynes' point is that when the appropriate price relation does *not* obtain, *it is in general not wages but asset demand prices that are out of line.*

The argument is that unemployment results from disequilibrium in the capital market which manifests itself as excess supply in the labour market, *even though the money wage and perhaps the real wage are at their full employment general equilibrium level.* In such a circumstance assigning the blame for unemployment to labour and prescribing a fall in money wages to rectify the situation involves a false application of partial equilibrium analysis to a general equilibrium system.[5] In one of the most insightful comments one is likely to encounter in book on neoclassical macroeconomics, Leijonhufvud (1968, p. 337) writes,

> [Keynes's] diagnosis [of unemployment] is not based on the naive presumption that the causes of macrodisequilibrium are to be found in the markets which at any time exhibit the most drastic symptoms of maladjustment. He approached the ('general *dise*-quilibrium') problem from a *general equilibrium* perspective.

Leijonhufvud is here making a point well-recognised in scientific enquiry, namely that things are not always what they appear to be. Even within the context of a neoclassical general equilibrium model, excess demand in the labour market is either a manifestation of *general* disequilibrium, or the result of some influence which prevents the money wage from adjusting to its general equilibrium level while all other markets are behaving properly along Walrasian rules. To assume that the latter is the case is completely arbitrary. In order that all other markets adjust in a Walrasian fashion, it must be assumed that False Trading never occurs in any commodity or money market except when forced upon agents by a failure of the money wage to 'properly' adjust. The cause of unemployment can be attributed to an inappropriate money wage only if it is assumed that all other markets function with Walrasian perfection.

There are persuasive theoretical reasons for predicting that false trading would be a general phenomenon characteristic of all markets. In order to clarify this point, the analysis will proceed by considering the neoclassical macro model in its most logically-defensible (if least credible) form. Let it first be assumed that money is strictly neutral, so the general equilibrium solution is not altered by changes in nominal variables; and, second, that there is only one commodity so that the possibility that *rising* wages will eliminate unemployment is eliminated. With these assumptions made, it is to be recalled that false trading is banished in general equilibrium theory by the intervention of the Walrasian auctioneer. This treatment ensures simultaneous market clearing, but does so by eliminating time from the analysis, for all exchanges occur at the same instant. Indeed, general equilibrium theory is the analysis of an economy without the time dimension, as one of the most distinguished practitioners of the theory makes clear.[6]

False trading is nothing more than trading in the context of chronological time. Once a model seeks to incorporate some concept of chronological time – i.e., all actions are not simultaneous – false trading is implied for all markets. If all exchanges do not not occur at the same time, then by definition some precede others. Unless one assumes perfect foresight (in which case simultaneity of exchanges has slipped in under a different name), it is completely arbitrary as well as hardly credible to proceed on the belief that a chronological sequence of transactions will produce the general equilibrium vector of prices. This is implicitly conceded in Walrasian general equilibrium theory, by use of the French word *tâtonnemont* to describe how equilibrium is reached, a word invariably translated to English as 'groping'. 'Groping' in markets in chronological time is false trading. The 'disequilibrium Keynesians' required no other defence of the superiority of their analysis over the traditional general equilibrium approach than to point out that chronological time is an inherent characteristic of all economic activity. General equilibrium solutions that exclude False Trading are of no practical or policy significance, nor is there any theoretical justification for such an approach.[7]

One would have thought that the obvious limitations of Walrasian general equilibrium theory would have resulted in the 'disequilibrium Keynesians' sweeping the field before them and winning a consensus around the view that disequilibrium is the general case and Walrasian market clearing the exceptional one.[8] Indeed, a disequilibrium analysis that incorporates false trading could be seen as a godsend to rescue the neoclassical macro model from its Walrasian vacuousness.[9] What has occurred in the profession is quite the contrary. Notwithstanding the fact that trading at non-equilibrium prices is implied by the placement of commodity exchange within chronological time, the burden of proof fell upon the disequilibrium Keynesians to explain why prices should not adjust instantaneously and, therefore, why false trading should occur. This is a strange demand, for it amounts to accepting an imaginary world (full employment general equilibrium) as the norm, and requiring the critics of that imaginary world to verify the existence of the real world.

Stranger still, the disequilibrium Keynesians have for the most part accepted such a definition of the debate, though Leijonhufvud is an exception (see next section). Rather than incorporating some concept of time into their analysis, which would automatically imply 'sticky' prices, the disequilibrium Keynesians have sought to establish their critique within a Walrasian world only slightly modified from the traditional neoclassical one. Specifically, they consider Walrasian markets 'without the auctioneer'. This leads them to place heavy emphasis on the cost of gathering information. The argument is that in the absence of the auctioneer, the general equilibrium solution can be known only at a cost of information gathering which no rational agent would incur.

While a reasonable enough argument, proceeding on this basis concedes the basic argument to the general equilibrium theorists. As Hahn points out, placing stress upon information costs implicitly accepts the principle that if information were readily and cheaply available, prices and wages would be perfectly flexible and there would be no problem of involuntary unemployment.[10] Further, invoking lack of information as the cause of unemployment disequilibrium permits the interpretation that unemployment in such a case is 'voluntary'. It could and has been argued that excess supply disequilibrium in the labour market is the result of workers chosing to wait for a more attractive offer which on the basis of information they suspect might come to them. Precisely to eliminate such an explanation (justification) for why some workers do not have jobs, Keynes excluded 'search unemployment' from his definition of 'involuntary unemployment' (see Keynes (1936), p. 15). In any case, placing emphasis upon information costs as the cause of unemployment renders the disequilibrium Keynesians particularly vulnerable to attacks from the new classical economics armed with the rational expectations hypothesis. While the NCE/REH mechanism by which agents acquire knowledge does not stand close scrutiny, it does offer a superficially compelling rejoinder to the information-cost disequilibrium analysis.

While one cannot offer a definitive explanation as to why the disequilibrium Keynesians have been willing to construct their critique upon such disadvantageous grounds, the proximate cause is clear. Like the general equilibrium theorists, the Disequilibrium Keynesians wish to retain the mathematical and analytical simplicity of market models without time. In doing so they abandon the fundamental and irrefutable justification of their approach. Once one enters a timeless world of the imagination, the general equilibrium theorists are quite within their rights to demand an abstract explanation for behaviour which is an inherent characteristic of the real world.

Finally, a quite disturbing aspect of the disequilibrium Keynesian approach needs to be mentioned. Particularly in the work of Leijonhufvud, there is a powerful critique of the use of a single-commodity supply side in the neoclassical model. However, the argument that one must consider aggregate adjustment in a multi-commodity context, when combined with a modified Walrasian analysis of markets, results in a *de facto* abandonment of macroeconomics as such.[11] The disequilibrium Keynesian approach becomes one of considering 'demand failures' with reference to specific markets, based upon the behaviour of individuals.[12] Such a treatment has considerably more in common with the economics of the new classical economics than with the economics of Keynes. By approaching their analysis along strict neoclassical rules of market clearing (without the auctioneer) in a multi-commodity context, the disequilibrium Keynesians perhaps earn the title 'neo-Walrasians'. What appeared as so promising and innovative in the early work of Clower and Leijonhufvud has now largely been swept aside by the rational expectations counterrevolution in macroeconomic theory. This is in no small part because the methodology of the disequilibrium Keynesians discards Keynes's most important innovation, macroeconomics.

11.3 LEIJONHUFVUD ON DISEQUILIBRIUM ADJUSTMENT

In terms of its scholarship and the profundity of its critique of the neoclassical macro model, Leijonhufvud's 1968 book, *Keynesian Economics and the Economics of Keynes* was perhaps the most important work on aggregate economic analysis since the end of the Second World War. Partly due to Leijonhufvud's own emphasis in subsequent work on the lack of full information as the cause of disequilibrium and unemployment, the best insights of the book have been lost. For a time after its publication the book was extremely influential, one of the key elements in what was called the 'Reappraisal of Keynesian Economics', but it quickly came under heavy fire from both the orthodox neoclassicals and the demand-side Keynesians. As said in the previous section, Leijonhufvud's attempt at reconstruction of aggregate analysis can be faulted on grounds that it abandoned macroeconomics all together. However, the opponents of Leijonhufvud, by focusing on his reformulation of aggregate analysis, largely missed the scientific content of his critique of the neoclassical macro model. The purpose of this section is to resurrect some of his arguments and to indicate their significance.

In previous chapters (2 and 8), we pointed out the obvious fact that unemployment is possible because of a particular institutional organisation of production. On the one hand, there are those who own the means of which production is carried out and whose decision to use those means of production is motivated by considerations of profitability. On the other hand, there are those who for all practical purposes have no commodity to sell except their ability to work. Unemployment is possible because the majority of 'agents' must sell their ability to work to the minority. Without a social division between employers and employees, a division based upon property relations, there is no labour market. With no labour market, there can be no unemployment. Leijonhufvud is one of the few theorists in the neoclassical tradition to recognise this, the social basis of unemployment.

> [T]he dynamic properties of an economic system depend upon what I will call its 'transaction structure'. That labor services are

sold for money and that households obtain their consumption goods in exchange for money is one aspect of the transaction structure in Keynes' system. In an economy of self-employed artisans [the problem of] unemployment cannot appear. (Leijonhufvud, 1968, p. 90)

Here Leijonhufvud has identified the class nature of production relations in capitalist society, an insight in the tradition of the nineteenth-century classical economists. Though Leijonhufvud employs his concept of the 'transaction structure' in a considerably more narrow way than Marx or Ricardo used the 'social relations of production' in their analysis, it serves him as a powerful tool for considering the essentially monetary character of a capitalist economy. The transaction structure of a capitalist economy implies that all exchanges must be treated as *monetary* exchanges and that 'real' solutions and 'real' calculations are largely irrelevant to the theoretical analysis or actual operation of such an economy. Some writers have taken issue with Leijonhufvud at this point, interpreting him as arguing that it is the *monetary* character of capitalist economies that makes unemployment possible, and countering with the contention that unemployment is just as much a logical possibility in a multi-product barter model as in a model with money.[13] The argument for unemployment in a barter economy is not difficult to make. In a multi-commodity world without money, individual workers will not in general barter their labour services against the commodity they produce. Rather, the capitalist must pay his workers in units of that commodity, which the workers then would have to barter for food, clothing, etc. In such a model there is a labour market, so unemployment is possible.[14]

However, it is incorrect to interpret Leijonhufvud as arguing that it is the money character of exchanges which makes unemployment possible. His orthodox neoclassical critics so interpret him because the use of social relations and classes as analytical tools are alien to them. Leijonhufvud's point is considerably more profound than the arid money-exchange/barter dichotomy. His argument is that it is the 'transactions structure' (property relations) of an economy which makes unemployment possible, and a secondary consequence of the transaction structure is that the exchange between capital and labour is necessarily a monetary exchange. One can conjure up imaginary examples of barter exchange between capital and labour. The relevance of such 'real' models to the problems of a money economy is not obvious (see Section 8.2). It reflects the scientific character of Leijonhufvud's methods that he wastes no time treating the metaphysics of barter models. Following this line of argument, that capitalist economies must be treated as money economies, Leijonhufvud is particularly scathing in his critique of the neoclassical practice of 'dividing through by the price level' to obtain a set of 'real' variables to work with. Like Keynes, he views 'the general price level' as a vague and imprecise concept (Keynes, 1936, pp. 40–43), and that its use as a deflator in theoretical models is a transparent attempt to avoid treating money exchange at all. The intrinsic role of money in capitalist economies and the complexities created by money calculations are what led him to conclude that the symptom of imbalance in an economy may not directly indicate the cause of that imbalance.

As explained in the previous section, the particular discordance between symptom and cause which Leijonhufvud stresses in non-clearance of the labour market, explained superficially by the orthodox neoclassicals as a result of an inappropriate real wage. Leijonhufvud finds the source of labour disequilibrium elsewhere: long-run interest rate is too high. This argument of Leijonhufvud's fulfils the promise made in the introduction to his book to interpret Keynes as seeking to integrate the theory of value (relative prices) with the theory of money. As shown in Chapters 1 to 7, no such integration is seriously attempted in the neoclassical macro model, for two reasons. First, the neoclassical approach raises the non-integration of value theory and monetary theory to the level of principle by constructing money-neutral models. Second, consistent use of one commodity models makes a theory of relative prices as unnecessary 'fifth wheel' in the system.

In Leijonhufvud's analytical model there are at least two commodities, one for investment and one for consumption. The interest rate then becomes a true price variable, not just the rate of transformation of present into future consumption. This approach has a strong kinship with the method of the nineteenth-century classical economists. Central to the theories of distribution and growth (accumulation) of Ricardo and Marx was the analysis of the relative values of consumer and producer commodities. However, Leijonhufvud encounters a serious difficulty: while he is interested in treating this problem stressed by the nineteenth-century political economists, he operates with neoclassical tools ill-designed to investigate it. As long as one holds to an analysis based upon the behaviour of individual agents, the analytical power gained from the division of output between consumer and producer commodities cannot be exploited.[15]

A final and extremely important characteristic of Leijonhufvud's book should be pointed out. One of the general conclusions of neoclassical economies, both micro and macro, is that capitalist economies tend to full employment equilibrium automatically under assumptions of perfect competition, and, therefore, the only possible causes of unemployment, fluctuations, and instability are exogenous influences, monopoly power, or state intervention in markets. Heaping ridicule upon such a sanguine view of *laissez-faire* ideology,[16] Leijonhufvud places himself in the camp of the handful of twentieth-century economists, such as Veblen, Schumpeter and Keynes, who were bold enough to argue that capitalist economies are inherently dynamic and unstable, not equilibrium systems. It is indeed a shame that Leijonhufvud's insights have been lost in a largely trivial debate over information costs and the value of disequilibrium versus equilibrium analysis. If his own writings have contributed to such an interpretation of his work, it none the less remains the case that his 1968 book borders on being a classic of economic analysis.

Part III

A Critique of Inflation Theory

12 Neoclassical Inflation: Aggregate Supply

12.1 INTRODUCTION

In previous chapters the focus has been on the neoclassical theory of employment. We began with a barter ('real') system, demonstrating that full employment is achieved in such a model by excluding the possible causes of demand failures. In subsequent chapters monetary models were investigated, with the conclusion that a number of theoretical difficulties and inconsistencies render automatic adjustment to full employment unlikely even as a logical possibility. Indeed, it is not clear that neoclassical theory has any consistent 'thought experiment' to take one from general disequilibrium with unemployment to general equilibrium with full employment (Chapter 8).

In this chapter we begin to investigate the neoclassical treatment of inflation. The purpose is to consider critically what might be called the fundamental neoclassical inflation parable. In most general form, the parable states that inflation is a monetary phenomenon.[1] More specifically, the allegation is that the rate of change of the price level is equal to the rate of change of the money supply. This hypothesis of proportionality (unit elasticity between prices and the money supply), and the real-wage/employment parable represent the two grand conclusions of neoclassical macroeconomics. It shall be argued that the inflation parable is as flawed as the real-wage/employment one.

The neoclassical theory of inflation has two basic characteristics. First, in the pure synthesis model inflation is a full employment phenomenon.[2] As shall become clear, mainstream economic theory has come to define full employment with reference to changes in the price level. Therefore, the analysis of inflation carries forward and incorporates all of the theoretical inconsistencies of Walrasian general equilibrium macro models. Second, inflation is a phenomenon of the money supply. When one puts these two characteristics together, the analysis of inflation is very simplistic indeed: if there is full employment determined by 'real' variables; if money is strictly neutral; if the demand for money is stable; and if the money supply is exogenously given; then the price level rises proportionally to an expansion of the money supply.

This simple story is the core of neoclassical inflation theory, presented in Section 12.2. Current neoclassical practice is to present inflation stories not in terms of IS and LM curves, but by use of 'aggregate demand' and 'aggregate supply' curves in which output is a function of price. Section 12.3 derives various versions of the 'aggregate supply' curve. In the next chapter 'aggregate demand' curves are treated.

12.2   THE SIMPLE INFLATION MODEL

The basic elements for treating inflation have already been presented, in Chapter 5. To keep matters simple, we shall begin with the false dichotomy model. So the reader does not have to turn back to that chapter, Figure 5.3 is reproduced with minor changes. To refresh memories, this model has a fixed supply of labour whose demand is derivative from an aggregate value added/ output function (Figure 12.1(a) and (b)); a commodity market in which consumption and saving are a function of income and investment a function of the interest rate (yielding the IS curve in Figure 12.1(c)); and a money market in which the demand for money is a function of the quantity of the single commodity to be exchanged (Figure 12.1(d) and (e)). The final part of the set of diagrams shows the money wage and the price of the single commodity, which are implicit in Figure 12.1(a).

The analysis begins at full employment equilibrium with a given money supply of $M*$. All markets are cleared at equilibrium levels, and the money supply dictates a nominal wage of $W(1)$ and a price of the single commodity of $p(1)$. At this point an issue of terminology should be clarified. Throughout the discussion of the neoclassical theory of inflation we shall deal with one commodity models, as is done in the standard textbooks (though rarely made explicit). Since there is only one commodity, it would be misleading to use the term 'price level', which by convention is a term implying a composite measure of many prices.[3] Since neoclassical theory prides itself on analytical rigour, one's terms should be precise and not incorporate unestablished propositions. We should not at this stage use a term which presupposes that the inflation theory developed for a single commodity model can be generalised to a multi-commodity system. The lengthy discussion of the aggregate production function showed

Figure 12.1   Price changes in the false dichotomy model

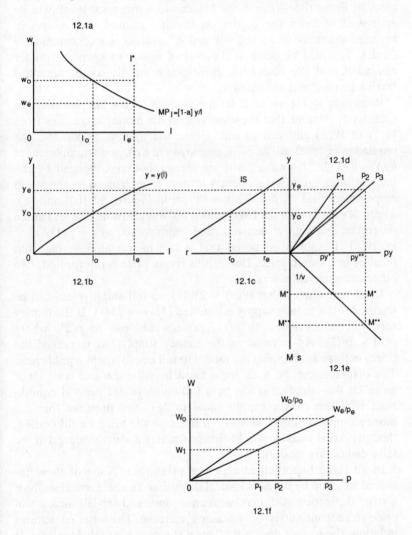

that the move from a one commodity model to a two commodity model is extremely problematical.

This same aggregate production function will play a central role throughout the discussion of inflation. Therefore, *price* rather than 'price level' is the precise and correct term to use in the present context. This usage may be unfamiliar to the reader who has repeatedly encountered 'price level' discussions in one commodity models. From time-to-time the inaccurate term 'price level' will be employed to keep the reader on familiar ground, but always in inverted commas when the discussion involves a one commodity model. This will be done at the cost of rigour to keep the reader reminded that the discussion corresponds strictly to the standard textbook treatment of inflation.

Returning to Figure 12.1, let the analysis follow the procedure in Chapter 5. Assume that for some reason the money wage rises from $W(1)$ to $W(o)$ and cannot fall. Given the money supply $M*$, the implied price level will be $p(o)$, employment $l(o)$, and unemployment $l(o) - l(e)$. In this model with no money holdings induced by the interest rate, aggregate monetary income is unchanged by the fall in employment and output. This is shown in Figures 12.1(d) and (e), where $M*$ along with the fixed velocity of money (note line $1/v$) alone determine monetary demand and supply, so $py* = p(1)y(e) = p(o)y(o)$. It should be noted that a rise in the money wage has resulted in a rise in price. Before this rise in price is interpreted, two other cases are considered.

Let it be assumed that $W(o) = 2W(1)$, so full employment can be restored if the money supply is doubled ($M** = 2M*$). If the money supply were increased to $M**$, price would rise to $p(2)$, where $p(2) = 2p(1)$. As increase in the money supply has increased the price, in this case bringing the model to full employment equilibrium. The diagrams can be used for a third hypothetical exercise. Once more let the initial situation be a full employment general equilibrium with the money supply equal to $M*$, and presume that the money supply doubles, to $M**$. In this case the price would double, though no real variable would change (money is strictly neutral in the false dichotomy model).

In all three hypothetical exercises price rose. None of these involved inflation by the neoclassical definition. In neoclassical analysis a strict distinction is drawn between a 'once-and-for-all' increase in price and a 'continuous' or 'sustained' increase. The latter constitutes inflation; the former does not.[4] This distinction is purely idealistic. It applies only to an abstract, timeless general equilibrium model under 'other things unchanged' assumptions and has no relevance to actual economies; nor has it empirical content. In actual economies there are periods when the measured composite index of prices rises; that is inflation. There are also periods when the composite index of prices falls (much rarer in the last half-century); that is deflation. Finally, there are periods when the price level is more or less constant.

By contrast, actual economies do not experience 'once-and-for-all-price-increases'; or if they do, no one could know it. To clarify the argument let us take an example. Assume that one observes an increase in prices. How would one know if this is going to be 'once-and-for-all' or 'continuous'? The question has no relevance unless the Quantity Theory is correct. If the Quantity Theory is correct, then the price level change will be once-and-for-all if the change in the money supply is once-and-for-all *and there are no parameter changes in the economy*. Under such conditions, after sufficient time of adjustment, the price level will stabilise in equilibrium and the process can be judged (*post-facto*) as once-and-for-all. If another increase in the money supply intervenes before equilibrium is reached, then the increase is a candidate for 'continuous'. But the distinction can have no impact on the behaviour of agents, since *ex ante* it cannot be known precisely what the monetary authorities will do, nor can it be known what parameter changes will occur. A 'one-shot' price increase can only be conceived of in a timeless model, since it refers to the comparison of two equilibrium states whose instantaneous adjustment interval involves no passage of time. In actual economies, prices rise (or fall) for a quarter, a year or several years. Whether any particular time period of price increase is defined as continuous or not is purely arbitrary.[5]

The issue here is not merely semantics. The distinction between 'one-shot' price increases and continuous ones involves assuming what the synthesis model seeks to prove; that inflation is a general equilibrium adjustment process provoked and necessarily facilitated by a change in an autonomous money supply. More rigorous than the unenlightening distinction would be to say: in a model in which money is neutral, the velocity of money is constant, the money supply is exogenously fixed, and output/income is at its full employment level, an increase in the money supply will provoke an increase in price, and price will stop rising when all of the increased money is absorbed into circulation. In such a model, further increases in price require further increases in the money supply; and under the assumptions made the elasticity of price with respect to the money supply is unity. Stating the proposition this way makes it clear that a 'continuous' rise in price is nothing but a series of 'one-shot' increases. The distinction between the two is arbitrary as well as ideal. One could

with complete theoretical rigour define inflation as as 'n-shot' increase in price, with n equal to or greater than some arbitrary number
of 'shots'.

Neoclassical analysis has a purpose in this arbitrary distinction
between 'once-and-for-all' increases and continuous ones. First, it
implies that inflation is always a full employment phenomenon:
increases in M which bring the model to full employment are 'shots',
not 'continuous'. Second, it lays the basis for a particular theory of
inflation, namely that inflation is the result of agents' expectations of
the future, in particular the expectation of inflation itself. In the
synthesis view inflation is largely the result of agents acting in a
manner which generates inflation *as a result of them expecting there to
be inflation*. Another aspect of this arbitrary distinction will be
stressed: the distinction between 'one-shot' and continuous price
rises is essential to sustain the argument that money is a neutral 'veil'
over the system of real variables. But before proceeding further, it is
necessary to develop additional concepts, the so-called 'aggregate
supply and demand curves'.[6]

12.3   THE AGGREGATE SUPPLY CURVE

In all previous diagrammatic presentations macroeconomic equilibrium has been presented in terms of real variables, with price
determined in the money market. Even where the real and monetary
values of the system were explicitly linked (see Table 8.1, models 2,
3, and 4), price was not presented in its relationship to the level of
output. In the last decade, an attempt has been made to derive
meaningful expressions of the type, $y(s) = y(p)$, and $y(d) = y*(p)$,
where s refers to the supply of the single commodity, d refers to
aggregate real expenditure, and $y(p)$ and $y*(p)$ are read as 'aggregate supply (demand) is a function of price'.

In macroeconomics, where supply is treated at the firm level,
output as a function of price is a familiar concept. If firms minimise
costs and sell in perfectly competitive markets (act as 'price takers'),
then the loss-minimising/profit-maximising level of output is set
where marginal cost equals price.[7] Therefore, the firm's marginal cost
curve is its supply curve (above the 'breakeven point'). For a homogeneous product the industry supply curve is the horizontal sum of
the supply curve of each firm. Despite allegations to the contrary in
some textbooks,[8] the aggregate supply curve cannot be constructed

by the argument just used to derive an industry supply curve. The most obvious objection to summing across industries to obtain an aggregate supply curve is that such a procedure only makes sense if the economy has a single commodity (one cannot add apples and oranges).

Even with only one commodity there is a fallacy of composition in the argument that the aggregate supply curve is the sum of firm supply curves. Firm-level supply curves (and therefore industry supply curves) are constructed on the assumption that the price of output is given or 'parametric'. The price of output is established by the intersection of the industry supply and demand curves. The price is treated as given because each firm is assumed to be too small for an expansion of one firm's output to result in a movement of any consequence down the industry demand curve. However, according to the rules of macroeconomic general equilibrium, *there is only one equilibrium price*, that associated with the clearing of the labour market. If there is excess supply in the labour market, price is falling; if there is excess demand, price is rising (recall that one is dealing with a one commodity world). Therefore, price will be stable – given to perfectly competitive firms – only if the labour market is cleared. In a one-commodity system only one real wage is consistent with market-clearing (recall from Chapter 10 that in a multi-commodity world there are multiple full employment real wages). If the money supply is given, only one money wage is consistent with market clearing (see previous section) and only one value for the price of the single commodity. Therefore, the neoclassical aggregate supply curve has only one point – full employment output offered at the price consistent with the money wage which clears the labour market. Graphically, the aggregate supply curve is vertical in the price–output/income space, and this is called the 'classical' case by some authors.[9]

This single-point aggregate supply curve (for a given price) implies that there is only one determinate consequence of the optimising behaviour of firms – general equilibrium full employment. Such a conclusion does not sit well with the more Keynesian-oriented neo-classicals. If one discards the assumption that the labour market is in continuous equilibrium and makes alternative supply- side assumptions, an aggregate supply curve of an opposite type can be derived. In the simplest 'Keynesian' version, the relationship between the 'price level' and output is a right-angle, and the two treatments of aggregate supply are shown in Figure 12.2. In the second version, as

Figure 12.2 General equilibrium and 'Keynesian' aggregate supply curves

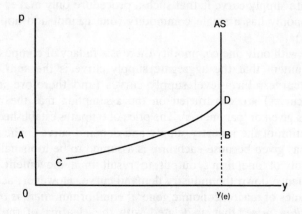

AB, B–AS – 'Keynesian' aggregate supply curve (constant marginal costs and rigid money wage); *CD, D–AS* – Keynesian-neoclassical aggregate supply curve (diminishing returns and rigid money wage); *y(e)–AS* – *general equilibrium aggregate supply.*

long as there is unemployment firms will be prepared to offer more output at a constant price. However, once one reaches full employment, firms begin to bid up wages and price increases with no change in the level of output. This is, of course, over-simplified, and the analysis could be rendered more in conformity with observed price behaviour by assuming that certain 'bottlenecks' such as shortages of skilled labour, raw materials, etc., begin to occur to an increasing extent as the economy approaches $y(e)$.

This second treatment of aggregate supply draws upon concrete experience and common sense more than high theory. Numerous writers have sought to provide theoretical foundations for such a view (see Eichner and Kregel, 1975). Involved is a 'mark-up' theory of pricing, in which firms are treated as having constant costs as long as there in unemployment (see Section 1.3), and cost is a constant proportion of price. Constant marginal costs can be justified on the grounds that production involves relatively little possibility of capital – labour substitution (i.e. switching of techniques), and the money wage is 'downwardly rigid'. The constant proportional mark-up is more difficult to justify, usually rationalised by the argument that the mark-up is primarily a function of the degree to which each industry deviates from perfect competition in the product market. Once full employment output is reached, the 'Keynesian' aggregate supply curve coincides with the general equilibrium supply curve. Assuming as it does constant marginal costs, this is a non-synthesis or non-neoclassical approach to the supply side. Authors favouring this right-angle aggregate supply curve are usually identified by the catch-all term for mainstream heterodoxy, 'post-Keynesianism'.

Another version of aggregate supply more in the neoclassical tradition but keeping the central Keynesian hypothesis of a non-clearing labour market can be constructed using an aggregate output/income function exhibiting diminishing returns, rather than governed by constant marginal costs. With the presumption of diminishing returns, assume a fixed money wage, which given the money supply implies less than full employment. With a fixed money wage (the hallmark of the Keynesian Neoclassical approach), labour market equilibrium no longer holds. The model is in a stable equilibrium with excess supply in the labour market dangling in mid-air, unable to exert downward pressure on the money wage and bring about a market-clearing real wage, However, were the price level to rise, other things equal, the real wage would fall, employment would expand, and output/income would increase. The fixed-money-wage aggregate supply curve is just such an 'other things equal' relationship between price and output/income. The curve would have a positive slope up to point $y(e)$ because of diminishing returns – a higher price with a given money wage implies a lower real wage, which is equated to a lower marginal product of labour. At full employment, $y(e)$, output/income cannot increase, so the aggregate supply curve becomes vertical. The curve CD, D–AS represents the Keynesian Neoclassical treatment of aggregate supply.

In order to use these aggregate supply curves to consider inflation, aggregate demand must enter the story. The aggregate demand curve has not yet been defined in terms of the price level, but the analysis can proceed for the moment without doing so. A given *monetary* demand will call forth a determinate price level if output does not vary (assume it to be at the full employment level) and other parameters remain unchanged. At full employment, increases in the money supply are necessary to generate inflation, either in the neoclassical or Keynesian case. In the Keynesian less-than-full employment range (on line AB in Figure 12.2), increases in the money supply increase output and move the system closer to full employment. Since most

Keynesians accept the assumption of an autonomous money supply, their view of aggregate supply requires increases in the government-generated quantity of money to provoke inflation just as the general equilibrium analysis does.

For current purposes, the principal difference between the general equilibrium and unemployment-fixed money wage analysis of inflation is that, from positions of unemployment, the real wage falls in the former and may be constant in the latter as full employment is approached (if marginal cost is constant). In neither case does the money wage rise when full employment is induced as a result of an expansion in the money supply (since less than full employment in both cases requires the assumption that the money wage is fixed). In subsequent analysis of inflation, we shall deal almost exclusively with modified versions of the general equilibrium aggregate supply curve, following the neoclassical view that inflation is a full employment phenomenon.

The reader should recall that the neoclassical model tends to treat the 'price level' as a derivative variable, somewhat of a theoretical afterthought which tidies up the analysis. If money is strictly neutral and the models are always in general equilibrium, then money is a 'veil', as Pigou put it. But if money is neutral so that the absolute price level makes no difference to 'real' decisions, and output is a function of real variables (e.g. the real wage), is it not a bit strange that the aggregate supply curve is a function of a purely monetary variable (price)? The enigma deepens when one recalls that neoclassical general equilibrium theory implies that the aggregate supply of output *is not* a function of the price level at all (the aggregate supply line is vertical in Figure 12.2). What then has one achieved by constructing a relationship between two variables ($y(s)$ and p) which is no functional relationship at all? And if one is to render this into a functional relationship, is it not necessary to abandon the neutrality of money? Answering these questions would move us ahead of a story developed in some detail in the following two chapters. We can anticipate those answers by saying that a *functional* relationship between aggregate supply and the price level (as opposed to a non-functional vertical relationship) is achieved by invoking the arbitrary distinction between 'once-and for-all' and 'continuous' increases in 'the price level'. This dubious distinction allows the theory to have its cake (neutrality) and eat it also (aggregate supply varies with 'the price level'). However, the argument must await a previous treatment of aggregate demand.

13 Neoclassical Inflation: Aggregate Demand

13.1 THE AGGREGATE DEMAND CURVE: NEW CLASSICAL ECONOMICS

The derivation of the aggregate demand curve in the price-output/income space is more problematical than doing the same for aggregate supply. In order that the aggregate demand curve be stable, it is necessary that at each point of the curve all variables affecting aggregate demand other than price be at stable, unchanging values. Perhaps the most important of these other variables is the interest rate. The interest rate will be stable only if the commodity market and the money market are in equilibrium. In other words, the aggregate demand curve in the price/real output space must connect points of intersection of the IS and LM schedules. It is to be recalled that the IS curve traces points of equilibrium between saving and investment, and the LM curve traces points of equality between the demand and supply of money. Thus, the aggregate demand curve is a 'reduced form' equation with a vengeance – a super-equilibrium locus constructed on the assumption that two markets are continuously and simultaneously in equilibrium.

Apparently the simplest rendition of the aggregate demand curve is that used by the new classical economists, sometimes called the 'monetarist' version. Parkin calls this approach 'the monetary theory of aggregate demand' (Parkin, 1984, p. 133). The approach assumes the interest rate to be constant, which reduces the demand for money to its transactions component. Then one can write,

$$M(d) = vpy(d)$$

This is pre-Keynesian, in which the demand for money is determined by agents' desired real expenditures ($y(d)$), the inverse of the velocity of money, and the 'the price level'. Next, one assumes that the money supply is exogenous and that the money market is in continuous equilibrium. This yields a very simple expression for real aggregate demand:

$$M* = vpy(d)$$

$$y(d) = \frac{M*}{vp} \tag{13.1}$$

One consequence of this formulation of the aggregate demand curve is the discovery that the elasticity of real expenditure with respect to the price of the single commodity ('the price level') is always unity – the curve is a rectangular hyperbola. Unit elasticity for nominal aggregate expenditure with respect to the price level should come as no surprise. In fact, this conclusion was demonstrated in Chapter 5 when dealing with the false dichotomy model.[1] At this point it was demonstrated that the simple quantity theory implied that the monetary demand for the single commodity is constant as long as the money supply is constant. Thus, the new classical theory of aggregate supply is but a manipulation of the quantity equation, $M = vpy$.

This new classical version of the aggregate supply curve is shown in Figure 13.1, along with the vertical aggregate supply curve. Constructing such an aggregate demand curve raises three problems, two of which we have encountered before. First, there is the difficulty raised by the logic of Walras' Law. If the money market and the commodity market are incorporated in the aggregate demand curve, then only one market is left out – the labour market. At point e on the aggregate supply curve the labour market is also in equilibrium. However, the aggregate demand curve is defined for all points along $AD–AD'$. This means that for every point except e, only one market is in disequilibrium. Such a situation, point b, for example, contradicts Walras' Law that the sum of excess demands must equal zero. As shown in Section 8.3, either the analysis must abandon Walras' Law, in which case general equilibrium and all that goes with it is abandoned (e.g. automatic adjustment to full employment), or the aggregate demand curve has only one point, namely e.

Second and no less problematical, this specification of aggregate supply and aggregate demand incorporates the false dichotomy. If the interest is constant and there is no real balance effect,[2] then the demand for money is simply the quantity theory. From Chapter 4, one knows that the quantity theory and Walras' Law combine to produce a theoretical inconsistency, two contradictory equations for the excess demand for money. The new classical theory of aggregate demand and aggregate supply is simple.[3] It is also theoretically invalid except at full employment (all excess demands are zero at full employment equilibrium, so the inconsistency is inoperative).

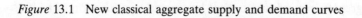

Figure 13.1   New classical aggregate supply and demand curves

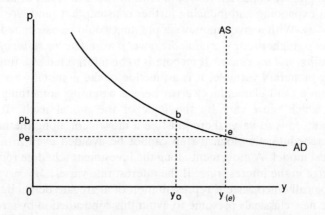

A third problem also involves logical inconsistency. While the commodity market does not appear explicitly in this formulation, it should be clear that it must be in equilibrium. If investment and saving are not equal, then income must be increasing or decreasing. If income increases or decreases, then the interest rate must change not only to equate saving and investment, but also to keep the money market in equilibrium (the latter only if the demand for money is interest elastic, of course).[4] But changes in the interest rate would alter $y(d)$ independently of p. Thus, expression (13.1) is consistent only for IS–LM equilibrium.[5] IS–LM equilibrium implies an internal contradiction if one defines aggregate demand as $y(d) = M*/vp$. Recall that the relationship, $M* = vpy(d)$ assumes commodity market equilibrium (points on the IS curve only) *and* a constant rate of interest. But if the interest rate is constant, then the level of real aggregate demand, $y(d)$, is uniquely determined. Since v and $M*$ are assumed constant, p cannot vary at all – the aggregate demand curve (like the aggregate supply curve) has only one point. Output demanded is not a function of price in the equation $y(d) = M*/vp$.

The inconsistency is worth elaborating for the insights it yields. Let the assumed constant interest rate be $r*$ and the implied level of real expenditure be $y(d)*$. That the first implies the second (ignoring labour market disequilibrium) can be verified by reference to Chapter 5. Consider the horizontal axis of the $y(d) = M*/vp$ function. For all $y(d) < y(d)*$, investment exceeds saving; and for all $y(d) > y(d)*$, saving exceeds investment. For both inequalities, real aggregate expenditure cannot be treated as a function of p. If $i > s$, then aggregate expenditure would tend to rise as a result of income/output expanding and inducing further consumption (and *vice versa* for $i < s$). With a given money supply, this would be associated with a lower p (higher for $i < s$), *but the lower p would be the result of $y(d)$ increasing, not the cause.*[6] If income is to be interpreted as a function of any monetary variable, it is a function of the nominal wage, W.[7] The basic (and elementary) error here is assuming something constant which must vary by the logic of the model itself. If real expenditure is to vary, there must be a movement along the investment schedule; this logical step cannot be avoided even in a new classical model. A movement along the investment schedule requires a change in the interest rate. If the interest rate varies, $M* = vpy(d)$ is a logically inconsistent representation of aggregate demand.

The new classicals presume to avoid this contradiction by a return to pre-*General Theory* models. Were neither saving nor investment a function of income and the demand for money determined by income alone, then the contradiction would seem to disappear. In such a formulation saving and investment would always be equated by a unique interest rate, and the interest rate would have no impact upon the demand for money. However, this is no solution at all, for the strict dichotomy in pre-Keynesian models between the determination of output/income on the one hand and savings and investment on the other *holds only at full employment*. The new classical aggregate demand curve seeks to pass through points at which output/income is less that its full employment value. If for all such values of output/income the level of saving and investment were equal and unchanging, this would imply the absurd result that, at very low levels of income, investment must exceed income. For this to be true with the interest rate equating saving and investment, consumption would have to be negative. Thus, either the new classical aggregate demand curve is trivial (reduced to a single point of full employment output/income), or it is logically inconsistent.

Escape from this internal contradiction is simply achieved: if the interest is allowed to vary, then one can derive, $y(d) = y*(p)$, such that the commodity and money markets are in equilibrium. However, then it would no longer be valid to treat the demand for money as interest-inelastic or to ignore the wealth effect. As we shall see, this progression takes one to more complicated models with the possibility of non-neutrality. The result plays havoc with the new classical approach to inflation, for simplicity and neutrality are at the heart of its stories.

In summary, what the new classicals have done is to attempt to resuscitate a version of the quantity theory that even those Keynes called the 'classics' would have rejected as invalid. At best, $M_* = vpy$ holds only in full employment, and then it is invalidated by the contradiction arising from Walras' Law except when all markets are in equilibrium. What the new classical theory of aggregate demand has demonstrated is that real expenditure *cannot* be written as $y(d) = M_*/vp$, and thereby provide a useful heuristic exercise. Money expenditure, $py(d)$, is not constant even in abstract models (its elasticity with respect to price cannot be unity).

We close this section by considering a different type of issue, the relevance of this internally inconsistent analysis to observed behaviour of economies. This is a dimension of neoclassical theory which we have given little stress, restricting the analysis to questions of logic. However, at this point allusions to actual occurrences become relevant. As shown in Chapter 9, the new classical economics makes strong claims for its relevance to observed events.

However, the aggregate supply and aggregate demand curves leave one with very few variables indeed to account for macroeconomic events. Were this partial equilibrium analysis, the model would not be so restrictive upon one's thinking. When considering supply and demand curves for a single commodity, for example, one holds certain things constant (money income, prices of other commodities, etc.). This *ceteris paribus* treatment is only an approximation, not an assertion that other things are in fact constant. The analysis is different in the case of aggregate demand and aggregate supply. Here, other things are not assumed constant but to be in equilibrium, which is a behavioural condition and not an assumption as such. In Figure 13.1 the analysis does not hold other variables constant in order that they might be considered at a later point. It presumes them to *vary such that they are always in equilibrium*. It is a short step to treating their equilibrium values as their natural condition,[8] and proceeding as if in actual economies aggregate demand and aggregate supply were a function of the price level alone (or at least primarily). As shown in Chapter 9 and again below, this is exactly the type of story the new classical economics wishes to tell about observed economic behaviour – that the 'real' variables of actual economies are in continuous full employment equilibrium. In order that subsequent analysis not be oppressively restrictive of thought, one must keep in mind that aggregate demand and aggregate supply are functions of many variables in the neoclassical model, and it is a theoretical simplification of an abstract model to treat them as varying with the price level alone.

13.2 AGGREGATE DEMAND AFTER THE NEOCLASSICALS

The new classical approach represents an extreme form of the neoclassical synthesis in which most of the contributions to macroeconomics inspired by the *General Theory* has been banished. The result is a number of internal contradictions. A more consistent aggregate demand curve is derived from the models presented in Chapter 6 and 7. What follows should be familiar, for nothing more is involved than an application of IS and LM curves. There are two basic versions, with and without the wealth effect. With the demand for money interest-elastic and/or the presence of the wealth effect, there is no false dichotomy. Considering first the 'complete Keynesian' model, one begins by writing commodity market and money market equilibrium (see pp. 81, 89 for derivation):

$$y(d) = \frac{c_* + i_* - dr}{l - b} \quad \text{(commodity market equilibrium)} \quad (13.2)$$

$$M_* = p[vy(d) + h - jr] \quad \text{(money market equilibrium)}$$

$$y(d) = \frac{[M_*/p + jr - h]}{v} \quad (13.3)$$

The aggregate demand curve subsumes equilibrium in both markets, so it is obtained by solving equations (13.2) and (13.3) for the interest rate and setting them equal to each other. This results in a rather complicated expression which has a simple form when the various parameters are combined. It can be summarised as follows.[9]

$$p = \frac{M_*}{a2[y(d) - a1]}$$

or (13.4)

$$y(d) = a1 + \frac{M_*}{a2}[1/p]$$

It will be recalled that the New Classical aggregate demand curve had an elasticity of unity – aggregate demand remained constant as the price level changed. Nominal aggregate demand in equation (13.4) varies with price, and its elasticity decreases as price falls. Unlike in the new classical case, the multiplier is allowed to operate in a logically consistent way. If one multiplies the second version of (13.4) by p, nominal aggregate demand becomes $py(d) = a_1p + M*/a_2$, whose elasticity is less than one – nominal aggregate demand decreases as price falls.[10]

The mechanics of the interaction of $y(d)$ and p in the complete Keynesian case can be summarised as follows: given the money supply and other parameters, a fall in price increases the real money supply; this prompts a fall in the interest rate in order to clear the money market, while simultaneously provoking a move down the investment schedule; a move down the investment schedule calls forth a higher level of output to equate saving and investment, keeping the money market in equilibrium; and, finally, nominal demand, $py(d)$, must fall because the lower interest rate has transferred money to idle balances (which is why elasticity of nominal aggregate demand with respect to price is less than unity).

When the wealth effect is included the algebra and the story become more complicated, though familiar. Let us assume that real balances affect only the demand for money and consumption. On these assumptions, the LM and IS curves are as follows (see Chapter 7).

$$M* = p[vy(d) + h - jr] + fM*$$

$$y(d) = \frac{[c* + i* + g\{M*/p\} - dr]}{1 - b}$$

When the two are combined to ensure equilibrium in the commodity and money markets and simplified by combining parameters, the result is equation (13.5).

$$y(d) = a1 + \frac{a3}{a2} M*[1/p] \tag{13.5}$$

This aggregate demand function differs from the previous by the term $a3$, which incorporates the parameters relating to the wealth effect (real balance effect in this case since to keep matters simple bonds are not included). The story with the real balance effect can now be told. From an initial position of IS–LM equilibrium a fall in price creates an excess supply of real money holdings. As a result, consumption is directly stimulated as agents relieve themselves of money by spending. At the same time, an increase in the real money supply also lowers the interest rate, which stimulates investment. Since agents are not victim to 'money illusion' and always hold the same proportion of the nominal money supply for a given interest rate, the marginal response of nominal aggregate demand to price is the same as in the complete Keynesian case, though the elasticity is lower.[11] As before, nominal aggregate demand falls when price falls because the interest rate drops, inducing additional idle balances.

When comparing the stories generated by these two aggregate demand curves, one must be careful not to confuse movements along schedules with shifts in schedules. In both stories real balances or the real money supply is key. In the complete Keynesian case, a change in $M*/p$ results in movements along schedules whose intercepts and slopes are unchanged except for the shift in $M*/p$ itself. This creates an excess supply of real balances. All other changes are the result of movements along schedules (presuming the saving schedule to be independent of the interest rate). In the second story, $M*/p$ creates an excess supply of real balances as before, but also enters the consumption function as a shift parameter. Assuming only the consumption function to be affected, the result is that a fall in price must provoke a greater increase in output/income than in the first story to maintain equality between savings and investment, for saving is lower for any given level of output/income. However, the complete result requires consideration of effects on the LM curve also, for it, too, shifts with changes in $M*/p$.

The effect of a change in price on real aggregate demand for the complete Keynesian and real balance effect cases can be clarified by first representing them in terms of IS and LM curves. This is done in Figure 13.2, with the initial equilibrium noted as Eo. Assume a fall in price, which would be provoked by a drop in the exogenous money wage, for example. In the complete Keynesian case, the IS curve is unaffected by a change in price. The consequence of a fall in price is movement along the investment and saving schedules. For the first schedule this results from a fall in the interest rate, and in the second the movement is generated by increase in the level of income. When the real balance effect is added to the story, consumption rises for any level of income as price falls. In consequence, there is a shift to the right for the IS curve (IS2). In the case of the LM curve, there is a shift to the right for both the complete Keynesian and real balance versions of the story. The shift is greater without the real balance

Figure 13.2   *IS* and *LM* equilibrium for an exogenous change in price
with and without the real balance effect

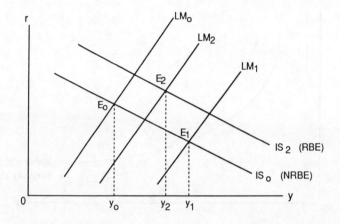

RBE – with real balance effect; *NRBE* – no real balance effect.

effect, since a real balance effect reduces the average velocity of
money (assuming the income velocity, v, to be the same in both
cases). The new equilibrium for the real balance effect is E2 (IS2 and
LM2), and for the complete Keynesian curves, E1 (IS0 = IS1 and
LM1). As a consequence of the price change, the new equilibrium
interest rate is lower if there is no real balance effect (the LM curve
has shifted to the right, but the IS curve has not). When the real
balance effect is operative, whether the interest rate rises or falls as a
result of a price decline is indeterminant, and this case implies the
larger increase in income is also indeterminant, depending on how
sensitive consumption is to real balances (how far IS2 lies to the right
of IS0) and the proportion of the money supply that agents wish to
hold at any interest rate (which affects how far the LM curve shifts).

Figure 13.2 can be used to demonstrate again the inconsistency of
the new classical aggregate demand curve. If the interest rate were
constant no point but Eo would be consistent with commodity market
equilibrium, and the aggregate demand 'curve' would be a single
point. Were there to occur an exogenous fall in price, the analysis
would become inconsistent, for it would be struck at some disequilibrium point directly to the right of Eo, off both the IS and LM curves.

The aggregate demand curve can now be transformed into the

Figure 13.3   Neoclassical aggregate demand curve and the false aggregate demand curve

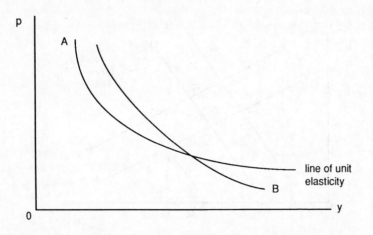

price/income space. In figure 13.3 an aggregate demand curve is drawn incorporating the real balance effect on consumption (equation (13.5)), and a second line with an elasticity of unity as a benchmark. The latter might be called the 'false aggregate demand curve' of the new classicals. The neoclassical aggregate demand curve, AB, has an elasticity less than unity because a lower price requires a lower interest rate, which reduces the level of active balances, so $py(d)$ declines.[12]

The purpose in going through this rather tedious discussion in order to draw Figure 13.3 is to demonstrate that the relationship between price and real aggregate demand is an extremely complicated one. One cannot merely write, $M = vpy$, assume the interest rate to be constant and re-designate y as $y(d)$; i.e., call income aggregate demand. As prices change, a complex set of instantaneous adjustments occur – income changes generate an increase in saving, which requires an equilibrating change investment implying a change in the interest rate; and if the real balance effect is at work, schedules shift. Further, the presence of the interest rate in the model implies the existence of bonds, in which case the wealth effect implies non-neutrality. Once money is no longer neutral, the analysis of inflation as a purely monetary phenomenon becomes extremely complicated, for it implies that a change in the money supply alters real variables.

As said before, the aggregate demand curve in the price/income space is a super-general equilibrium construction. Most of the adjustments which characterise the operation of a capitalist economy are hidden from view, lost in arbitrary assumptions of continuous market clearing.

14 Expectations, Inflation and Full Employment

14.1 INFLATION AND UNEMPLOYMENT

As so far developed, aggregate demand and aggregate supply curves are of limited interest. They come into their own when 'augmented' with price expectations. The vehicle for moving to expectations augmented aggregate supply and demand is the Phillips curve, which summarises the relationship between unemployment and the rate of inflation via the intermediary of money wage changes. First we consider the alleged trade-off between the level of unemployment and the rate of inflation (the 'Phillips curve'), which allows one to derive the 'expectations augmented' versions of aggregate demand and supply. Section 14.2 puts together the aggregate supply and demand curves in their expectations-augmented versions to tell inflation stories, with emphasis on the new classical parables. Section 14.3 retells the stories with a fixed money wage.

The relationship between unemployment and money wage changes (and unemployment and prices) is easily investigated empirically. This was probably done first by Fisher in the 1920s, but the empirical relationship is universally known as the Phillips Curve, after an article published by A. W. H. Phillips in 1958.[1] Phillips' hypothesis was a simple one: a low rate of unemployment is associated with excess demand for labour; excess demand for labour generates upward pressure on money wages; and rising money wages provoke entrepreneurs to raise prices.

The Phillips hypothesis is shown in Figure 14.1(a), with the rate of change of the price level measured on the vertical axis ($\dot{p}$) and unemployment on the horizontal axis. There are two important points to make. First, with regard to causality, the hypothesis postulated that tight labour markets were the cause of inflation; i.e., higher money wages lead to higher prices. As shall be shown, in the current rendition causality is reversed. Second, the original analysis was strictly *empirical*. Indeed, Phillips came under sharp criticism for allegedly not supplying an adequate theoretical explanation of the empirical results he obtained. If we treat Figure 14.1(a) as an empirical relationship, we can say that there is by definition an excess demand for commodities to the left of unemployment rate u_* (where prices rise), and an excess supply to the right of that rate (where prices fall); i.e., a rising or falling price level is by definition evidence of positive or negative excess demand.

However, positive or negative excess demand for commodities *does not in itself imply what conditions prevail in the labour market.* Wage increases may not be the cause of price increases, but both the result of the operation of some third variable not represented on the two-dimensional diagram (such as a temporary shortage of some non-labour input). The presumption that wage increases are the only possible cause of price increases requires specific assumptions. The argument is sometimes made that price inflation can be reduced to wage inflation because 'labour costs represent a fairly stable proportion of total costs' (Parkin, 1984, p. 300), but this is an *ad hoc* justification with no obvious theoretical basis. In fact, the link from wage increases to price increases is strictly valid only in a one commodity model with no non-labour inputs.

However, arguments over causality have been swept aside by the practice of *assuming* that only wages and prices are the relevant variables. The bottom diagram, Figure 14.1(b), represents the hypothesis put forward by Friedman. The analysis begins by assuming there to exist a unique and stable rate of unemployment for which the rate of change of inflation is zero; i.e., such that any given inflation rate has no tendency to increase or decrease. This level of unemployment was called by Friedman 'the natural rate', and was treated in Chapter 9.[2] Let this 'natural' rate be $u*$ or point A in Figure 14.1(b). Through $u*$ passes line SFC1, a short-run Friedman curve. This curve, SCF1, has the characteristic that economic agents anticipate a zero rate of inflation. Next, assume that workers individually or through their trade unions bargain for a money wage which clears the labour market.[3] Finally, define the unemployment rate associated with a zero rate of change of inflation to be the unemployment rate consistent with a 'cleared' labour market. In other words, $u*$ is the full employment rate of unemployment. We return to this apparent contradiction in terms after treating the mechanics of expectations-generated inflation.

Let the analysis begin at point A where the labour market is in equilibrium (along with all other markets) and a zero rate of inflation is anticipated for the future. The story now introduces an *ex machina* unanticipated increase in the price level. Since money wages are given, the real wage falls. The fall in the real wage induces firms to increase employment, reducing the unemployment rate to a u1 (a

Figure 14.1   (a) Inflation as a function of unemployment (the Phillips hypothesis)

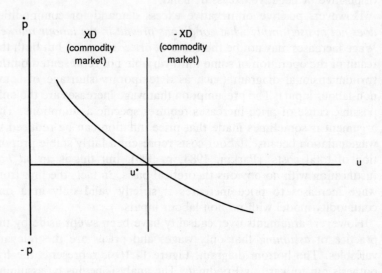

(b) Unemployment as a function of inflation (the Friedman hypothesis)

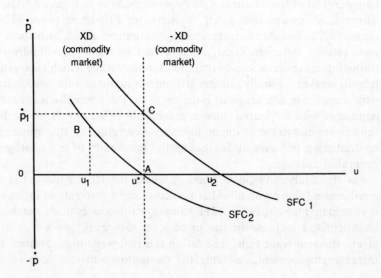

movement along SPC1). However, dissatisfied with a lower real wage, workers demand a higher money wage to compensate them for the higher price level. The story concludes that the new money wage will be such as to regain the 'natural rate of unemployment', $u*$. A new short-run Friedman curve is established, $SFC2$, based on the expectation of a rate of inflation of p_1. This adjustment process is summarised by the movement from point A (zero inflation equilibrium) to B (disequilibrium) to C (equilibrium at inflation rate p_1). The implication is that any rate of inflation will eventually result in a return to the 'natural' rate of unemployment.

The purpose of this story is to undermine the basis for government policy intervention to reduce the unemployment rate. If one assumes that the *ex machina* appearance of inflation was the result of the government expanding demand *at full employment* in order to reduce the rate of unemployment, then it can be concluded that such intervention is ineffective. By stimulating inflation and thus lowering the real wage, expansion of aggregate demand will lower the unemployment rate (to u_1), but only temporarily. Further, lower unemployment was purchased by inflation and to keep the rate at u_1 accelerating inflation is required.[4] Each successive rate of inflation calls forth a rate of money wage increase to match it, so the SFC shifts continuously upwards. This process is summarised by the statement that 'the long-run Phillips [*sic*, Friedman] curve is vertical'.

The Friedman hypothesis would seem to offer a devastating critique of expansionary fiscal and monetary policy – such interventions at best reduce unemployment momentarily at the cost of inflation. However, the result is a rather trivial statement of a special case. The result is trivial because the analysis assumes from the outset that the labour market clears. If the economy is continuously regaining full employment equilibrium, then it is obvious that expansionary policies are ineffective. There is an absurdity here: presumably the purpose of policy intervention is to reach full employment, yet the Friedman hypothesis assumes that the economy is already there.

The result is a special case in that the 'long-run' relationship is vertical if and only if money is neutral. If money is not neutral, then demand expansion by increasing the money supply will change the full employment rate of interest. This in turn can affect the supply curve of labour, shifting point $u*$ even if the 'natural rate' hypothesis is accepted as valid (see Chapter 8).[5]

It is important to note that in the Friedman analysis causality runs from inflation to unemployment, not *vice versa*. Beginning from a position of 'full employment unemployment', the government unwisely generates inflation in hopes of reducing unemployment. This inflation then alters the level of unemployment, though temporarily. Were the government to refrain from intervention, the labour market would be in a continuous equilibrium with no inflationary pressure. In the next section this full employment/money neutral story is pursued in terms of aggregate supply and demand curves.

14.2 EXPECTATIONS AUGMENTED AGGREGATE SUPPLY MECHANICS (NEW CLASSICAL)

In the previous section the money wage played a central role in the mechanics of inflation, though it did not appear explicitly in the diagrammatic analysis. This omission is rectified in Figure 14.2, showing a single commodity model labour market with the money wage on the vertical axis and the level of employment on the horizontal. In order to incorporate the real wage into the analysis, each labour supply and labour demand curve is drawn for a given price of the single commodity. As in previous chapters, the demand for labour is derived from a single commodity output/value added function. Unlike in most of the previous models, the supply of labour is assumed to be a positive function of the real wage, which rises as the nominal wage rises with a given price of output. Only one labour supply curve is drawn (for price equal to p_0), along with three labour demand curves. If the price of the single commodity is p_0, then the labour market is in equilibrium at employment level of $l0$ and a nominal wage of W_0.

Our purpose now is to analyse how changes in price affect the equilibrium in the labour market. For the moment let it be assumed that changes in price are *ex machina*, unexplained and exogenous, and that economic agents form expectations of the future price. Consider first the case in which expectations prove correct. Anticipating a price of the single commodity of p_1, capitalists shift their notional demand curve for labour upwards to $l(d)$, p_1. If money is strictly neutral, the point on this new labour demand curve corresponding to full employment equilibrium (l_0) will be at a money wage which has increased by the same proportion as the price of the single commodity; i.e., at the same real wage. Similarly, workers will change their offerings of work with respect to the *money wage* (unchanged with respect to the *real wage*) such that the aggregate

Figure 14.2   Labour market equilibrium and money wages

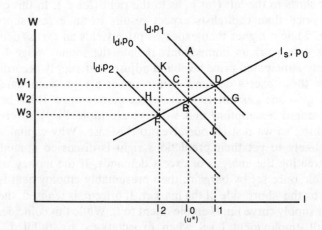

supply curve of labour shifts upwards until it intersects the new labour demand curve at the same real wage as before. If price expectations are continuously fulfilled, the locus of equilibrium points in Figure 14.2 is vertical, shown by line *AB*. This is the long-run Friedman curve charted in terms of money wage *levels* rather than money wage *changes*.

If expectations are not always correct, then the multiple results are possible. First we consider the case in which capitalists always are correct in their expectations, but workers sometimes err. To consider this case in Figure 14.2, let workers have an expectation of price p_0, yielding curve l_s, p_0, which may or may not prove correct. Assume that the actual price that comes to prevail is p_1, correctly anticipated by the capitalists. In this case, labour is supplied along curve l_s, p_0, and demanded along l_d, p_1. This implies that workers have negotiated in the previous period a money wage of W_0, which would have called forth an equilibrium employment of l_0 had price p_0 prevailed. But with price p_1 ruling, the real wage has fallen and capitalists desire a level of employment at point *G* (with an excess *demand* for labour at money wage W_0). If the realised price proves to be p_2 (lower than p_0 and correctly anticipated by capitalists, then the labour demand would be point *H* (yielding an excess *supply* for labour at money wage W_0). Thus, when capitalists get their expectations right and workers do not, a realised price below the expected price *by workers* results in an excess supply of labour and *vice versa*.

If on the other hand, workers are invariably correct and capitalists err, the demand for labour remains at point B while the supply of labour shifts to the left (for p_1 as to the right (for p_2). In this case, a lower price than capitalists expect results in an excess supply of labour, while a higher than expected price yields an excess demand. In this case workers immediately deflate the money wage by the correctly-anticipated price level and adjust their supply accordingly.

How these excess demands and supplies are accommodated depends upon one's assumptions about the money wage. It has become the standard assumption that workers are more likely to err than capitalists, so we restrict ourselves to this case. Why capitalists are more likely to get their predictions right is discussed immediately after treating the analysis of excess demands. If the money wage is inflexible once set by bargain, then presumably employment is governed by the 'short' side of the market. If price p_1 is realised, then the labour supply curve limits employment to l_0. While this coincides with the full employment level when expectations are fulfilled, some capitalists are left discontent. If price p_2 is realised, then employment is set by labour demand at point H, with HB workers unemployed. By definition this would be 'involuntary' unemployment, since the unemployed workers are willing and able to work at money wage W_0.

To avoid the conclusion that involuntary unemployment is possible even as a temporary phenomenon, the new classical economists arbitrarily assume that the labour market always clears no matter what money wage is reached in the hypothetical bargaining. They go on to apply this assumption of market clearing to real economies. If the money wage does adjust, then Figure 14.2 allows for multiple full employment equilibria. If capitalists predict a price of p_1 and workers p_0, the realisation of p1 as price along with a money wage W_0 results in excess demand of BG. In response, the money wage rises to W_1, clearing the labour market at employment level l_1. It is to be noted that though the money wage is higher at W_1, the real wage is lower. Conversely, a price of p_2 (correctly foreseen by capitalists and overestimated by workers) results in a fall in the equilibrium level of employment to l_2, where the money wage is lower but the real wage higher.

This analysis supports an important political conclusion now familiar to us: unemployment is voluntary. Indeed, in the current story unemployment is non-existent. What looks like unemployment is the labour market clearing at lower levels of employment. Figure 14.2 and the assumptions necessary to construct it imply that declines in the level of employment are the result of workers over-estimating the coming price level – excessive inflationary expectations depress employment (though no unemployment results). However, this conclusion requires the assumption that capitalists tend to be right in their predictions more often than workers. If the reverse were true, then excessive inflationary expectations by capitalists would lead to levels of employment in *excess* of l_0.[6]

The assumption that capitalists are more successful in making predictions than workers is the way one obtains a positively sloped aggregate supply curve. Recall that the aggregate supply curve presumes that the labour and commodity markets are cleared. Therefore, a positive slope requires that there be multiple full employment equilibria. Such a supply curve is constructed in Figure 14.3. In Figure 14.3(b) is the aggregate value added function and the labour market below it. These are linked to the price-output/value added space via a 45 degree line in Figure 14.3(c). As in Figure 14.2, the labour market is treated in terms of the money wage, and capitalists are assumed to predict correctly and workers to err. The resultant curve in Figure 14.3(d) might be called the 'workers' erroneous expectations aggregate supply curve'. It is to be recalled that the positive slope results from the correct-expectation demand curve for labour shifting with the erroneous-expectations labour supply curve remaining fixed. If workers got their expectations right and capitalists erred, then in Figure 14.3(a) l_d, p_0 would be treated as fixed with l_s shifting, yielding a set of equilibria such as points *J–B–K*. When followed around to Figure 14.3(d), these points would result in a *negatively* sloped expectations augmented aggregate supply curve.

The neoclassical inflation story with a flexible money wage and the neutrality of money can now be told, beginning at general equilibrium with an expectation by workers and capitalists of no change in the price of the single commodity; i.e., at money wage W_0, employment level l_0, output/value added as y_0, and price of P_0 (points indicated by *B* in all four parts of Figure 14.3). Let the 'authorities' increase the money supply by an amount which would raise price to p_1 when all timeless Walrasian adjustments are complete. Capitalists correctly predict the coming price level, so the demand for labour curve shifts to l_d, p_1; workers underestimate the price increase, retaining their notional supply curve l_d, p_0. Thus, the labour market clears at a money wage of W_1, which implies a fall in the real wage and a higher level of employment l_1. This higher level of employment

Figure 14.3 Expectations-augmented aggregate supply (From Parkin, 1984, p. 361.)

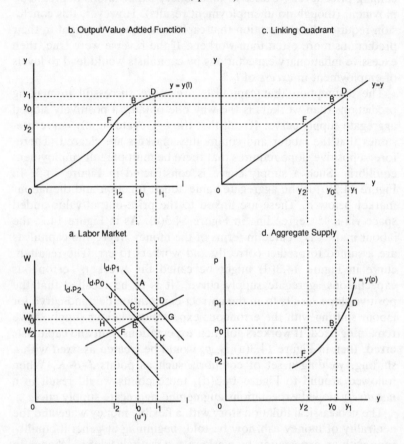

b. Output/Value Added Function

c. Linking Quadrant

a. Labor Market

d. Aggregate Supply

brings forth a higher level of output, and the aggregate supply curve is positively sloped (Figure 14.3(d)). If a fall in the money supply had been assumed, then the new equilibrium would have been those levels noted by the letter '*F*'.

The first point to note about this analysis, which is the essence of the new classical approach, is that it is no theory of inflation at all. The inflation itself is the result of an increase in the money supply, something one knew from the quantity theory without going through the tedious derivation of aggregate supply and demand curves. Further, the story is one involving continuous full employment equilibrium even though price is rising. In other words, points *F*, *B*, and

D represent labour market equilibrium, so there are no excess demands in the system. For this reason it is unnecessary to represent in Figure 14.3(d) the aggregate demand curve we laboured so hard to derive; however constructed (consistent with the neutrality of money), it must intersect the aggregate supply curve at points of general equilibrium. Stripped of all of its unnecessary complications, the analysis says that inflation is a full employment phenomenon resulting from increases in the money supply, which will come to an end when monetary expansion ceases, hardly a step forward from the simple quantity theory.[7]

The analysis offers a hypothesis that full employment, defined as no *involuntary* unemployment, can occur at different levels of output and employment. This conclusion is important for its political implications, and sweeps away the negative aspects of what used to be commonly called 'the business (or trade) cycle'. Up until the 1970s, most neoclassical economists would have conceded that actual capitalist economies tend to evolve through time in a cyclical pattern – periods of relative expansion followed by periods of relative contraction. Such a view implies that at best capitalist economies are characterised by a *tendency* to full employment, but the tendency is perfectly consistent with extended periods of involuntary unemployment. On the basis of this view, one could go on to argue that while eventually the economy would equilibrate itself to full employment, government intervention is justified to speed and smooth the process of adjustment. This minimal argument for counter-cyclical fiscal and monetary policy is strengthened if one believes that capitalist economies are subject to frequent unanticipated disruptive events (usually called 'shocks').

It is this minimal justification for government intervention which the new classical inflation story seeks to refute. If the economy is always at full employment general equilibrium, then there is no reason for intervention. However, the cyclical movement of capitalist economies provide *prima facie* evidence that such economies were always in some stage of expansionary or contractionary disequilibrium. In brief, for generations most economists looked at actual economies and concluded that periods of full employment were the exception rather than the rule.

The new classical inflation story is an attempt to demonstrate that not only full employment but full employment general equilibrium is the rule and deviations from it the exceptions. The argument is that the movements one observes in output and employment (abstracting from any trend) *are to be interpreted as variations in an economy in continuous general equilibrium*, provoked by expectational errors with regard to the coming price level. What looks like an expansionary period is in fact a temporary rise in the equilibrium level of employment as a result of prices rising faster than anticipated by workers. Similarly, what appears as an increase in involuntary unemployment does not involve unemployment at all, but rather a labour market in equilibrium in a moment when workers' price expectations are above the realised price level.[8] One can conclude from this line of argument that there is no 'business cycle' in the sense of periods of greater and less unemployment of labour, but only equilibrium movements in response to incorrectly anticipated variations in the price level.

Any pretensions to relevance to actual economies for this new classical story rests on the ability of the model to predict 'procyclical' movements in the price level and employment – when unemployment falls prices rise, and when unemployment rises prices fall.[9] Put another way, the new classicals must show how a positive relationship between prices and employment is consistent with no involuntary unemployment. This theoretical prediction is achieved in Figure 14.3, for the aggregate supply curve is positively sloped, a construction based upon the assumption that workers are more likely to err in their expectations than capitalists.[10] If the reverse were the case the aggregate supply curve would be *negatively* sloped, and the new classical story would predict that inflation should be abating when employment rises.

This assumption about the expectations of workers as opposed to capitalists is arbitrary. To demonstrate the arbitrariness of treating workers' expectations one way and those of capitalists another, it is useful to review the hypothetical bargaining process postulated by the new classicals. Workers are assumed to seek a money wage which when combined with the expected 'price level' will yield a real wage that ensures full employment (clearing of the labour market). Capitalists are assumed to seek the same labour market result. Further, if either party proves wrong in its expectations, it is assumed that the money wage, even though it has been set by bargaining, is flexible and will adjust upwards or downwards to clear the error-in-expectations-ridden labour market. Why rational agents would bother to waste the time to bargain over the money wage when agreed-upon bargains are ineffective is not obvious, but this inconsistency is a small point given other logical problems.[11]

In order that the workers set the real wage that will call forth the full employment general equilibrium supply of labour, they must predict all relevant prices for their consumption commodities (there being only one in a one commodity model). In order that capitalists predict their labour demand, they must also anticipate price, in their case the price of their product. The new classical justification of greater probability of error for workers' predictions is based on an alleged greater intrinsic difficulty involved in their formulation of expectations. It is argued that capitalists ('firms') have only to predict the prices of the products they produce in order to formulate an expectation of the coming real wage. Workers (euphemistically called 'households') on the other hand must predict all the prices of the commodities that comprise their 'consumption basket'. Since workers have more prices to predict, they are more likely to err, the new classicals conclude.[12]

A moment's reflection shows this asymmetric treatment of expectations to be arbitrary, an *ad hoc* assumption inserted to reach a prearranged result rather like taking 'back-bearings' in sailing. When the asymmetry is considered as a purely theoretical result, it is absurd, since the New Classicals usually work with a one commodity model. In a one commodity model there is only one 'price' to anticipate on the part of any agent. If the theoretical result refers to an multi-commodity model, then in general the demand curve for labour is not downwardly sloped with respect to the real wage, as shown in Chapter 9. Alternatively, the asymmetry might be interpreted as an *empirical* generalisation, that in practice it is harder to get a lot of prices right than a few. This argument, however, contradicts a general law of random events. It is to be noted that in practice workers are predicting the general price level. If changes in relative prices are assumed to be random, then it is reasonable to assume that expectations errors will tend to cancel each other out. That is, some predictions will be too low, others will be too high, and the more prices that are predicted, the more likely it will be that the prediction of the *general price level* will prove close to the mark every time. On the other hand, precisely because capitalists are predicting a few prices, this class of agents are more likely to come up with results different from the actual outcome.[13] This variant of the 'law of large numbers' must be repealed by the new classicals in order to obtain their positively sloped aggregate supply curve even as an *ad hoc* empirical relationship. Further, since the new classicals presume money to be neutral, changes in the money supply should leave relative prices unchanged, making prediction of a collection of prices equivalent to predicting a single price.

One can conclude that the new classical story of continuous full employment general equilibrium predicts pro-cyclical movements in prices (if workers err more than capitalists), *and* counter-cyclical movements in prices (if capitalists err more than workers), *as well as* a random relationship between prices and employment (if workers and capitalists predict with equal accuracy on average). A theory which predicts all possible outcomes in practice predicts none. The conclusion follows that there is little empirical support for the continuous full employment story.

14.3 A FIXED MONEY WAGE AND THE 'NATURAL' RATE OF UNEMPLOYMENT

The analytical difficulties of the new classical macroeconomics largely derive from an attempt to defend the ideological position that capitalist economies do not in practice suffer from unemployment. Once the defence of this position is no longer paramount, the relatively less problematical models of Chapters 6 and 7 can be used to tell a more familiar neoclassical story. In these models unemployment in excess of the 'natural rate' is a theoretical possibility; i.e., the labour market need not always clear. This non-clearing is always the result of a rigid money wage, which allows for equilibrium at less than full employment. The problem arises when one tries to establish the logical conditions under which a rate of unemployment *less* than the 'natural' rate can prevail.

A central element in the disequilibrium treatment of inflation (which might be called Keynesian–Neoclassical) is again the real wage. As long as one works with an aggregate output/value added function, a necessary condition for a positively sloped aggregate supply curve is that the real wage falls as price rises. It is the fall in the real wage which calls forth a greater demand for labour, which gives the $y = y(p)$ function its positive slope. A fall in the real wage implies that price rises faster than money wages, which the new classicals achieved by arbitrarily treating the predictions of workers and capitalists differently. The more Keynesian neoclassicals tend to justify prices rising more than money wages as an empirical relationship. If one thinks that wage contracts are effective, it follows that unexpected increases in the price level will depress real wages and unexpected declines will raise the real wage. In this case as before workers err in their predictions, agreeing to a money wage which yields the 'wrong' real wage (i.e. not the real wage that produces $u*$). Presumably capitalists also erred, since the hypothetical bargain was mutual, and their labour demand is adjusted to the commodity wage which actually prevails ('actually' in the context of the model, for one is not referring to observed behaviour).

However, variations in the real wage are not *sufficient* to yield a positively sloped aggregate supply curve. Let us return to the one commodity model in Figure 14.3 and inspect the labour market on the assumption that there is an invariant money wage W_0 (representing a collective bargain struck for the period). If the price of the single commodity proves to be p_2 instead of the anticipated p_0, then the real wage will rise and the demand for labour will be H, with HB workers unemployed. Thus, for price below p_0, the aggregate supply curve in Figure 14.3(d) is upward-sloping, from a point to the left of F and through point B (i.e. more elastic than the new classical segment FB). The problem arises for price above p_0. In such a case, the demand for labour is a point such as G, but this lies beyond the labour which will be offered at money wage W_0. Without further assumptions, the aggregate supply curve of the Keynesian neoclassicals is of the shape HBB' in Figure 14.4 (adapted from 14.3(d)).

Unless the concept of the supply curve of labour is abandoned, the disequilibrium aggregate supply curve cannot logically extend to the right of the point of 'natural' full employment.[14] If one assumes a fixed money wage, there is a very restricted sense in which one can construct an aggregate supply curve that lies to the right of the level of output implied by the 'natural' rate of unemployment. From a point of full employment ($u*$) in a one-commodity model, if the money wage is fixed, a rise in price will increase the amount of labour which firms wish to hire (shown by point G in Figure 14.3(a)). To the right of the level of output implied by $u*$ one gets an ultra-notional supply curve of output. The supply curve is notional in the now-familiar sense that it assumes no sales constraints. It is ultra-notional in that such levels of output require an amount of labour which workers are unwilling to supply.[15]

By accepting the natural rate hypothesis[16] Keynesian neoclassicals produce a logical story which is perhaps more radical than some would wish. The desired end-product of the Keynesian neoclassical treatment of inflation is to justify policy intervention. As in the rest of their analysis, a fixed money wage is the critical assumption. This

Figure 14.4   Aggregate supply curve constrained by the supply of labour

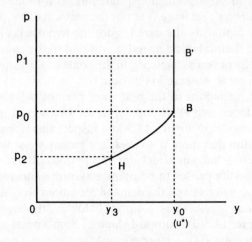

allows for less-than-full-employment solutions if money wages rise more than price in a one-commodity model. In such solutions, an expansionary monetary or fiscal policy allows the model to regain full employment u_* by raising price. However, there is no obvious scenario by which unemployment could drop below the 'natural' rate. The empirical implication follows that capitalist economies suffer from unemployment except in brief moments when these economies are pushed to their 'natural' limit; i.e. they are economies typically characterised by a waste of human resources.

15 The 'Natural' Rate, Neutrality and Monetary Inflation

15.1 A NON-NEOCLASSICAL LABOUR MARKET

Central to the neoclassical treatment of inflation is the concept of the 'natural' rate of unemployment, which proves to be another term for labour market equilibrium. The 'natural-ness' of this rate derives from its characteristic of being consistent with a zero rate of change of the price level. The hypothesis that there is a rate of unemployment which does not provoke inflation is the heart of the Phillips curve relationship. This hypothesis need not be based on notional supply and demands nor on a concept of equilibrium. A quite convincing non-neoclassical argument can be made in terms of excess supply and demand in the context of a non-homogeneous labour force.

When the rate of unemployment is high, it could be argued that firms will find little difficulty in matching their job vacancies with applicants, and under such circumstances employment and output can expand without the need to raise money wages to attract workers. Unemployment is serving a disciplining function to discourage workers from demanding higher wages. As the rate of unemployment falls, the likelihood of firms finding workers who match the qualifications of the available openings declines, and wages must be raised, either to bid workers away from other firms or to draw more workers into the labour market.

It can be imagined that at some stage the pool of the unemployed is reduced to those whose qualifications are so limited or work habits so unsatisfactory (perhaps because of long-term unemployment) that further increases in money wages have little impact on the level of unemployment. While the economy may not be at full employment in that there are people seeking work, the labour market would have reached a point at which the remaining pool of the unemployed are unemployable from the standpoint of potential employers. In the

211

1950s and 1960s economists told stories like this in terms of a distinction between 'cyclical unemployment' (that which could be reduced by demand-expansion) and 'structural unemployment' (that which could not).[1] Phillips had such a story in mind to explain the shape of his famous curve.[2] We shall refer to it as the 'cyclical unemployment story'. In this story there is no difficulty constructing a positively sloped relationship between output and the price level, though the result is not an aggregate supply curve in the sense of the previous two chapters. In the cyclical unemployment story increasing output as unemployment falls is associated with excess demand in the labour market. This excess demand pushes up the general level of wages, which on the assumption of a fixed mark-up over cost results in rising commodity prices. In this case, increased output calls forth a higher price level,[3] while for the aggregate supply curve the causality is reversed.

While this story appeals to commonsense and has considerable empirical support, it is inconsistent with the neoclassical treatment of labour markets, even if general equilibrium theory drops the assumption of homogeneous labour. Central to the cyclical unemployment story is 'false trading', since full employment comes only at the end, if at all. Further, no concept of labour market equilibrium is necessary. Empirically there may be discovered a rate of aggregate unemployment associated with price stability, but the desirability of maintaining that rate rather than one higher or lower is purely judgemental. The arbitrariness of any particular level of unemployment as a target was encapsulated in the economic literature of the 1960s and early 1970s by referring to the 'dilemma of the trade-off between unemployment and inflation'.

In the context of general equilibrium theory the causality in the cyclical unemployment story must be completely rejected, for strange as it may seem, *ceteris paribus*, a rising money wage (and therefore price) cannot be the result of an excess demand for labour. In the neoclassical model, unemployment is the result of the money wage being *too high*. Given the money supply, a decline in the level of unemployment is associated with a *fall* in the money wage (and price), not an increase. Only if 'the authorities' expand the money supply can the model produce a scenario in which unemployment declines and the money wage rises, but this is not the result of an excess demand for labour pushing up the wage, but the result of a rising price reducing the commodity wage ('real wage'). In other words, the model cannot produce a story in which there is an excess demand for labour that generates inflation by inducing employers to bid up the money wage. The inflation must always come first, to lower the commodity wage which creates the excess demand for labour.

The difficulty of producing a story in which excess demand pushes up money wages generates alternative stories in which the rate of inflation is autonomously determined and wage increases are the expectational response. In general equilibrium the labour market is neither 'tight' nor 'loose', but continuously cleared. Money wage increases do not reflect the pressure of excess demand, but attempts by workers to maintain a cleared labour market at a higher anticipated price level. The entire analysis of inflation and expectations is based upon the premise of labour market equilibrium, which itself requires the Walrasian auctioneer.

15.2 MONEY-NEUTRAL INFLATION STORIES

In the neoclassical treatment of inflation, the auctioneer oversees bargaining in a money-neutral model, and the cause of inflation itself, increases in the money supply, goes largely unexplained. The basic neoclassical model establishes the general equilibrium conditions for a one commodity system, conditions dependent upon the arbitrary assumption of Walrasian market clearing. Additional arbitrary assumptions render this model neutral with respect to changes in the money supply (no bonds or counter-empirical restricts on bonds such as indexing). On this creaky façade, one rests the conclusion that under conditions of perfect foresight *ex machina* increases in the money supply leave all real variables unchanged, so inflation of price has no impact on agent's behaviour. In order to avoid the conclusion that inflation has no consequences worth mentioning, expectations are introduced in an arbitrary way (workers are more likely to err than capitalists in their predictions) to derive a positively sloped aggregate supply curve that extends beyond what previously was defined as maximum (full employment) output. Through all of this, the basic question, why do prices rise faster during some periods than others, is begged by attributing inflation to changes in the money supply; and the possibility of inflation occurring at less than full employment never seriously considered.

The vacuousness of this approach is unavoidable because of the manner in which real variables and monetary variables have been

Figure 15.1   Aggregate supply and demand with a fixed money wage

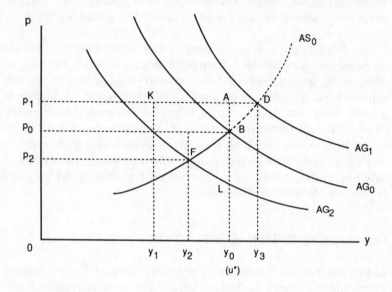

analytically linked but not integrated. Since neoclassical theory did not successfully construct a model of a money economy on the basis of its a priori method, it does not successfully treat the phenomenon of inflation. The failure to produce a satisfactory model of a money economy was explained in some detail in Chapter 4. At this point the relevant aspects of that discussion are further developed with the aid of Figure 15.1, where aggregate supply and demand curves are employed. The aggregate demand curve is of the complete Keynesian type – an interest elastic demand for money but no real balance effect. The aggregate supply curve is drawn for a fixed money wage and shown as a dashed line beyond the level of output/income associated with full employment (the 'natural' rate of unemployment). This dashed portion will be ignored in what follows due to the logical inconsistencies involved in its construction.

Consider first the aggregate demand curve AG_2, which intersects the aggregate supply curve AS_0 at point F. An old-fashioned Keynesian neoclassical would say that aggregate demand is too low to achieve full employment, $u*$, and this could be rectified by monetary expansion which would shift the aggregate demand curve up to AG_0, with a full employment intersection at B. A newfangled Keynesian neoclassical who has taken rational expectations on board would come to a similar conclusion in a more complicated way.[4] First, and unlike their counterparts a generation before, they would usually feel obligated to explain why the model ever reached a point like F instead of the full employment level L, B, or A. Obviously a point like F involves a money wage that is too high. In the new view it is too high because while workers wished to strike a bargain for the general equilibrium real wage, they over-estimated the coming price level. They anticipated the aggregate demand curve AG_0, which in combination with the aggregate supply curve AS_0 (based on an anticipation of price level p_0) would yield full employment at point B. However, the estimate of aggregate demand was too optimistic, and AG2 was realised. This results in an intersection at F, where workers are 'locked into' contracts at too high a money wage. Such a result would be interpreted by the previous generation of neoclassical Keynesians as 'temporary money illusion', in which workers were seduced by the lure of higher money wages only to fall victim to less than full employment. New neoclassical Keynesians (committed to the assumption of downwardly-rigid money wages) would say that expansion of the money supply would be necessary to reach full employment at point B. Others, more influenced by the New Classicals, would tell a story in which a lower money wage bargain was struck once existing contracts expired if aggregate demand remained AG2, and full employment would be achieved at point L. In both versions unemployment appears as a temporary phenomenon at point F.

A new classical economist would say that the labour market was cleared at F (on the arbitrary assumption that workers anticipated the wrong price level but capitalists got it right). The labour market was cleared at F by the following process: workers had mis-predicted the price level (guessing too high); this error had resulted in instantaneous excess supply at the bargain-struck money wage; the money wage fell from this level to instantaneously clear the labour market. This is a temporary equilibrium, however. Soon workers will correct their error and the supply curve will shift out to intersect aggregate demand at some point such as L. At point L both workers and capitalists anticipate correctly the price that actually prevails and the real wage is such as to clear the labour market at output level y0 (implying u_*).

All three stories would agree that sustainable full employment points lie on the vertical line y_0A. Increases in the money supply which shift the aggregate demand curve out further, AG_1 being an example, substantiate the conclusion that 'policy cannot permanently bring the economy above the natural rate of unemployment (or income)'. The stories are obvious deductions from the following premises:

(1) **If** *all* markets clear according to Walrasian rules;
(2) **If** money is strictly neutral;
(3) **If** the money supply is autonomous with respect to output; **then**
(4) Output will be at its full employment value and increases in the money supply will have no effect but to raise the price of the single commodity.

As shown in previous chapters, the three premises upon which the conclusion is based are each flawed. First, there is considerable reason to doubt that Walrasian market-clearing is an appropriate analogue for the actual behaviour of agents. If markets do not clear, then the concept of the 'natural' rate of unemployment, on which the inflation stories are based, is an unverified theoretical hypothesis. If money is not neutral, which in general it is not if bonds are included in the model, then increases in the money supply affect real variables and the 'natural' rate is not unique. If there is interaction between the supply of money and its demand, then the entire analysis is called into question.

The introduction of aggregate demand and supply curves has done little to enhance the Keynesian Neoclassical 'demand-pull' inflation stories of the 1950s. The effect has been to render those stories static by limiting the analysis to the special case in which the commodity and money markets are in equilibrium. The new classical story would seem to trivialise the analysis of inflation by making it a phenomenon of continuous general equilibrium. The overall effect of both types of stories is to imply that inflation does not matter, since any level of price and any rate of inflation yields full employment. Why, then, has so much analytical effort been expended?

15.3 COSTS OF INFLATION AND 'SUPER-NEUTRALITY'

If one surveys currently used textbooks in macroeconomics, one finds a common tendency for the costs of unemployment to be understated. While the new classical argument that involuntary unemployment neither exists nor can exist (since labour markets continuously clear) is apparently an extreme view, it is accepted as a respectable position within the economics profession. One of the most widely-used intermediate texts, by an author far from the new classicals in his orientation, warns the reader in strong terms against the danger of pushing the unemployment rate too low.[5] On the other hand, virtually all mainstream economists are negatively disposed to inflation.

This is a rather strange set of split-judgements for neoclassical economists, since the pure theory would suggest that neither unemployment nor inflation should be a source of preoccupation. With regard to unemployment, there are only two theoretical possibilities for those who avert their eyes from the neoclassical model's internal inconsistencies: (1) if labour markets continuously clear, then what appears as unemployment is voluntary leisure; and (2) if unemployment is the result of rigid wages (the older view), then workers have only themselves to blame. The non-problematic character of inflation would seem even more obvious. As Pigou argued, money is a 'veil' over the real system (the neutrality hypothesis), so the price level and its rate of change should be a matter of small import. Yet warnings about the dire consequences of inflation are common among economists.

The Keynesian neoclassicals tend to justify their concern about inflation in terms of the social and economic cost of controlling it. The argument is that if a high rate of inflation is 'built into' workers' expectations, then wage bargaining will produce high money wages at the same time that the monetary authorities are reducing the rate of growth of the money supply. As a result, real wages will rise, and output and employment will decline until workers incorporate into their wage demands the new and lower rate of inflation targeted by policy-makers. This transition to a lower rate of inflation which generates wage-expectation unemployment is called 'stagflation'.[6] The argument involves a *non sequitor*. The *non sequitor* arises for the following reason: if money is neutral and inflation makes no difference, why should the authorities be concerned with reducing the rate of price increase?[7] Before one can convincingly warn against the adjustment costs of deflation, it must be demonstrated that inflation *should* be reduced. But the reasons for 'combating' inflation derive from non-neutrality, distributional effects, and destabilising consequences of inflationary expectations, all of which have been assumed away in constructing the aggregate demand/supply model.

The Keynesian neoclassicals may be quite sensible in their concern about the practical consequences of inflation. However, as in the

1950s and 1960s, they are caught in a logically indefensible intellectual position: on the one hand, they accept the basic money-neutral model as the theoretical benchmark; on the other hand they wish in practice to stress those problems which are denied in theory. The basic theory of inflation reduces to the statement that increases in the money supply result in proportional increases in price, which have no impact on real variables (even expectations if inflation is anticipated).

The unimportance of inflation implied by the neutrality of money has prompted some neoclassicals (particularly the new classicals) to stress a distinction between neutrality and 'super-neutrality'. The former term is used to refer to consequences for real variables of a 'one-shot' increase in the money supply, and the latter to the consequences when the money supply expands 'continuously'. Money is said to be 'super-neutral' if the values of all real variables are independent of its continuous expansion.[8] The point of this distinction is to have one's cake and eat it also – yes, money is neutral with respect to an increase in the price level, but not with respect to inflation (money is neutral but not super-neutral).

The first step involved in investigating super-neutrality is to assume that real variables are in general equilibrium, which sets the level of the 'real' interest rate, r. The nominal interest rate (R) is then defined as the real interest rate plus the rate of inflation. Neutrality will be maintained but super-neutrality contradicted by specifying agents' desired real money holdings (cash balances) in terms of the nominal interest rate.

To proceed, assume that all markets instantaneously clear (general equilibrium), that the rate of price increase equals the rate of growth of the money supply, which in turn equals the difference between the nominal and real rate of interest. Let these rates be constant and noted as $q*$ (rate of exchange of money supply, price, and the difference between the nominal and real interest rates). For purposes of review, consider a one-off increase in the money supply of proportion $q*$. The result would be an immediate excess supply of money (excess real balances). Agents would seek to rid themselves of this excess money by spending it on the single commodity (it is assumed that there are no bonds to purchase). Output is at its full employment maximum, so price would rise to reduce real balances to their original level. Since instantaneous market clearing is required to avoid false trading, it is illegitimate in this example to consider transitional disequilibrium events.

Now assume that the model is in initial equilibrium with a given money supply, and suddenly the money supply begins to grow continuously at a rate correctly anticipated by all (at rate $q*$). In this case the increase in price provoked by excess demand (itself the result of the excess supply of money, the real balance effect) cannot bring cash balances into equilibrium. Each price increase at rate $q*$ is followed by another increase in the money supply of $q*$. The rate of return on investments has risen to $(r + q*)$, while the pre-inflation market cost of borrowing was r. As a result, the market (nominal) rate of interest must rise. The nominal rate of interest rises until it exceeds the real rate of interest by the rate of inflation, $q*$. This exactly compensates lenders for the loss of purchasing power due to inflation. As a result of the increase in the nominal rate of interest, desired real cash balances fall; in other words, the excess demand continuously generated by growth of the money supply is eliminated by an increase in the nominal rate of interest. Thus, while money is neutral (proportional increases in M result in equal proportional increases in p), it is not super-neutral since one real variable, real cash balances, has changed.

As it stands this inflation story seems hardly more interesting than the tales of 'one-shot' price increases. The only difference between the two is that in the 'inflation' case the proportion of the nominal money supply held as cash balances falls. Every variable that would seem to matter – output, employment, real wages, and the real interest rate – remains the same.

If indeed the main consequence that neoclassicals obtain from their continuous price increase model is a fall in the proportion of cash balances, inflation does not seem a very serious problem. However, the neoclassical view is that a decline in real balances is itself a cause for concern. The allegation is that 'an increase in the expected rate of inflation tends to reduce the average household demand for real money balances, a reduction that imposes a welfare cost by making everyday transactions more inconvenient' (Gordon, 1981, p. 334). The argument is that as the nominal rate of interest rises, the resultant reduction in cash balances implies an increase in 'transactions costs', such as trips to the bank, shifting money from deposit to current accounts, and in general from less liquid assets to money when purchases must be made. Frequently this argument is buttressed by reference to examples of cases of hyperinflation. A particularly favourite example to cite is the rampant inflation in Germany after the First World War for which there is a wealth of anecdotal horror stories.

It is difficult to make this argument about the transactions costs of inflation too seriously, especially since the spectre of hyperinflation is singularly inappropriate. Drawing conclusions about the actual consequence of inflation from periods of hyperinflation (which have been extraordinarily rare in developed capitalist countries, associated with wars and general social breakdown) is rather like seeking lessons for conventional warfare from nuclear holocaust. If inflation were to reach triple or quadruple digit level in some developed country, it would be disastrous, but transactions costs would be a minor irritant compared with other consequences. The stress given to transactions costs by neoclassicals is further evidence of the trivialisation of the inflation phenomenon. Given the range of inflation rates which developed countries have experienced since the end of the Second World War and the institutional changes in credit systems, the welfare consequences of transactions costs would seem minor.[9] The trend in the last three decades has been for fewer transactions to be carried out in what is normally defined as money (cash plus demand deposits). For example, credit cards are used as means of payment and debts subsequently cancelled by payments from interest-accruing bank accounts and 'money market funds'. In most developed capitalist countries there has been a decline in idle balances as a proportion of GNP since the end of the Second World War. This could be explained as a secular tendency responding to institutional changes, not a response to high nominal interest rates and inflation (implying 'warfare losses' due to increased transactions costs as some have suggested).[10]

Perhaps recognising that the transactions costs argument is a little limp on its own, one finds the suggestion that increases in such costs may have indirect effect on real variables.[11] If such indirect effects are allowed, the implication is that money is not neutral after all, which is a contradiction of the premise upon which the inflation model was constructed. Further, if one remains in a model in which markets are always cleared, these effects must be consistent with full employment and general equilibrium for real variables. As long as money is neutral for 'one-shot' increases in the money supply and merely 'not quite super-neutral' for continuous increases,[12] and markets are cleared, it is impossible to relate inflation to the principal 'welfare cost' of capitalist economies, unemployment. In attempting to generate an anti-inflation judgement, neoclassical theory is hoisted upon its own theoretical petard. Having argued in its defence of capitalist economies that the system is automatically self-regulating and money is only a veil over the real system, it is forced to introduce *ad hoc* arguments about transactions costs and the possible impact of infla- tion on expectations in order to justify the desirability of a stable price level.

We can sum-up the discussion of inflation theory with three points. First, all of neoclassical inflation theory is based upon a motley collection of theoretical fictions, or 'parables' as Samuelson calls them.[13] The most important at this point is parable of the 'the money supply', which as demonstrated in Chapter 4, remains at the level of an unverified hypothesis. It has not been established theoretically nor empirically that one is justified in treating the quantity of the circu- lating medium as something under the control of government (or any other institution). If the quantity of the means of circulation is to some degree endogenous to the operation of the economic system, then the inflation parables must be reformulated.

Second, the analysis of inflation employs in a relatively uncritical way Walrasian general equilibrium theory. If markets do not clear and unemployment results, then either (a) there can be no inflation since increases in the money supply stimulate increases in ouput; or (b) some fundamental theoretical revision is necessary to account for acceleration of the price level when there is an excess supply of labour.

Third, if one accepts the two previous fictions (the autonomous money supply and Walrasian market clearing), the possibility of non-neutrality renders the neoclassical inflation stories indeterminant and void of normative judgements about the desirability of price stability. Welfare judgements in neoclassical theory derive from comparisons to a hypothetical optimal state, derived at the level of firms and agents, called Pareto Optimality. This optimum is estab- lished in terms of relative prices and is unique only if money is strictly neutral. Non-neutrality yields multiple states of optimality, among which no judgement can be passed as to which is more efficient or involves the highest level of community welfare.[14] Further, if money is non-neutral, then the expansion or contraction of money even in general equilibrium results in fluctuations in real variables. All of these fluctuations represent outcomes which may be optimal.

It must be stressed that treating money as neutral is singularly inappropriate in the context of the analysis of inflation. Recall from the discussion at the end of Chapter 7 that including bonds in the neoclassical macro model would seem to preclude neutrality.[15] If at the starting point in the analysis there is some given ratio of bonds to money, *ceteris paribus* expansion of the money supply must necessarily alter this ratio. A change in the ratio of money to bonds must at the very least alter the general equilibrium interest rate and therefore saving, investment, and real bond prices. In other words, assuming increases in the money supply results in non-neutrality; inflation renders the neoclassical model non-neutral.[16]

Finally, it should be noted that even if one ignores the problem of bonds and accepts the neutrality of money, the stories produced by the neoclassical model are rather bland and uninteresting. With full employment assumed to prevail, the major negative consequence of inflation proves to be transactions costs, a form of 'welfare loss' that except in catastrophic times seems to be of little concern to anyone save neoclassical economists themselves. The appropriate conclusion to draw from neoclassical models is that inflation is a phenomenon of little consequence and certainly nothing for governments or private agents to worry about.

16 The Critique of Neoclassical Macroeconomics Summarised

16.1 THE PURPOSE RESTATED

The purpose of this book has been to analyse critically neoclassical macroeconomics *as it is taught*. The presentation has gone into considerable detail, and the reader might have lost track of the basic purpose of the critique. The basic purpose has been to refute the fundamental macroeconomic 'parables' of neoclassical theory: (1) other things equal, more employment requires a lower 'real wage' (commodity wage); and (2) other things equal, increases in the price level are proportional to increases in the money supply. Each parable can be restated in the more journalistic and ideological form in which one frequently encounters them: (1) cutting wages will bring full employment; and (2) inflation is the result of increases in the money supply.

Before summarising the critique, it should be made clear exactly what is meant by 'refute'. No attempt has been made at an empirical refutation. Whether in practice increased employment can be found to be associated with a reduced value of price-deflated wages (for example) is largely irrelevant to the issue considered here: can it be demonstrated in theory (logic) that the former follows from the latter? If a theory is logically flawed, empirical support for its predictions is no support at all – the implication is that the theory (at least on occasion) yields the correct prediction but has the wrong explanation. Geocentric celestial theory yielded roughly accurate predictions of major astronomical events, but it was wrong. More important, it was the wrong framework in which to consider those events. In a sentence, the purpose of this book has been to provide *prima facie* logical evidence that the basic neoclassical model is the wrong way to think about economies in the aggregate. This is not to say that the theory is totally wrong or that it does not provide useful insights. But notwithstanding advanced and esoteric qualifications, the heart of

223

standard macroeconomics, as evidenced by the way its wisdom is distilled and passed on to each new generation, is the single commodity supply side, neutrality of money, and Walrasian market clearing. These were the basic principles of pre-Keynesian ('classical') economics, and remain the core of synthesised macroeconomic wisdom to this day. Any textbook, undergraduate or graduate, which does not base itself on these principles is considered an eccentric curiosity.[1]

16.2 CRITIQUE OF SELF-ADJUSTING FULL EMPLOYMENT

In Chapter 1 the critique began with the manner in which neoclassical economics conceives of the circulation of commodities and money in a capitalist society – 'the circular flow of income'. The subsequent treatment of the supply side as consisting of only one commodity has its basis in this stylised interpretation of the economy. Ignored here is all intermediate production, a necessary step towards justifying an aggregate production function.

Perhaps more important in ideological terms, the circular flow model initiates at the outset a parallel and symmetric treatment of the two major classes in capitalist society, those who own productive property (capitalists and rentiers) and those that do not (blue- and white-collar workers). This counter-factual treatment of social and economic relations is a fundamental characteristic of all neoclassical theory, microeconomic as well as macroeconomic. The interpretation is that households supply a variety of services, corresponding to factors of production: services which allegedly flow from labouring activity, the ownership of capital, the ownership of land, and the abstinence from consumption. The symmetry is fallacious. In order to obtain a claim on income, wage and salary workers must sell their ability to work and do so repeatedly. 'Capital services', by contrast, are not for the most part bought and sold. What is bought and sold is a claim on income from the ownership of capital. Presumably the service sellers in the case of capital are stockholders. While a business firm must continuously enter into transactions with its workers in order to obtain a labour force, no exchange in the usual sense of the term is required to set its machinery in motion.

This strongly ideological treatment of capital and labour plays a subsidiary role in the neoclassical model as long as the analysis is restricted to the demand side. The stress upon demand as the determinant of national income allows for considerable flexibility of analysis and ideological orientation, for integral to this emphasis is the view that the economy is typically at less than full employment. An obvious line of inquiry is to place heavy emphasis upon the social and economic cost of unemployment, as Keynes did. A somewhat more radical approach has stressed the fundamental distinction between consumption and investment, the former being what workers do and the latter what capitalists do. Since in a demand-determined system the level of national income is determined by the level of capitalist spending (investment), one can come to Nicholas Kaldor's famous aphorism that 'workers spend what they get and capitalists get what they spend'.[2]

However, these left-wing tendencies have had limited respectability within the neoclassical tradition, and the vehicle for writing them out of the distilled wisdom of the mainstream[3] has been the introduction of a supply side for the model (Chapter 2). The heart of the supply side is the aggregate production function, and rare is the textbook that omits it.[4] The only consistent way in which to construct this aggregate relationship is by assuming a single commodity, which has a number of fundamental implications. First, it eliminates much of the meaning of the distinction between consumption and investment, which is formally completed by use of the IS (commodity market equilibrium) curve.

The most profound effect of the aggregate output/value added function is to introduce a stylised labour market into the analysis. The familiar parable that more employment requires a lower real wage derives from the introduction of this aggregate function, giving it a central analytical and ideological role in the model. Once an aggregate labour market is included, all else in the model is purely derivative: the values of all variables are unique once the real (commodity) wage is determined. The real wage is determined either by the 'clearing' of the labour market or by assigning an arbitrary lower limit to this key variable, with the lower limit given the ideological interpretation that it reflects trade union monopoly or state intervention. The clearing of the labour market establishes an imaginary result called the 'real solution', which serves as a benchmark for all more complicated models. The allegation is that agents make their decisions in relationship to 'real' (price-deflated) variables, and to do anything else would result in irrational behaviour (to suffer from 'money illusion').

The critique of this hypothesis – that the economy has a full employment set of real values which agents seek through a veil of nominal values – was critiqued on two grounds. First, the 'real' solution is largely trivial, because it lacks the *diferentia specifica* of a capitalist economy: that workers must sell their labour services for money and capitalists must sell their output. To represent these exchanges as barter is to misrepresent the basic nature of a capitalist economy. Second, subsequent chapters demonstrate that even were the 'real' solution relevant to decision making, it does not exist even in theory in any meaningful sense. Once one moves beyond the internally contradictory world of the false dichotomy all solutions are nominal solutions from which real values of variables are derivative.

Central to the neoclassical macro model is a particular concept of equilibrium (Chapter 3). Much confusion results from utilising this concept in a loose and momentarily convenient manner. Neoclassical macro models involve *short-run general equilibrium*. One can specify the reactions of agents in disequilibrium, but disequilibrium states as such cannot be treated without allowing for exchanges at disequilibrium prices ('false trading'), in which case general equilibrium is ruled out. In other words, the model is rendered extremely restrictive of thought because it limits itself to the special case when all variables are at rest. In formal terms the special case results from specification of agents' behaviour in terms of notional (general equilibrium) supply and demand. The manner in which markets clear in the model is extremely stylised and even bizarre: general equilibrium is the right answer and agents are prohibited from making mistakes in their trades. The allegation that in the real world unregulated markets will result in socially desirable outcomes derives from this extraordinarily fragile special case.

In Chapter 4 the critique took up the issue of money, introducing the concept of *neutrality*. Sometimes presented as an inherent characteristic of valueless (non-produced) money, neutrality is correctly seen as a hypothesis. The essence of this hypothesis is that there is a unique set of full employment values for the real variables in the model, and that this set is independent of the money supply. The implication of this hypothesis is that the 'real' system is primary and the set of nominal values of variables of limited analytical significance. Essential to the neutrality hypothesis is the further hypothesis that money available for circulation in an economy is exogenous with respect to the real variables in the system. The most simplistic form of this second hypothesis is what is called the quantity theory of money, in which a constant velocity of circulation is assumed. The quantity theory, Walras' Law and the output/value added function produce a simple and compelling parable, which was explored in the next chapter. However, these elements cannot be logically combined, for the first implies a demand for money function which is inconsistent with that implied by the second. The importance of this inconsistency is that it demonstrates that the neutrality hypothesis cannot be established by superimposing nominal values upon predetermined real values.

The inconsistency between Walras' Law and the quantity theory can be resolved in a number of ways, one of which is by introduction of the real balance effect, which grants to money a function in addition to means of circulation, namely store of wealth. The real balance effect resolves one difficulty at the expense of creating additional more serious ones. First, it is difficult in theory to establish that there exists a form of money which when held by agents could represent net wealth in the neoclassical model. To a great extent, the real balance effect is an *ex machina* appendage to the model designed not to illuminate any important aspect of economic behaviour, but rather to salvage the neutrality hypothesis. Perhaps the central message of this chapter was that the hypothesis of an exogenous money supply is unsustained in theory; and even if one proceeds upon this hypothesis quite arbitrary assumptions are required in order to avoid logical contradictions.

In Chapters 5 to 7 the fundamental (and flawed) building blocks of neoclassical macro theory – the aggregate output/value added function, Walras' Law, and an exogenous money supply – were combined to produce formal models. The first of these models incorporated the false dichotomy between real and nominal variables. The purpose of presenting an invalid model, other than that it is encountered in most textbooks without its internal inconsistency noted, was to derive certain parables which the more complex models seek to duplicate. The basic parable is that the only source of deviation from full employment is the labour market: if money wages are flexible, then there can be no unemployment ('rigid' money wages are the cause of unemployment). The false dichotomy model does not quite achieve this conclusion, for it incorporates the logical possibility that saving might exceed investment for all positive interest rates, in which case there would be excess supply in the commodity market which could not be cleared.

The possibility of an 'inconsistency' between saving and investment provides the rationale for taking up a real balance effect model next, in Chapter 6. If one makes the arbitrary assumption that money represents net wealth, one can unambiguously come to the conclusion that rigid wages are the only logical cause of unemployment; in addition, the model sustains the neutrality hypothesis. Thus, it can be concluded that flexible wages will ensure full employment, and that this full employment is unique for all assumed levels of the money supply. No other version of the neoclassical model can make both of these claims without assumptions considerably more arbitrary than those of the real balance effect model.

An alternative manner to resolve the false dichotomy (and much preferred in textbooks) is to introduce an interest-elastic element in the demand for money, which yields what in the past was called the 'complete Keynesian system'. In this model the link between real and nominal variables (the absence of which is the source of the false dichotomy) is achieved by making the demand for money a function of the interest rate, which produces the LM (money market equilibrium) curve. Keynesian in form, the LM curve is neoclassical to the core, since all distinction between more or less volatile elements of the demand for money is eliminated, as the IS curve eliminated any meaningful difference between consumption and investment. It should be remembered that Keynes himself placed considerable stress upon the instability of the demand for money as a cause of unemployment. Money is neutral in the complete Keynesian model, but the model's tendency to automatic full employment is ambiguous. As before, an inconsistency between saving and investment is a possibility, as well as a demand for money which becomes infinitely elastic with respect to the interest rate ('Liquidity Trap'), as is stressed in the standard presentations. In Chapter 7 the complete Keynesian model was expanded to include a wealth effect (the real balance effect generalised to non-money assets). The result was to again produce an unambiguous tendency to full employment (via Walras' Law, of course), but to preclude the neutrality of money unless one entertains extremely contorted arguments.

The implication of loss of neutrality was explored in Chapter 8. The ideological importance of neutrality cannot be stressed too much. It is not too much to say that the entire argument against state intervention in capitalist economies rests upon the hypothesis of the neutrality of money. If money is non-neutral, then there is no 'natural' full employment equilibrium which the economy seeks, but an endless number of these, each unique for a given level of the exogenous money supply. Non-neutrality implies that there is no neutral monetary policy, and every full employment equilibrium is one that results in part from state action ('the monetary authorities'). Put succinctly, if money is non-neutral, then there is no real solution, only price-deflated values of nominal variables. Even if one grants that capitalist economies have an automatic tendency to full employment, most of neoclassical macroeconomics as it is taught and passed on to the new generation deals with the special case of that tendency when it produces a unique outcome. But there is no compelling reason to accept the argument that capitalist economies automatically tend to full employment, for in the standard models there are no tendencies at all, only equilibrium outcomes. This myopic restriction was mentioned earlier, and in the second half of Chapter 8 the point is elaborated. Walras' Law is the mechanism of general equilibrium full employment market clearing, yet Walras' Law only applies to a situation in which the labour market is in equilibrium. That is to say, if the labour market is in equilibrium but all others in excess demand and excess supply, the bizarre mechanism of Walras' auctioneer can produce a general equilibrium solution. However, when not in general equilibrium, neoclassical models typically deal with the case in which there is excess supply in the labour market and all other markets cleared (a rigid wage-constrained less than full employment equilibrium). In this most common case Walras' Law proves of little use, for its axiom that the sum of all excess demands must be zero is violated.

Chapter 9 deals with a development in macroeconomics of the last twenty years which required a wholesale rewriting of textbooks – the rational expectations 'revolution'. It is likely to prove a transitory fad which will drop out of macroeconomic textbooks of the coming generation just as today's texts allocate little space to the rigid-coefficient accelerator models of investment which were found so compelling in the 1940s and 1950s. In the interim this bit of pseudo-science requires serious treatment. The rational expectations hypothesis (REH) is pseudo-science because it is premised upon a metaphysical proposition that no other science, social or natural, would seriously entertain – the full range of future outcomes is known, as well as the probability of each outcome occurring. The functional role of the REH has been to provide a new respectability to the pre-Keynesian economic ideology of the 1920s, but to carry that ideology a step further. While the pre-Keynesians argued that capitalist economies tended to full employment 'in the long run' and could manifest short-run unemployment (caused by rigid wages), the new classical economics has discovered that capitalist economies are in continuous short-run equilibrium and any unemployment is voluntary or an illusion of mis-measurement.

For this book the REH is important in two ways: (1) by carrying the logic of the neoclassical macroeconomic model to its extreme it unwittingly provides a parody of the synthesis school considerably better than any strawman a critic could create; and (2) it indicates clearly the extent to which full employment general equilibrium is a special case. The central conclusion of the new classical economics, that agents armed with rational expectations will behave in such a way as to nullify any policy action by governments, is a special case in the extreme: it assumes that the economy is continuously in full employment general equilibrium, and that money is neutral so that the equilibrium is unique. Involved here is avoiding all of the difficulties associated with adjustment to equilibrium and the theoretical problems with assuring neutrality. That such a special case based upon the pseudo-science of complete knowledge of future outcomes could be influential in the economics profession indicates the intrinsically conservative nature of the discipline.

Chapter 10 took up an issue which had been lurking in the background throughout the critique: the severe limitation placed upon the neoclassical model by virtue of assuming a one-commodity supply side. A bit of simple algebra and graphics demonstrates that the hypothesis that a lower real wage calls forth a higher level of employment cannot be generalised even to the two commodity case. In general, multi-commodity models yield multiple full employment real wage levels, so it is not true even in theory that an excess supply of labour implies that the return to labour should fall in order to clear the labour market. Perhaps the most inexplicable aspect of this conclusion is that it is so patently true, yet goes unmentioned in virtually all standard presentations of macroeconomics; on the contrary, the parable that more employment requires a lower real wage is repeated as if it were a natural law of economics.

The purpose of Chapter 11 was to indicate the dissatisfaction in the economics profession with Walrasian general equilibrium analysis by reference to seminal works critical of this approach. Important as the anti-Walrasian critique was its reception in the profession, which has been to trivialise it. Again, the conservative nature of economic science is indicated by a comparison of the reception of the disequilibrium Keynesian critique and the rational expectations 'revolution'.

The insights of the former contribution are rarely incorporated into textbooks, implicitly judged as insufficiently important to be passed on to students of macroeconomics. The latter, for all of its theoretical problems and narrow attention to a special case, can be found in most standard works.

The entire purpose of the first eleven chapters of this book has been to undermine the generally-presented judgement that capitalist economies tend automatically to full employment. This judgement was undermined by several basic arguments, all of which one can find in the more advanced economic literature: (1) that the mechanism of Walrasian market clearing is no guide to the operation of real economies (there is no 'good theory', as Hahn puts it, of the movement from less than full employment states to full employment); (2) that if there were a satisfactory theory of disequilibrium adjustment, it would not necessarily imply that moving to full employment involved a reduction in the real wage (parables based on a single commodity model do not survive the test of multi-commodity models); and (3) were there an automatic tendency to full employment and were this associated with a lower real wage, the result would not be unique (in real economies money is not neutral).

Of course, all textbooks do not take as a serious practical conclusion the argument that capitalist economies tend automatically to full employment. But virtually without exception standard undergraduate and graduate works repeat the view that such is the case in the abstract: that the pure theory is correct in logic and if nothing else provides an optimal benchmark against which the second-best achievements of the real world can be judged. This compromise position perpetuates an unsubstantiated dogma and its powerful ideological message. It is an ideological incantation, unsupported empirically and a special case in logic. It is grist for the mill of right-wing ideologues and a barrier to the development of theory which would address the fundamental problems of a capitalist economy.

16.3 CRITIQUE OF MONETARY INFLATION

With regard to aggregate utilisation of resources, neoclassical theory has a simple parable: any unemployment state can be eliminated by falling real wages. With regard to the other great scourge of capitalist economies, inflation, it has an equally simple parable: inflation cannot occur if the 'monetary authorities' do not expand the monetary supply. High wages cause unemployment; too much money causes inflation. These are powerful and intrinsically conservative messages. In Chapters 1 to 11 the first was shown to be at best a very special case.

The inflation parable is also false in as far as it posits an inevitable causality or necessary condition. The first and most fundamental difficulty with the inflation parable is that it is based upon an unsubstantiated hypothesis: that the amount of money available for commodity transactions is independent of the level of output. Simply put, the inflation parable requires that there be an exogenous money supply under the control of the monetary authorities. To begin by assuming this to be the case ('let the money supply be . . .') is to assume what must be proved.

In Chapter 12 the critique began with the basic neoclassical treatment of inflation. In the synthesis model increases in the money supply always result in increases in the price of the single commodity ('price level'), but all increases in price are not inflation. This apparent paradox, some increases in the price level are not inflation, is rationalised by a distinction between 'one-shot' and 'continuous' increases in the price level. This is a distinction with more form than content. The basic neoclassical inflation story is extremely simple and a variation on the tale of Pigou in which money is a 'veil' over the real system. If the economy is at full employment, if the demand for money is stable, and if the money supply is autonomous, then increases in the money supply will call forth equal-proportional increases in the price level. This is, of course, a money neutral story.

Chapter 12 also introduced the 'aggregate supply curve', which attempts to summarise the relationship between the price level and the amount of output in the aggregate which firms wish to sell. This apparently simple relationship, aggregate output is function of the 'price level', is fraught with difficulties. If the labour market is assumed to clear, the aggregate supply curve is vertical at full employment; if one assumes a rigid money wage, then increases in price call forth more aggregate supply as long as there is unemployment, but again the curve is vertical at full employment. Both imply that nothing very interesting happens as a result of inflation, for all real variables would appear to be unaffected as the price level rises (i.e. one is in a money-neutral world with no distributional effects).

The 'aggregate demand curve' was presented in Chapter 13, where one encountered the strange tale of the new classical 'theory of monetary demand'. Through a manipulation of the familiar quantity equation ($Mv = py$), the new classicals seek to establish an aggregate demand for output function. However, the function is internally inconsistent, requiring the interest rate to vary (to equate saving and investment) while assuming it to be constant. It also incorporates the false dichotomy, which is the source of its internal inconsistency. Aggregate demand curves derived from the real balance effect model or the complete Keynesian model (explained in Chapter 6) are internally consistent. However, they are extremely restrictive of thought, for they presume all markets to be in equilibrium. In other words, if one works with aggregate supply and aggregate demand curves, one is treating inflation as a general equilibrium full employment phenomenon. The possibility that inflation might be a disequilibrium process which manifests itself when the labour market is in excess supply, or even when the commodity market is in excess supply,[5] is not seriously treated. This is a good example of how excessively formalistic and rigid theory can be a barrier to innovative thinking.

The extent to which conservative ideology gained ascendancy in neoclassical macroeconomics in the late 1970s and 1980s was indicated in the treatment of expectations in Chapter 14. Central to the role of expectations is the value-laden concept, 'the natural rate of unemployment', which is nothing more than an attempt to apply to actual situations the abstract and problematical hypothesis that capitalist economies tend toward full employment general equilibrium. Neoclassical theory predicts that inflation should only occur at full employment. Therefore, the typical neoclassical inflation story involves explaining the existence of inflation at various levels of unemployment without abandoning the tenet that inflation is a full employment phenomenon. Achieving this unlikely goal involves invoking expectational errors. If one arbitrarily assumes that workers are more likely to err in predicting inflation than capitalists, it is possible to produce a story which the rate of price increase is inversely related to the rate of unemployment. Economic theory has had a quite passable explanation of this relationship for quite a long time, so what has the new approach achieved? Its achievement is not to cast any new light upon the inflation process, but to show circumstances under which continuous price changes can be interpreted as *a general equilibrium phenomenon*.

There is a problem here, however: if inflation can rage when the economy is at full employment and in general equilibrium why should it be of any concern? The final analytical chapter investigates this question, which is particularly pertinent when one recalls that the neutrality of money implies that the increases in the price level should have no impact on any real variable. Full employment/money neutral stories are ill-designed to illuminate the social costs of inflation. The negative effects of inflation identified by the theory, 'transactions costs', would seem minor indeed compared with costs of eliminating inflation: increased unemployment and falling real output. Would one rather be employed and forced to make more frequent trips to the bank, or unemployed and fewer ones (fewer partly because of the meagre balance to be found in one's account)? Invoking transactions costs and irrelevant alarmist references to periods of hyperinflation, which are basically *ad hoc* arguments, indicates that the neoclassical objection to inflation is essentially ideological.

The fundamental problem is that neoclassical theory has no explanation for inflation. Once one assumes an exogenous money supply and a stable demand for money, the only possible cause of increases in the price level is an increase in the money supply. The only avenue for further inquiry with regard to cause is to speculate about what motivates the monetary authorities to increase the money supply. This does not add to knowledge of the inflationary process if its basic premise is invalid: that the necessary condition for inflation is an increase in the autonomous money supply.

In summary, the neoclassical inflation parable is that inflation is the result of increases in the money supply, and a given proportional increase in the money supply will result in an equal proportional increase in prices. This basic parable, endorsed by virtually all textbooks as correct at least in the 'long run', is a very special case, the case in which money is neutral. Since there is little reason to think that money is neutral in actual economies, there is little reason to think, for example, that a 10 per cent increase in the money supply (were it exogenous and capable of discretionary manipulation) would result in a 10 per cent increase in the price level, in the short, long or any run. When it is assumed that the money supply is exogenous and the velocity of circulation is constant, one does not have be an economist to conclude that inflation is a monetary phenomenon. However, breaking away from this simple and stylised inflation story is vigorously resisted by neoclassical macroeconomics.

16.4 THEORY AND IDEOLOGY

It is not uncommon to find neoclassical economics presented as 'value free', encapsulating eternal truths of economic behaviour and natural law which are as independent of human perception and volition as the law of gravity. The fact of the matter is that economics as a discipline has always been highly political, and modern mainstream theory no less so than theory in the past. Recognising that neoclassical theory is heavily laden with ideology does not invalidate its insights, but it does require one to make a serious attempt to distinguish that portion of the theory which is scientific and that portion which is essentially propaganda. One example demonstrates the distinction: the hypothesis that there exists a rate of unemployment in the aggregate for which the rate of change of the price level would be zero (and that this relationship is stable) is a scientific proposition in that it can be justified theoretically and empirically verified or rejected; calling such a rate of unemployment 'natural' and associating it with full employment is propaganda, theory in the service of ideology.

As it is taught in the 1980s (with notable exceptions) neoclassical macroeconomics conveys the following messages to the student: capitalist economies are essentially self-regulating, with major problems resulting from mismanagement by governments. Further, inflation is to be feared more than unemployment, because the self-regulating economy will tend to eliminate unemployment automatically, but one must be eternally vigilant against the inflation-producing errors of governments. Along with this distrust of government intervention goes a negative assessment of the role of trade unions in capitalist societies, which are viewed as instruments to create monopoly power in labour markets rather than the historical vehicle by which workers have collectively protected themselves against the power of capital. While many mainstream economists would disagree with this crude characterisation of the political message of mainstream economics, it is none the less what the pure theory teaches.

Due to its methodology economics is the most conservative of the social sciences. For the first one hundred years of its existence (*circa* 1750–1850), conservatism was not inherent in the methodology due to the importance of the hypothesis that labour was the only source of expanded value. During this period the advocates of unregulated markets, such as Ricardo, could operate within the same broad framework as critics of capitalism, such as the Ricardian socialists, the French socialists (Proudhon and Sismondi), and Marx. After a few decades of theoretical turmoil, the discipline coalesced around a new paradigm based upon individual optimising behaviour, marginal productivity theory of production, and Walrasian general equilibrium. For the last one hundred years economic inquiry has largely dedicated itself to demonstrating the inherent stability of capitalist economies and the tendency of such economies to generate socially optimal outcomes if the system is left unregulated. The Great Depression briefly undermined that sanguine approach, with the attack led by Keynes. However, Keynes's basic message, that capitalist economies tend to produce socially unacceptable outcomes if not controlled and regulated, found a receptive audience in the profession for only a brief period. The traditional free market conservativism of the profession had reasserted itself by the early 1970s. If there was a consensus in the profession in favour of intervention in markets and the necessity for macroeconomic management by the state, it lasted for no more than 25 years.

The conservatism that characterises mainstream economics is not based upon unimpeachable theoretical foundations. The models from which the two fundamental macroeconomic parables derive, that unemployment is a real wage phenomenon and inflation a monetary phenomenon, suffer from serious flaws of internal logic. Accepting these models and proceeding as if they were analytically sound is essentially an act of politically-motivated faith. That is the basic message which this book seeks to convey to students of economics.

Appendix: Keynes and Aggregation

1 INSIGHTS FROM THE PAST

The text of this book provided a critique of the main aspects of neoclassical macroeconomics. The purpose of this appendix is somewhat different, to indicate from the work of Keynes an alternative approach to aggregate economic problems. If nothing else, this appendix seeks to encourage the reading of the work of Keynes, above all *The General Theory of Employment, Interest, and Money*. The vehicle to achieve this purpose is the demonstration that a number of the critiques of neoclassical macroeconomics presented in this book were made by Keynes over fifty years ago. In the 1950s almost all students of macroeconomics were required to read Keynes; in the 1960s most were; by the 1980s few if any. Much is lost by not reading Keynes, for even those who disagree with him fundamentally (and the author of this book falls into that category) will find important insights in his work (as well as being charmed by his wit and humour).

The tendency in all the social sciences to assign students interpretations of great figures in place of the writings of the great figures themselves is insidious. In economics this practice partly reflects a fervent belief that knowledge accumulates and discovery proceeds in a strictly linear fashion. By this view each succeeding generation of economists culls the wisdom and discards the errors from the work of the previous, so at each successive moment of time we are at a new peak of knowledge and understanding. Every day in every way theory becomes better and more complete.

While few sophisticated economists would explicitly voice such a naïve and self-serving view of the profession's progress, the vast majority would judge that fifty years of sifting through *The General Theory* must have resulted in the discovery of all that is valuable in it. Indeed, those few who continue to seek insights from the work of Keynes risk the danger of being accused of ancestor worship.[1] Why read *The General Theory* after fifty years of progress in theoretical macroeconomics? Keynes himself provided an answer to this type of question: economics is a science which can accumulate knowledge without gaining wisdom or understanding. Because of its ideological element, economics is not a science which proceeds primarily on the basis of formulating hypotheses and testing the validity of these against observed phenomena.[2] Different social groups in society find it in their interest to portray capitalist economies in varying manners. Perhaps the most difficult task in understanding economic phenomena is trying to separate the scientific content of each theory from its ideological message.

Because of the strong ideological component in economics, theories which contain valuable insights may be discarded for a considerable length of time because the general orientation of those theories is at variance with the

237

prevailing political climate. The economics of Marx is an obvious victim of political prejudice. Whatever the failings of Marx's analysis may be, it contains a number of important contributions to cycle and growth theory, yet few respectable orthodox economists would explicitly admit to being influenced by the nineteenth-century revolutionary writer.[3] Many of Keynes's basic insights have also been discarded for largely political reasons. In particular, his conviction that capitalist economies do not automatically tend towards full employment and that it is wishful thinking to treat them as doing so[4] made Keynes theoretically suspect in the profession.

In this appendix no attempt is made to present the reader with an interpretation of the 'real Keynes', but rather to bring together some of his more unorthodox arguments which directly relate to the theoretical critique of neoclassical macroeconomics developed in previous chapters. It must be confessed that in part the following reinvestigation of Keynes is an unabashed attempt to lend authority to the arguments of this book. But the more important motivation is to indicate the exciting possibilities opened up for aggregate economic analysis when one breaks from the confines of the single commodity, general equilibrium macro model.

2   THE CENTRAL THEORETICAL PROBLEM OF MACROECONOMICS

In the preceding chapters a critique was made of the neoclassical approach to macroeconomics, with the purpose of logically refuting two basic parables: that increased employment is achieved through a lower real wage, and that increases in the price level are the consequence of increases in something called the money supply. The critique has dealt in detail with a number of issues and concepts judged as crucial to the neoclassical argument: general equilibrium adjustment, the aggregate single commodity, the autonomous money supply, and the neutrality of money. While the critique has at times been complex and involved, all of the arguments made in this book stem from a very fundamental theoretical problem which the neoclassical approach fails to resolve in a satisfactory manner.

No matter what methodological approach one takes, *the fundamental problem of all aggregate economic theory is to relate the money value of production to the material quantity of that production.* The basic characteristic of an economy in which monetary exchange is the dominant form of distribution is that products have a monetary value as well as their diverse material forms. These two aspects of commodities we will call their *monetary form* (or value form) and their *material form*. The essence of macroeconomics is specifying the relationship between the two. This specification involves discovering a way in which the total collection of commodities in their material form can be consistently related to the monetary value of those same commodities. The problem can be illustrated with an apparently trivial example. Assume that an economy produces only two commodities, wheat and beer. Let the production of wheat and beer in the first period be four units and three units, respectively, and three units and four units, respectively, in the second period. In which period is output greater? This difficulty in comparing different collections of commodities we shall call the *valuation problem*.[5]

In microeconomics this question never arises, for each market and each price (value form) refers to a single commodity. For a single homogeneous commodity output can be measured in physical units of the product. Many markets can be treated simultaneously by use of partial or general equilibrium analysis, but the issue of expressing production or value as an aggregate need not concern the theorist. Macroeconomics *is* the analysis of aggregates; therefore its basic foundation is the manner in which many things of great diversity (the material form of commodities) are related as an aggregate to the monetary form of those things. Involved here are three different aggregates, two of which are strictly empirical. First there is the collection of commodities produced in its material form. This collection exists as a real world phenomenon and is an aggregate in the sense that one can conceive of it as such (all the economy's commodities brought together in a great pile), but an aggregate number cannot be assigned to it (one cannot add tons of wheat and bottles of beer).[6] Second, there is a monetary form of these commodities, which also exists as an observable phenomenon and can be measured in a single number (one can add the price of wheat and price of beer).

The *sine qua non* of macroeconomics is the discovery of a third aggregate which is the expression of the collection of diverse commodities in homogeneous units, these homogeneous units being independent of the prices used to compute the total monetary value of commodities. In the most general terms, this third aggregate has the purpose of allowing for quantitative comparisons of different combinations of commodities. One aspect of such comparisons is being able to assign a unique value to a given collection, so its quantitative assessment remains unchanged whatever set of market prices may prevail for it. To avoid the ambiguous modifier 'real', we shall refer to this third aggregate as the 'price-independent' measure of output. The need for such an aggregate in order to create a field called 'macroeconomics' is so obvious that elaboration of the concept may seem trivial. However, modern economics hardly deals with this issue at all, or does so only at the most superficial level.

This third aggregate allows one to construct short-run macro models and models of economic growth. It is on the basis of it that one is allowed to make statements about the rate of flow of production and changes in society's productive assets. However, unlike the first two types of aggregates *the third is not directly observable*. A beer can be drunk and its price paid, but beer measured in homogeneous units that allow it to be added to other commodities similarly measured can only be inferred. In essence, this third aggregate is an analogue of the material form of commodities, but cannot itself be measured in the physical units one uses to measure each commodity taken alone.

Several great economists sought to specify the nature of this third aggregate with varying degrees of success. Ricardo was the first to treat the problem systematically, with the purpose of deriving a theory of the distribution of income and long-term accumulation. In attempting to solve the problem of 'an invariant measure of value', Ricardo can be assigned the distinction of being the first macroeconomist. His solution involved measuring the output of a diverse collection of commodities in terms of their labour content, though theoretical difficulties which he found insurmountable drove him to use a one commodity model at critical points in his analysis.

The neoclassical treatment of the valuation problem is not without its sophistication and complexity, but either trivial or irrelevant to short-run models. The valuation problem is trivialised by the assumption of a single commodity, as was explained in some detail in Chapter 2. The construction of a one commodity supply side ignores the valuation problem rather than confronting it, creating a system in which there are no relative prices or relative costs. Neoclassical theory offers another approach to the valuation problem which is not trivial, but has no relevance to aggregate analysis. Assume a two commodity system with fixed resource endowments. Following neoclassical logic, one can say that output is less than maximum if all resources are not fully used (or fully in a manner which does not involve cost minimisation). In this case, more of both commodities could be produced with the given resources. However, maximum output is not unique: output is at its maximum if all resources are devoted to wheat, all to beer, or all to the infinite possible combinations of wheat and beer.

The analysis need not stop at this point. On extremely restrictive assumptions, one can construct a 'community utility map' (or 'community indifference curves'), which shows all combinations of wheat and beer which all economic agents taken together find equally desirable (for each curve the level of community welfare is constant).[7] One can then say that at the point where the wheat/beer production transformation curve (or 'production possibilities curve', fixed by technology and the given factor endowments) is tangent to the highest community indifference curve production maximises community welfare. Even if one accepts the extremely dubious and rather jerry-rigged idea of aggregating individual preferences, the result is of little relevance to macroeconomics. With regard to comparisons of less than full employment to full employment, all has been said is that more complete use of resources results in increased output (though one cannot quantify the increase unless production remains in the same proportions). With regard to full employment positions, all output combinations look alike empirically because even in principle there is no way to know if the community is in equilibrium in its consumption choices.

During the 1950s and 1960s when Neoclassical Keynesians dominated the profession, there was a tendency to create a compartmentalisation between macroeconomics and microeconomics (which the anti-Keynesians such as Friedman quite correctly found unsatisfactory on grounds of theoretical consistency).[8] Along with this compartmentalisation frequently went a judgement that macroeconomics was 'more realistic' and 'more relevant to the real world' than microeconomics, since the latter seemed bogged down in a number of dubious and non-empirical concepts such as utility, perfect competition, and subjective optimisation. It would seem, however, that despite all the failings one might find in microeconomics, it has always been on stronger theoretical ground than macroeconomics. Even in its early origins as part of monetary theory, neoclassical macroeconomics has never resolved the central issue of aggregate analysis: the valuation problem. This failing did not go unnoticed by Keynes. In the section that follows Keynes's incomplete and sometimes confusing approach to the problem of aggregate valuation is analysed. The purpose is not to offer a general interpretation of the work of Keynes (of which there are many). Rather, I demonstrate the profound doubts held by the century's greatest economist with regard to the basic building blocks of neoclassical macroeconomics, doubts which are quite similar to those raised in this book.

3   KEYNES'S VIEWS ON 'REAL VARIABLES'[9]

In a comment that has gone relatively unnoted, Keynes tells the reader of *The General Theory* that it is his goal to provide an integration of the theory of money and the theory of value, a task he felt that his 'classical' opponents had failed to achieve or had not seriously attempted. At one level his objection was that Classical economics had by virtue of the dichotomy between real and monetary variables failed to integrate the theory of relative prices with the theory of money.[10] A close reading of *The General Theory*, particularly those parts largely ignored by mainstream economics, suggests that he had ambitions to do something considerably more fundamental: to provide a general theory of a money economy based upon a radically different solution to the valuation problem. It is this more challenging task that is discussed below.

Among the least read parts of *The General Theory* are its passages that grapple with the problem of valuing aggregate output both in monetary and in price-independent terms. The lack of attention to Keynes's discussion of the aggregation and valuation problem is in contrast to his own statement that deciding upon the proper choice of units to measure his aggregate concepts was one of the 'three perplexities which most impeded my process.' (Keynes, 1936, p. 37). It is to be recalled that throughout this book we have dealt with models specified in terms of 'real' variables – real income, consumption, investment, etc. At an early stage in *The General Theory* Keynes explicitly rejected such concepts as inappropriate for the construction of economic models.[11] Real concepts play two quite different roles in macroeconomics which must be distinguished in order to grasp the significance of Keynes's objections. First, there is their role as empirical measures: at one point in time one measures a certain level of money GNP, say, and at a subsequent point in time another level; which involves the greater level of production? Answering this question involves the construction of *index numbers* about which there is a large and quite technical statistical literature. While no method of construction is ideal, some can be judged as providing more accurate answers to the question than others. Keynes considered this use of 'real' variables – more precisely, *price-deflated* variables – to be quite valid. However, he warned (and any economic statistician would endorse this) – that these were 'vague concepts', 'avowedly imprecise and approximate', and their use should be limited to cases 'when we are attempting historical comparison'.[12]

Second, there is the use of 'real' categories as elements in an abstract economic model, and to this Keynes objected vehemently; particularly to 'real income', whose 'precise definition is an impossible task'.[13] In the construction of his model, Keynes abandoned all 'real' variables, choosing instead to employ only two units of measure, 'quantities of money-value and quantities of employment', and concludes his discussion by saying,

> It is my belief that much unnecessary perplexity can be avoided if we limit ourselves strictly to the two units, money and labour, when we are dealing with the behaviour of the system as a whole. (Keynes, 1936, p. 43)

If one does require models to be formulated in terms of units of money and labour, then a complete and radical break has been made with the prevailing economic wisdom of Keynes's time and subsequent neoclassical macroeconomics (though it is not clear whether Keynes realised this). Keynes's objection is to the use of a spurious aggregate measured in 'physical' units. If his objection is sustained, then the aggregate production function must be abandoned. With the aggregate production function gone, capital-labour substitution must also be dropped from the analysis.[14] As we shall see, Keynes did not draw these conclusions from his 'choice of units'.[15]

Before proceeding with the implications of the choice of labour and money as sole units of measure, one should note Keynes's method of abstraction or theory-building. At this point the reader might wish to refer back to Section 2.1 and the discussion there of two theoretical methods, 'abstract ideal' and 'abstract simplified'. In the first, the theorist begins with mental constructions which need have no direct analogue in the phenomena to be explained. In effect, the theorist reduces complexity ('abstracts') by creating a simple fictitious world of his or her own construction. This is the method of neoclassical economics, referred to in the profession as *a priori* reasoning. Output measured in physical units is a purely ideal concept, for it has no analogue in a functioning economy. In all economies there are physical inputs and physical outputs and a more-or-less established technology that links the one to the other. However, in no economy except a mythological one is there an aggregate homogeneous commodity which is both the system's input and output.

Keynes recognised this indisputable fact and quite sensibly concluded that it would be ridiculous to assume the existence of that which cannot be. His choice of money and labour as theoretical quantities indicates use of the abstract-simplified method. These are not concepts created by the mind of the theorist, but categories of actual economies. While neither is a simple category – many things can serve as money and labour comes in many varieties – for all their complexities they are 'real' categories in the dictionary sense of the term. In other words, Keynes did not create these two abstractions, money and labour, but drew them out of the confusing complexity of reality and assigned them simplified definitions.

4 KEYNES'S MONEY AGGREGATES

Whether or not Keynes was aware of the distinction between ideal abstractions (creations of the mind) and abstractions drawn from reality is difficult to judge, for he gives little explicit treatment of methodology in his writings. However, there is considerable textual evidence in *The General Theory* to suggest that at the very least he had a strong intuition that reality should inspire theory. One of the clearest examples is his treatment of aggregate income, which is in sharp contrast to the neoclassical approach. All the models treated in this book begin with homogeneous value added or income, then reach money income as a variable derivative from the price level. In Keynes's view, money income could not be decomposed into the product of 'physical output' and 'the general price level'. In order to understand Keynes's treatment of national income, we must consider the institutional context of his abstract model.

Recall from Chapter 1 that the neoclassical macroeconomic model is formulated in terms of households (or individuals), with all national income representing personal income. This is one of the most fundamental characteristics of the neoclassical macro model, a not very subtle ideological obfuscation of the economic power of business enterprise. Keynes rejected the view that economic models should be formulated in terms of socially undifferentiated economic actors, be they called 'agents' or 'households'. At the outset of his analysis *a money economy is treated as a capitalist economy, whose most important actors are business enterprises, not households*. There is a quite clear reason for this difference between neoclassical models and the model of Keynes. In neoclassical theory economies are treated in terms of notional demand and supply curves, so the system is not demand-constrained. In the absence of demand constraints, the relevant constraints refer to individual choices between income and leisure. In Keynes's demand-constrained system, the crucial actors become business enterprises, and in particular their expectations with regard to the future are crucial.

Having conceptualised a money economy with business enterprise at the centre of it, Keynes proceeds to define the components of national income in terms of the cash-flow or net worth position of these enterprises.[16] By this procedure Keynes seeks to extract from the complexity of real business transactions that part of cash-flow which represents the net addition to society's production during the time period; i.e., the value added created by the process of transforming intermediate products.

It might be thought that this is an extremely tedious method. Why cannot one just begin with a concept of value added in production ('payments to factors') and ignore intermediate costs altogether, since we know that these cancel out in the aggregate? The answer to the question is that the workplaces of business enterprise do not produce value added, but produce *commodities* in which value added is embodied, and the sales revenue from these commodities only in part becomes factor incomes. By treating income in the context of the cash-flow of enterprises, Keynes's analysis incorporates fact that money economies are characterised by the production of commodities. Neoclassical theory, on the other hand, treats economies as systems which produce value added.

It is perhaps necessary to elaborate this point, for habits of neoclassical thought are so ingrained that its significance could easily be lost. In neoclassical macroeconomics, costs of production other than those that correspond to factor payments are not merely netted out, they are assumed not to exist. In Keynes's approach, there is an explicit analysis of the netting-out process that allows one to reach, rather than begin with, factor payments. Taking Keynes's route to the concept of income results in quite subtle insights which could make a neoclassical economists feel like a Euclidian lost in a non-Euclidian world.

To demonstrate the theoretical implications of Keynes's procedure, the steps he takes to obtain factor incomes will be briefly pursued. Beginning with gross receipts of the enterprise, Keynes subtracts out purchases from other firms. This subtraction eliminates the money value of intermediate inputs. Next Keynes adjust for changes in the valuation of the enterprise's capital stock, which accounts for that part of the sales revenue which covers depreciation. The result of these *theoretical* calculations (which could also be carried out in practice) is to obtain the net sales revenue which accrues to factors of production. As a result of proceeding in this way, Keynes has broken the definitional equality found in neoclassical macroeconomics between value added and the aggregate production of final commodities (consumption commodities and investment commodities). In neoclassical theory these two must be equal *because there are no intermediate commodities and no changes in the valuation of the capital stock*. In practice they are never equal except by chance. In Keynes's analysis the principal reason the two can differ arises from changes in the valuation of the capital stock. Prior to explaining this, let the three money aggregates be clearly defined:

(1) total factor income, equal to sales minus intermediate cost, with adjustment for equipment and stocks due to price changes;
(2) aggregate supply of final commodities, equal to the market value of consumption and investment commodities; and
(3) aggregate final demand, the expenditure by workers and capitalists on consumption commodities, and the expenditure of capitalists on investment commodities.

Keynes argued that the aggregate supply and aggregate demand for commodities (numbers 2 and 3) could differ because of insufficient aggregate demand (some final commodities go unsold). Implicit in his analysis is the possibility that factor income and the aggregate supply of final commodities could differ. The implications of this second inequality are considerably more interesting theoretically than the first.

Assume that a major technical change, such as computerised automation, renders a significant proportion of the economy's capital stock obsolete. Part or all of the depreciation of the obsolete capital stock which is embodied in commodities as money costs cannot be recaptured in the commodities' selling price if factors of production continue to receive their previous (pre-innovation) income payments. Though the depreciation of the capital stock as such cannot be recaptured in the selling price, money must be set aside by enterprises in order that at some future date the productive stock be replaced with new plant and machinery. The money to do so must be deducted from factor incomes. In the short term the money will be taken from profits and in the longer term perhaps by forcing wages down. The effect of shifting money from factor payments to the depreciation account is to make disbursed factor payments less than the money value of final commodities. With disbursed factor incomes less than the value of final commodities, some final commodities will go unsold even if all income is spent. This provides an explanation of demand failures somewhat more convinving than Keynes's emphasis upon a declining average propensity to consume.[17] Further, recognising the possible incongruity between final commodity supply and factor income provides a convenient vehicle for treating economic relationships dynamically, particularly the dynamic effects of technical change. While he lays out the possibility of an inequality between aggregate supply and factor incomes in some detail,[18] Keynes does not employ it as an analytical device in his discussion of the determinants of effective demand.

The discussion so far has demonstrated how Keynes sought to define his national income aggregates with reference to the commodity-producing nature of money economies. This attention to commodities also manifests itself in his treatment of the apparently simple category 'price'. As explained above, Keynes derived factor incomes by taking gross receipts of the enterprise and subtracting out intermediate costs (including depreciation). The part of gross revenue which does not accrue to factors of production Keynes called 'user cost'. As any student of first year economics knows, in neoclassical microeconomics, like at the macro level, output is treated as produced without intermediate products – with capital and labour alone. As a consequence, 'marginal cost' is really 'marginal labour cost'. At the micro level firms are treated as producing value added, not commodities. Referring to his concept of user cost, Keynes proceeds to take issue with the orthodox treatment of price theory:

> The concept of user cost enables us, moreover, to give a clearer definition than usually adopted of the short period supply price of a unit of a firms' saleable output. For the short period supply price is the sum of the marginal factor cost and the marginal user cost.
> . . .
> Whereas it may be occasionally convenient in dealing with *output as a whole* to deduct user cost, this procedure deprives our analysis of all reality if it is habitually (and tacitly) applied to the output of a single industry or firm, since it divorces the 'supply price' of an article from any ordinary sense of its price . . . (Keynes, 1936, p. 67)

Keynes is here making a point which would be quite obvious were it not for habits of thought induced in economists for generations: the price of a commodity includes all of the elements which go to produce it, be they factor services or inputs of materials. Consider any commodity, such as beer. The price of beer includes labour cost, other factor payments, depreciation on equipment, and commodity inputs such as the bottle, hops, and electricity. Keynes's recommendation is that the production of the beer industry be treated as what it is – the amount of beer produced in a time period, embodying non-factor costs as well as factor costs. This is in sharp contrast to neoclassical microeconomics, where for purposes of analysing price behaviour, the production function for beer is written, $q(b) = q(k,l)$, and $q(b)$ refers to that amount of beer which corresponds to the value added embodied in beer, not the actual production and sale of beer.[19]

The implication of treating prices as what they are (inclusive of all costs) rather than as what they are not (factor costs only) is quite radical. Pursuing this sensible approach leads one to abandon marginal productivity analysis in favour of some version of the labour theory of value for commodity-production models set within an input–output framework. Once there is explicit consideration of intermediate costs, a part of the money value of every commodity is not created in the production of that commodity. Intermediate commodities arrive at the production process with their money value already determined, and this money value is passed on to the final item ('final' with respect to the production process in question). To put the matter simply, the electricity used to heat the vats in a brewery does not *create* value added, but only represents a cost of production. Once one includes a category of inputs which merely pass their money value on in production without expanding value, the *raison d'être* of a value-expanding capital input is lost. Machinery can also be treated as passing its money value on to the final product through use (what Keynes called the 'sacrifice' of equipment). It is not obvious why a vat which lasts several production periods should not be treated similarly to electricity and hops in its role in the production of beer. This was the argument of Ricardo and Marx – that only the labour input generates value added (expands value),[20] and Keynes endorsed this view:

> I sympathise . . . with the pre-classical doctrine that everything is *produced by labour*, aided by what used to be called art and is now called technique, by natural resources which are free or cost a rent according to their scarcity or abundance, and by the results of past labour, embodied in assets, which also command a price according to their scarcity or abundance. It is preferable to regard labour . . . as the sole factor of production, operating in a given environment of technique, natural resources, capital equipment and effective demand. (Keynes, 1936, pp. 213–14)

Since Keynes does not formulate a theory of price on the basis of the labour content of commodities, it is more precise to say that he is endorsing a labour theory of production and aggregation rather than a labour theory of value.[21] It is by use of labour as a unit of measure that he seeks to relate the money aggregates to material production.

5 KEYNES'S PRICE-INDEPENDENT AGGREGATE

As explained before, the production of commodities results in the output of a heterogeneous collection of useful products, on the one hand, and an aggregate value that represents their market value, on the other. Keynes discarded a concept of 'real' variables, implicitly measured in physical units, as a valid tool for constructing economic models. His solution to the problem was the 'labour unit'.

Keynes defines a labour unit to be homogeneous labour performed for a standardised amount of time, one person-day, for example. With this unit he proposes to construct his theory of effective demand. Analytically verifying the hypothesis of homogeneous labour is a problem which has plagued practitioners of the labour theory of value for over one hundred years. The first difficulty is that labour is not in fact homogeneous. In order to render labour homogeneous, Keynes proposes that different types of labour be evaluated on the basis of their remuneration.[22] This is an appealing and simple solution which is adopted by most Marxists and Ricardians. There is very little theoretical justification for it. At the outset it would seem to fail the test which Keynes himself has used to flunk 'real income'. This latter concept was ruled out-of-court by Keynes because of the '. . . grave objection . . . that the community's output of goods and service is a non-homogeneous complex . . .' and the same is true of the community's labour force. If this labour force can be aggregated on the basis of relative wages for some base period, why is not one justified in aggregating commodities using relative prices? Keynes's main defence of the labour unit, that wage differentials are more or less fixed by comparison with commodity prices, is both empirically suspect and suspiciously *ad hoc*.

Keynes's labour unit was from its inception a non-starter, rarely employed even by those most in sympathy with the innovative aspects of his work.[23] The basic problem with the labour unit is that it offers an alternative aggregate measure to that of the neoclassicals but keeps the same method. Like the neoclassicals, Keynes in effect created by assumption the element central to his aggregate analysis (homogeneous labour). As a consequence, use of the labour unit appears quite arbitrary – as long as one is assuming labour to be homogeneous, go on and 'resolve' all the aggregation problems by assuming output to be homogeneous also.

The attempt by Keynes to provide a fresh solution to the valuation problem immediately runs into trouble when he attempts to relate employment in labour units to money output. In specifying the output side of his model, Keynes defines an industry supply curve as follows:

$$Z = Z(N)$$

where N is employment in labour units, Z is the sales revenue,[24] or $Z = pQ$ and Q is the output in physical units.

The aggregate supply function is defined for levels of sales revenue. While by definition sales revenue equals price times the quantity of output, $Z = pQ$, output can only be assigned a number in the case of an industry which produces a homogeneous output. Keynes's case for the adoption of his version of the industry supply curve[25] in place of the familiar neoclassical supply curve is that it can be aggregated across industries to obtain an aggregate supply curve. The usual supply curves cannot be added because they are measured in physical units. The aggregation is achieved, Keynes argues, by summing labour units across industries.

In fact, Keynes's aggregate supply curve is no improvement upon the neoclassical assumption of a single commodity; indeed, an equivalent assumption, plus additional restriction, is required to construct it. In order that Z, sales revenue, be unique with respect to the level of employment, at least two assumptions are necessary. First, the price of each commodity produced by the industry must be constant. This Keynes achieves by assuming constant returns to scale and a constant money wage. More important in terms of the aggregates Keynes seeks to discard, his supply function requires that commodities always be produced in the same proportion. If an industry produces more than one commodity, the amount of sales revenue generated by a certain level of employment will depend upon how much of each commodity is produced. The same restriction carries over to the aggregate supply curve – given the set of commodity prices, the aggregate supply curve is unique with respect to the number of labour units if and only if the composition of output remains unchanged. Yet if the composition of output remains unchanged, there is no difficulty in measuring 'real' output, since such a situation is equivalent to a one commodity system. In the construction of the aggregate supply function the labour unit becomes superfluous. After an exciting start in his formulation of money aggregates, Keynes provides little insight into solving the aggregate relationship between the material production of commodities and their market value.

Notes and References

INTRODUCTION

1. Marx's theory of aggregate economic activity will be treated in John Weeks, *Capital and Circulation: Macroeconomics after Marx* (London: Macmillan, forthcoming).
2. I shall take Frank Hahn's definition of neoclassical economics.

   I have frequently . . . been classified as a neo-classical economist . . . There are three elements in my thinking which may justify it:

   1) I am a reductionist in that I attempt to locate explanations in the actions of individual agents.
   2) In theorising about the agent I look for some axioms of rationality.
   3) I hold that some notion of equilibrium is required and that the study of equilibrium is useful. (Frank Hahn, *Equilibrium and Macroeconomics* (Oxford: Basil Blackwell, 1984), p. 1)

3. This analysis is found in Volume II of *Capital*. This has been justifiably called the 'lost' volume, and the analysis found there is the basis of the reconstruction of aggregate analysis in *Capital and Circulation*.
4. Axel Leijonhufvud, *Keynesian Economics and the Economics of Keynes* (Oxford: Oxford University Press, 1968) p. 7–8.
5. 'Few economists would argue with the general proposition that lower real wages will mean higher employment . . . The debate is not over whether such a relationship exists but how strong it is.' *The Times*, 12 Nov 1985.
6. Relevant to this plea is a comment by Hahn,

   The most strongly held of my views I have left to the last. . . . It is that neither is there a single best way for understanding in economics nor is it possible to hold any conclusions, other than purely logical deductions, with certainty. (Hahn, 1984, p. 7)

1 THE DEMAND SIDE OF THE NEOCLASSICAL MODEL

1. Many, if not all of the neoclassical terms have meaning only within the model; i.e., they are theoretical abstractions not necessarily descriptive of empirical relationships. 'Services' as in 'labour services' is one of these. However, from this point on we shall not put all of these in quotation marks. It should be kept in mind, therefore, that use of these terms does not imply anything more than their role in the model.
2. Throughout this book we shall avoid use of the term 'goods', which has a strong normative connotation, derived from subjective utility theory in

which anything one buys is by definition a source of pleasure and therefore a 'good'. Instead, we use the neutral term 'commodity' or 'product'.

3. One is Chick, who writes, '. . . I came to realize that the circular flow and Keynes's treatment of finance and money were not really compatible.' (Victoria Chick, *Macroeconomics after Keynes* (Oxford: Philip Allan, 1983) p. v.)

4. The method of these economists is critically treated in Alan Coddington, *Keynesian Economics: The Search for First Principles* (London: George Allen & Unwin, 1983) ch. 6.

5. 'The aggregate procedure is . . . as important in determining the properties of an economic model as are the assumptions made about the relationships between the aggregates . . .' (Leijonhufvud, 1968, p. 111).

6. In the appendix on Keynes it is shown that these are not true identities.

7. In this and all subsequent algebra in this book, parentheses will enclose identifying notation or functional relationships of general form. Brackets, of the form [ ] and { } , embrace algebraic operations.

8. Introduction of this lag requires a redefinition of terms so that aggregate demand and aggregate supply can assume different values. For example, $Z(t) = C(t) + I(t)$, where consumption is $C(t) = C(Y(t-1))$, and the equilibrium condition, $I(t) = S(t)$ implies $Y(t) = Y(t-1)$.

9. One exception is Allen, who suggests the possibility of a production lag, but does not pursue it. See R. G. D. Allen, *Macro-Economic Theory* (London: St Martin's Press, 1968) pp. 16–18.

10. See Alfred Eichner and J. A. Kregel, 'An Essay on Post-Keynesian Theory: A New Paradigm in Economics', *Journal of Economic Literature*, Vol. XIII, p. 4 (December 1975), where this is defended, and Coddington (1983), ch. 6, where it is critiqued. Macroeconomic treatments with constrained variables are sometimes called 'fixed price models'. See John Muellbauer and Richard Portes, 'Macroeconomic Models with Quantity Rationing', *Economic Journal*, vol. 88 (December 1978).

2 THE NEOCLASSICAL MODEL WITH A SUPPLY SIDE

1. Robert J. Gordon, *Macroeconomics* (second edn) (Boston: Little, Brown, 1981) p. 176. The aggregate supply curve Gordon refers to here is the aggregate production function translated into a price/output space from a labour/output space. Aggregate supply curves are treated in the discussion of inflation, Chapters 12 and 14.

2. After making no mention of any aggregation problem, Parkin writes, 'This completes the definition of the short-run aggregate production function' (Michael Parkin, *Macroeconomics* (Englewood Cliffs, New Jersey: Prentice-Hall, 1984)) p. 112. Dernburg is considerably more careful. (Thomas F. Dernberg, *Macroeconomics* (New York: McGraw-Hill, 1985) pp. 145–8.) Bronfenbrenner, whose text includes non-neoclassical treatments of macroeconomics, makes no mention of the aggregation problem when he presents the aggregate production func-

tion. (Martin Bronfenbrenner, *Macroeconomic Alternatives* (Arlington Heights, Illinois: AHM Publishing Company, 1979) pp. 52, 220–21.)

3. Neoclassical theory does consider relative commodity prices at the microeconomic level, which falls within our discussion of Walras' Law.

4. If all income is made up of wages and profits, then obviously it follows that $Y = Wl + rK$ (wages plus profits measured in current prices). The neoclassical adding-up condition asserts more than this definitional identity. Its assertion is that the equality will hold if one substitutes for the commodity wage, w, the value which brings equilibrium to the labour market ($ls = ld$) and the interest rate uniquely implied by that equilibrium w. It is this conditional equality which requires the assumption of constant returns to scale.

5. The anomaly that the interest rate is absent from the supply of labour function was pointed out to me by Ben Fine.

6. In the early 1950s, two pioneers of econometrics, Lawrence Klein and Arthur Goldberger, estimated consumption functions in which income data were divided by functional groups – employees, entrepreneurs and farmers. Such studies subsequently were victim to considerable ridicule, with it suggested that distinguishing consumption behaviour by economic class was no more theoretically valid than doing so on the basis of hair colour.

7. While what follows is in terms of the wage measured in the single commodity, the neoclassical labour market analysis is not amended when one moves to money wages, as we do in Chapter 5.

8. See the seminal article by Smith and a similar treatment by Ackley. In both of these the commodity market equilbrium is treated by use of 'IS–LM' curves (see Chapter 5). (Warren L. Smith, 'A Graphical Exposition of the Complete Keynesian System', *The Southern Economic Journal*, vol. 23 (October 1956); and Gardner Ackley, *Macroeconomics: Theory and Policy* (New York: Macmillan, 1978).)

9. The market-clearing difficulty presented here ignores the equally problematical restriction that any exchanges at non-equilibrium prices preclude an equilibrium solution. This difficulty, involving the intervention of the 'Walrasian auctioneer', is considered in the next chapter.

10. Overtime work does not contradict the all-or-nothing character of employment contracts, since one must work full-time before one can work overtime. Part-time work characterises a minority of the labour force in developed capitalist countries, occuring primarily in the service and trade sectors.

11. The usual way of writing the 'IS' curve is $y = c(y, r) + i(y, r)$. Chick comments, '. . . the distinction between consumption and investment . . . was virtually obliterated . . .' in the neoclassical model (Chick, 1983, p. 4).

12. In other words, that it is an object of utility, which we have presumed throughout the discussion.

13. For an elaboration of the implications of this definition, see John Weeks, *Capital and Exploitation* (New York and London: Princeton University Press and Edward Arnold, 1981), ch. 2.

3 COMPARATIVE STATICS AND EQUILIBRIUM

1. Referring to Roy Harrod's definition, Baumol writes, 'dynamics should be confined to the analysis of continuing changes as against once-and-for-all changes,' and goes on to say, 'Economic dynamics is the study of economic phenomena in relation to preceding and succeeding events' (W. J. Baumol, *Economic Dynamics* (New York: Macmillan, 1959) p. 4).
2. Rudiger Dorbusch and Stanley Fischer, *Macroeconomics* (New York: McGraw-Hill, 1983) p. 367.
3. '. . . [T]here is no theoretical evidence to suggest that the invisible hand performs better "asymptotically" than it does "momentarily" . . .' (Frank Hahn, *Equilibrium and Macroeconomics* (Oxford: Basil Blackwell, 1984) p. 98). 'Momentarily' refers here to instantaneous market clearing.
4. Some would say 'none', arguing that the synthesis model is formulated in a way which makes money useless as a theoretical concept. See Laurence Harris, *Monetary Theory* (New York: McGraw-Hill, 1981) pp. 289ff.
5. Once we explicitly introduce Walrasian general equilibrium mechanisms into the model, it will no longer be possible for only one market not to clear.
6. One might argue that the disappointment of buyers takes the form of labour services which go unsold, since a shortfall in the barter of the single commodity must correspond to a shortfall in the barter of labour services to produce the unbartered commodity. However, this ignores the notional demand of employers for the single commodity, as an item of present and future consumption.
7. For this interpretation of the multiplier, see Leijonhufvud (1968) pp. 52ff; and Harris (1981) ch. 13.
8. See David K. H. Begg, *The Rational Expectations Revolution in Macroeconomics: Theories and Evidence* (Oxford: Philip Allan, 1982), where 'continuous market clearing' is used throughout.
9. See J. R. Hicks, *Value and Capital* (Oxford: Oxford University Press, 1939) pp. 119ff.
10. Axel Leijonhufvud, *Information and Coordination: Essays in Macroeconomics Theory* (New York: Oxford University Press, 1981) ch. 7.
11. See Stephen Toulmin and June Goodfield, *The Fabric of the Heavens* (New York: Harper Torchbooks, 1961) ch. 7.
12. See Harris (1981) pp. 51–8. Also useful is Leijonhufvud (1981) ch. 5, where he treats what he calls 'Say's Principle'.
13. One must keep in mind that disequilibrium does not refer to a situation in which trades have taken place, but to a situation in which some agents are dissatisfied, but no one has committed himself or herself.
14. Leijonhufvud persuasively argues that Walras' Law and Say's Law (Walras' Law defined over commodity markets only) do not imply anything about market clearing. However, if the Law is accompanied by the omniscient auctioneer, market clearing is implied.
15. A number of these papers are reprinted in Hahn (1984).

16. '. . . [T]he recent meaning given to equilibrium (and disequilibrium) has had quite disastrous effects. Equilibrium is defined as Walrasian competitive equilibrium or a rational expectations equilibrium. All other states are said to be in disequilibrium.' (Hahn, 1984, pp. 8–9.) Rational expectations is treated in Chapters 9, and 14.

17. See, for example, K. J. Arrow and G. Debreu, 'Existence of an Equilibrium for a Competitive Economy', *Econometrica* (1954); and G. Debreu, *Theory of Value* (New York: John Wiley, 1959). Hahn has written, 'The main conclusion [about Walrasian general equilibrium dynamics] is rather pessimistic: we have no good reason to suppose that there are forces which lead the economy to equilibrium. By that I mean we have no good theory.' (Hahn, 1984, p. 13.)

18. In the companion volume to this book it will be argued that aggregate economic behaviour does not require a concept of equilibrium; at least, equilibrium in the neoclassical sense (John Weeks, *Capital and Circulation*).

19. It is called the 'homogeneity' postulate because of the mathematical relationship between the demand for commodities and services with respect to the absolute price level, which is *homogeneous of degree zero*. That is, the price level enters into the demand functions with an exponent of zero, and a variable raised to the zero power yields the number one regardless of its numerical value.

20. Except in rare cases, the utility functions of consumer theory invoke the homogeneity postulate, as does the theory of the firm. Aggregates based upon such micro foundations must also incorporate the postulate. While Walras' Law need not involve the homogeneity postulate, if it does not it is inconsistent with the usual supply and demand analysis.

21. Despite the artificial and ideal character of the Walrasian solution to market clearing, the mechanism is treated with considerable respect in the economics profession. Leijonhufvud, a severe and sometimes polemical critic of Walrasian general equilibrium models, writes, 'Walras, Marshall, *et al.* had left a by-and-large satisfactory solution to the problem of the determination of prices for "final" outputs and factor services and the allocation of resource flows under the (arbitrary) condition of "fixed" resource endowments.' (Leijonhufvud, 1968, p. 214.)

4 MONEY IN THE NEOCLASSICAL MODEL

1. The definition is taken from Harris (1981) p. 43. We have added only the words 'full employment' to make more explicit the nature of the equilibrium state.

2. Frequently neoclassical writers define money as anything generally accepted as *means of payment*. We do not employ this term in this book, for it will be used in the quite different classical (Ricardo and Marx) sense in the companion volume, *Capital and Circulation*.

3. Harry G. Johnson, *Macroeconomics and Monetary Theory* (Chicago: Aldine Publishing Company, 1972) ch. 7.

4. See Victoria Chick, *The Theory of Monetary Policy* (Oxford: Basil Blackwell, 1979) pp. 13–14; and Harry G. Johnson, *Essays in Monetary Economics* (London: George Allen & Unwin, 1974) pp. 41ff.

5. This one can refer to various textbooks, current and past. In Ackley (1978) one finds only passing reference to any controversy over the money supply. In Branson (1972) there is a three-page treatment of the relationship between central bank lending and commercial bank response, a method of approach a leading monetary theorist called 'a mechanistic analysis of the determination of the money supply, very similar to the outmoded treatment of velocity' (Johnson, 1974, p. 41). No reference to the controversy is to be found in Edward Shapiro, *Macroeconomic Analysis* (third edn) (New York: Harcourt Brace Jovanovich, 1974) or in Gordon (1981).

6. See the report commissioned by the British government on the effectiveness of monetary policy, Radcliffe Committee: *Committee on the Working of the Monetary System: Report* (London: Her Majesty's Stationery Office, Cmnd, 827, 1959).

7. As will be seen later in this chapter, the proportional relationship between prices and the money supply need not imply that the homogeneity postulate holds.

8. '. . . a theory of money, if it is to be consistent, requires that supply be determined independently of the demand for money, and if the theory is to be of use, it must allow that the central bank ["monetary authorities"] can control the quantity of money in the hands of the public.' (Johnson, 1972, p. 136.) This independence of supply and demand is necessary for a theory of *valueless* money, not a general requirement of a theory of money.

9. If capital is mobile across industries, then there will be a tendency for the rate of return to equalise for all commodities. This theoretical rule would also apply to the commodity serving as money. Thus, all other commodities would have to exchange against the money commodity such as to bring about this equalisation. An increase in the cost of producing money would then lower all prices and vice versa.

10. The contradiction between Walras' Law and the quantity equation was first pointed out by Patinkin. See Don Patinkin, *Money, Interest and Prices: An Integration of Monetary and Value Theory* (New York: Harper International Editons, 1965) ch. VIII.

11. See the discussion of the debate over the real balance effect in Johnson (1974) pp. 17–21. Notwithstanding the virtually universal agreement among neoclassical monetary theorists that the real balance effect in some form (e.g. as the Pigou effect, considered in Chapter 4) is critical for logical consistency in adjustment to equilibrium, it is not unusual for textbooks in macroeconomics to ignore it and proceed on the basis of internally inconsistent models. See Branson (1974) pp. 107ff, where the demand for cash balance is defined in real terms ($M*/p$), but consumption and investment are functions of the level of output/income and the interest rate only.

12. Branson (1972) p. 62. This quotation is a latter-day version of Pigou's

famous reference to money as a 'veil'. (A. C. Pigou, *The Veil of Money* (London: Macmillan, 1941) pp. 20–27.)

13. For a review of the empirical literature, see Harris (1981) ch. 20.
14. For a clear explanation of inside and outside money, see Harris (1981) ch. 3.
15. J. G. Gurley and E. S. Shaw, *Money in a Theory of Finance* (Washington: The Brookings Institute, 1960).
16. B. P. Pesek and T. R. Saving, *Money, Wealth and Economic Theory* (New York: Macmillan, 1967).
17. And the inconsistency takes yet a third form when the Pigou effect replaces the real balance effect.
18. 'The definition of the money supply . . . is neither a question of abstract principle, to be decided by theoretical controversy, nor an empirical matter, to be decided on the basis of statistical estimates of substitutability [among different empirical categories of money]. It is a practical matter, a free and always somewhat arbitrary choice, based on the judgement of the investigator, of the aggregate most relevant to the problem he is attempting to answer.' (Chick, 1979, pp. 13–14.) Among books on monetary theory, Chick's provides the clearest and most thorough treatment of the controversies surrounding the presumption of an autonomous money supply.

5 THE CLASSICAL FALSE DICHOTOMY MODEL

1. See, for example, Gardner Ackley, *Macroeconomic Theory* (New York, Macmillan, 1961) ch. VI; and Shapiro (1974) ch. 17. The inconsistency goes unmentioned in more recent textbooks as well, as shown in the treatment of inflation.
2. Since the exponents add to one, $[1 - a] + a = 1$, the function is characterised by 'constant returns to scale'; i.e. if from any initial level, the inputs are doubled, output/income also doubles. This implies $y = wl + rk$, and that $py = Wl + rk$. Refer back to the discussion of the 'adding up' equation in Chapter 2.
3. A firm takes the market price as given if there is perfect competition. Walrasian markets presume perfect competition.
4. The simplicity of the solution derives in large part from the special property of the Cobb–Douglas function that the exponents are equal to the income shares of the variables they are associated with; i.e., $wl/y = Wl/py = [1 - a]$, and $rk/y = rK/py = a$.
5. Also implied is a negative relationship between employment and the money wage. This 'trade-off' is the result of diminishing returns combined with the quantity equation.
6. This has been established in the Cambridge Capital Controversy, which is treated in Chapter 10.
7. The new classical economics would appear to deny that increasing the money supply can raise the level of employment. However, their conclusion is the result of arbitrarily assuming that all markets quickly and

instantaneously equilibrate. Obviously, if the labour market is always in full employment equilibrium, increasing the money supply will not increase employment. This approach is dealt with in Chapter 9.
8. The other two exceptions are rigid money wages, considered above, and the 'liquidity trap', considered in Section 6.3. Leijonhufvud has argued that neither of these two can be found in *The General Theory* (Axel Leijonhufvud, *Information and Coordination: Essays in Macroeconomic Theory* (New York: Oxford University Press, 1981 pp. 53–4)).
9. In Figure 5.4 it is assumed that saving is interest inelastic and investment is unrelated to current income. The same point can be demonstrated if both saving and investment are interest elastic. A clear, if rather old, treatment is found in Ackley (1961) pp. 193–5.

6 LOGICALLY CONSISTENT MONEY-NEUTRAL MODELS

1. 'Money illusion' is defined as behaviour by an agent in which a real variable (M_*/p in this case) is affected by a change in a nominal variable (p or M_* in this case). Leijonhufvud has a low opinion of the concept of money illusion, calling it a 'fudge-phrase'. His objections are treated in Chapter 11.
2. To refresh memories, the difference between the excess demand functions in the previous and present models can be summarised algebraically. Below, the function implied by the money market function is on the left and that implied by the commodity market on the right.

   Classical (false dichotomy) case:

$$M(d) = vpy \qquad\qquad y(d) = c + i$$
$$M(xd) = vpy - M_* \qquad M(xd) = -py(xd)$$
$$\qquad\qquad\qquad\qquad\quad M(xd) = py - p[c + i]$$
$$M(xd) = p[vy] - M_* \qquad M(xd) = p\{y[1 - b] + [c_* + i]\}$$

The two are clearly inconsistent, since the one on the right increases proportionately with the price level, while the one on the left does not.
3. The consistency is demonstrated below for the Real Balance Effect model, using the same notation and framework as in note 2, above.

   Classical (real balance effect) case:

$$M(d) = vpy - fM_* \qquad\qquad y(d) = c + i$$
$$M(xd) = vpy + fM_* - M_* \qquad M(xd) = -py(xd)$$
$$M(xd) = vpy - [1 - f]M_* \qquad M(xd) = py - p[c_* + by + gM_*/p + i]$$
$$M(xd) = p[vy] - [1 - f]M_* \qquad M(xd) = p\{y[1 - b] + [c_* + i]\} - gM_*$$

Now in both cases a change in the price level affects the first term and leaves the second term (involving M_*) untouched.
4. Clower and other post-Keynesians go on to argue that in disequilibrium unemployment can result even when the real wage is at the level

consistent with full employment general equilibrium (i.e. where notional supply and notional demand are equal). This is explained in Chapter 11.

5. Recall that $p(e) = [1 - f]M*/vy(e)$. The intercept of the consumption function can have only one value given the marginal propensity to consume (its slope). This is shown below.

$$c(e) = c_* + by(e) + gM_*/p(e)$$
$$c_* = c(e) - by(e) - gM_*/p(e)$$

The intercept of the saving function is $-[c_*]$, which is not a true parameter. It changes with the variables of the model and has a unique (non-arbitrary) value in equilibrium.

6. The model presented in this section is virtually identical to that in Warren Smith, 'A Graphical Exposition of the Complete Keynesian System', *Southern Economic Journal*, vol. 23 (October, 1956). Smith's diagrammatic technique subsequently became common usage. The model is neither complete nor Keynesian, as will be shown in this section.

7. Assume one buys a bond for $100 that has a yield of 5 per cent. If the interest rate on bonds rises to 10 per cent, then one can purchase a 5 per cent yield for $50. As a consequence, the owner of the original 5 per cent bond will find that while that bond has a face value of $100, it will fetch only $50 when sold in competition with 10 per cent bonds. This assumes all other factors unchanged, of course.

8. The modern analysis is cast in terms of what is called 'portfolio theory', which involves a priori determination of the optimal composition of an individual's wealth holding (money, bonds, etc.) on the assumption of utility maximisation. See Harris (1981) ch. 10, for a treatment of the transactions, precautionary, and speculative demands for money within this framework.

9. See Harris (1981), pp. 196–203, for an elaboration of this argument in terms of utility theory.

10. Sometimes, particularly in older textbooks, this relationship is written,

$$M(d) = pvy + (h - jr).$$

This implies 'money illusion', for a nominal variable ($M[d]$) is determined by a real variable (r). Harris (1981) pp. 246–7.

11. Just as in the case of the familiar supply and demand curves for a single commodity, the stability of an equilibrium point for the IS and LM curves depends upon the slope of each (presuming the parameters to be given). If one curve is downward sloping and the other upward sloping, the equilibrium is stable without qualification. If both have a positive slope or both have a negative slope, stability depends upon the slope of one curve relatively to the other.

12. Keynes explicitly deals with the fundamental differences between a barter system and a money economy in Chapter 17 of *The General Theory*. Some would argue that this is the most important chapter of the book.

13. As in the previous section, the two are compared below. The demand for

bonds is $B(d)$ and the supply B_*, where the latter is given, for a fixed money supply implies a fixed supply of bonds.

$$M(d) = pvy + p[h - jr]$$
$$M(xd) = pvy + p[h - jr] - M_*$$
$$M(xd) = pvy - p[jr + h] - M_*$$

$$p[y(d) + B(d) = p[c + i] + B(d)$$
$$-\{p[y(xd)] + B(xd)\} =$$
$$py - p[c + i] + [B_* - B(d)]$$
$$M(xd) = p\{y[1 - b] - [c_* + i_*]\}$$
$$+ pdr - B(d) + B_*.$$

In the last expression on the left and the right each equation for the excess demand for money has three elements: one which varies with the level of income and price, one which varies with the interest rate and price, and one which is constant. Both respond in the same way to changes in the price level, the interest rate, and the supply of money (for a change in M_* is the result of a change in B_*).

14. The algebraic solution begins by substituting the demand for labour equation, $l(o) = [1 - a]y(o)[p(o)/W_*]$ into the production function, thus eliminating $l(o)$ for the moment. With $y(o)$ a function of a number of parameters and the yet-to-be-determined price of the single commodity, one moves on to the IS curve where $y(o)$ is eliminated. The IS curve provides the substitution for the interest rate, with the result that the LM curve directly yields price as a function of many parameters, among which M_* and W_* are the most crucial.

15. The inequality of saving and investment does not directly bring about a rise in the interest rate in this model. Interest rate adjustment is elaborated below in the discussion of the liquidity trap.

16. The Liquidity Trap concept is commonly attributed to Keynes. Leijonhufvud argues that it is not to be found in *The General Theory*. Be that as it may, its inspiration comes from Keynes's stress upon the volatility of the demand for money. See Leijonhufvud (1981) p. 53.

17. For a detailed discussion of the Liquidity Trap in the context of modern monetary theory, see Harris (1981) pp. 183–6.

7 THE 'COMPLETE' MODEL WITH A WEALTH EFFECT

1. Central to the debate is whether economic agents discount the future stream of taxation necessary to finance the interest payments on state bonds. If so, bonds are 'inside'. Such an analysis involves a truly heroic presumption about the absence of distributional effects, since in general bond holders (the wealthy) are better at evading taxes than non-bond holders.

2. If the supply of labour were a function of the interest rate it would be no less valid to presume full employment, but full employment output/income would no longer be unique. This point will be clear later in the discussion of neutrality.

3. To reduce complications, we have ignored the impact of price upon the demand for money and bond schedules.
4. 'Allegedly', because it has not been established theoretically that the supply of money should be treated as exogenous with respect to the level of output/income. See Chapter 4.
5. The normal operation of a capitalist economy no more dictates that bonds be indexed than that money itself should be. Were a government to pass a law making the issuance of non-indexed outside bonds a criminal offence, the wealth variable would be as follows:

$$q = M*/p + pB*/rp$$

In this case in which the state attempts to legislate the neutrality of money, a doubling of the nominal money supply and price leaves q unchanged. However, if $M*$ is increased by the purchase of bonds, then $B*$ decreases (people sell them to the state), so q is changed by virtue of increasing the money supply. To legislate neutrality, the state must not only prevent the issuance of non-indexed bonds, but amend the charter of the Central Bank to restrict 'open market operations'.
6. Hahn provides a clear and concise discussion of the implications of bankruptcies. At the end of the treatment, he writes, 'I conclude from all this that the assertion that the "Pigou effect" ensures the existence of an equilibrium is unproven' (Frank Hahn, 'Some Problems of Proving the Existence of Equilibrium in a Monetary Economy', in F. H. Hahn and F. P. R. Brechling (eds), *The Theory of Interest Rates* (London: Macmillan, 1965 p. 135).

8 NEUTRALITY AND FULL EMPLOYMENT

1. The references here to empiricism and below to the 'test of empiricism' do not refer to statistical testing in the context of econometric models constructed on the basis of neoclassical models. Empiricism here refers to observation of what actually occurs, not its interpretation through a theoretical filter.
2. See Keynes (1936) ch. 19, 'Changes in Money Wages'.
3. Actually, uniqueness requires additional assumptions. But for sake of argument, I concede uniqueness.
4. By definition in this argument markets are 'unregulated'and 'free' in the absence of state intervention.
5. The full employment values $y(e)$ and $l(e)$ need not be unique. As noted in the previous section (and discussed in Section 2.2), it would be reasonable to assume that the supply of labour is influenced directly by the interest rate. If this were the case, $l(e)$ would no longer be unique nor would $y(e)$.
6. In the examples given we make the invalid but simplifying assumption that the state acts autonomously of economic agents.
7. In the models developed in the previous chapters, no action by the

'monetary authorities' can change the functional distribution of income. This is because the production function used (Cobb–Douglas) implies constant factor shares no matter what the values of y, w, and r. With a more general functional form, even of the Constant Elasticity of Substitution type (of which the Cobb–Douglas is a special case), a change in r would change the distribution between wages and profits. It should be kept in mind that this discussion of distribution refers to points of full employment equilibrium and ignores the impact of fiscal policy, particularly taxation.

8. Patinkin's claim is assessed in light of modern economic theory in Harris (1981) pp. 84–90.

9. The problem of a dangling excess supply is not restricted to the labour market. Recall that the demand for labour schedule is constructed on the assumption that firms plan their supply with no demand constraint. This implies that the notional supply of output is full employment output. Thus at less than full employment equilibrium, there is a second unrequited excess supply, for the single commodity. See Harris (1981) p. 259.

10. Among various proposals is the suggestion that unemployed workers have an excess demand for money balancing their excess supply of labour. Apart from the tautological aspect of this proposal – for it is nothing but an obscure way of saying each potential sale would be for money if effected – it would require a complete reformulation of the demand for money function.

11. This is in fact recognised by the new classical economics school, which argues that deviations from full employment do not occur even in the short run. While this position is perhaps the most faithful to the logic of the neoclassical model, one is reminded of Oscar Wilde's observation that madness is anything carried to its logical conclusion.

12. Now it is not justified to refer to r as 'the interest rate'. Indeed, it has not been valid throughout the discussion so far to proceed as if there were no difference between the rate of return and the interest rate. In doing so we have been following rather sloppy convention. In the factor markets, maximising behaviour involves the rate of return, while in the market for investment it is the lending rate which is relevant. In general the two are not the same in the short run, even in full employment equilibrium. Rather than showing this algebraically, one can demonstrate the divergence of the two with a 'thought experiment'. Assume that any of the models of the previous chapter are at less than full employment equilibrium in the short run (i.e. money wages are initially assumed rigid). Let money wages fall to clear the labour market. Since employment will rise, the commodity wage must fall and the rate of return must rise. The latter must rise because more labour combined with a given capital stock results in a rise in the average and marginal products for capital for any level of k. However, over in the other markets, the lending rate (interest rate) must fall, because the IS curve is downwardly sloped – greater output/income requires a lower interest rate. Only by coincidence will all of the functions of the model be such that the rate of return and the interest rate are the same at full employment equilibrium. Static general equilibrium analysis is not designed to treat this inequality of the rate of

return and the interest rate. They are brought into equality by adjustment of the capital stock, which lies in the domain of growth theory. With the interest rate not equal to the rate of return, interpretation of the 'adding up' equation becomes problematical ($y = wl + rk$, see Chapter 2). We make no attempt to tidy up this loose end of the neoclassical model.

13. The discussion which follows is not contradicted if the supply of labour is a positive function of the commodity wage. This can be seen by inspecting Figure 8.1. If the line l_* in Figure 8.1(a) is positively sloped with respect to w, the only consequence for the solution noted by (1) is that the level of employment at which the labour market is cleared is slightly lower.

14. The point holds if dividend payments are interpreted as reflecting the flow of 'capital services' and common stock shares as ownership of productive capital. What is 'owned' in this case is a claim on income. No shareholder in IMB can identify his or her fragment of the company's plant and equipment, much less choose to hold it out of production.

9 EXPECTATIONS AND FULL EMPLOYMENT

1. Friedman's argument is treated in many places. See, for example, Harris (1981, ch. 21) and G. K. Shaw, *Rational Expectations: An Elementary Exposition* (Brighton: Harvester Press, 1984). Friedman's argument is relevant to our discussion of inflation in Chapters 12–15.

2. The REH is a deterministic theory by the definition employed in the physical sciences. Max Born, the famous physicist, wrote, '*Determinism* postulates that events at different times are connected by laws in such a way that predictions of unknown situations (past or future) can be made.' He distinguishes determinism from causality, defining the latter as follows, '. . . there are laws by which the occurrence of an entity B of a certain class depends on the occurrence of an entity A of another class, where the word "entity" means any physical object, phenomenon, situation, or event. A is called the cause, B the effect.' He goes on to argue that causality does not imply predictability (determinism). The REH makes no reference to this fundamental distinction (Max Born, *Natural Philosophy of Cause and Chance* (Oxford: Clarendon Press, 1949) p. 9).

3. By neoclassical rules it may not be rational for all economic agents to form their expectations in this manner, because of information costs. The REH explicitly recognises this point, but incorporating it into the analysis proves of no consequence. It is assumed that virtually all agents form their expectations rationally either from their own complete knowledge or via intermediaries. See discussion of wage bargaining below.

4. And apparently has existed for some time, since the new classical economists have used the REH to analyse the Great Depression of the 1930s.

5. The defenders of the REH might ponder the following statement by a mathematician.

All science is full of statements where you put the best face on your ignorance, where you say: true enough, we know awfully little about this, but more or less irrespective of the stuff we don't know about, we can make certain useful deductions. Now, my view is that any theory which pretends to comprehend everything breaks down on this point. It will be a uselessly rigid theory because it won't have a place into which to put new things. . . . [W]e ought to so shape our theories that new discoveries won't upset *every* theory we have and for that purpose we must have plenty of *open* theories. (H. Bondi, *Assumption and Myth in Physical Theory* (Cambridge: The University Press, 1967) p. 11).

This view directly contradicts the neoclassical obsession with ensuring that all models are 'closed', with no loose ends. Hahn takes the sensible and modest view that in economics understanding does not imply precognition. 'It is plain that we can claim understanding of an event without claiming that we can predict it. Geophysicists, for instance, believe that they understand earthquakes but cannot predict them . . .' (Hahn (1984) p. 4).

6. Hahn, for example, writes, '. . . [I]t is by no means the case that [economists] are agreed that the IS–LM cross is a generally accepted theory of the economy' (F. H. Hahn, 'Monetarism and Economic Theory', *Economica* (February 1980) p. 1). Shaw offers an ingenious solution to this problem.

If professional economists can disagree as to what should constitute the appropriate definition of the money stock, how does the proverbial man in the street determine whether a money supply change has occurred or not? . . . Unable to understand or fathom the all-important changes occurring in economic variables, [the men in the street] fall back upon the consensus of opinion [*sic!*] in the news media. (Shaw (1984) p. 54)

So while professional economists cannot agree, financial journalists can produce the correct model out of the controversy!

7. In one important branch of science, quantum theory, the inherent indeterminacy of the material world is central to the analysis. Referring to the treatment of quantum theory by Heisenberg, Bohm writes,

The *fact* that quantum theory implies that *every* process of measurement will be subject to the same limitations on its precision led Heisenberg to regard the indeterminacy relationships . . . as being a manifestation of a very fundamental and all-pervasive general principle, which operates throughout the whole of natural law. Thus, rather than consider the indeterminacy relationships primarily as a deduction from the quantum theory in its current form, he postulates these relationships directly as a basic law of nature and assumes instead that all other laws will have to be consistent with these relationships. (David Bohm, *Causality and Chance in Modern Physics*

(London: Routledge & Kegan Paul, 1957) p. 83, referring to W. Heisenberg, *The Physical Principles of the Quantum Theory* (New York: Dover Publications, 1930) p. 3)

The particular indeterminancy relationship referred to in the quotation is the problem of simultaneously measuring the position and momentum of sub-atomic particles. Emphasis added to word 'fact'.

8. 'Nor is it necessary for economic agents to know the true model of the economy. All that is required is for them to form their expectations in the aggregate *as if* they did know it.' (Shaw, 1984, p. 57) Emphasis in original.

9. '[The REH] does not imply that individuals should not make systematic errors. This does not imply that individuals invariably forecast accurately . . . [but] rather the assertion is that guesses about the future must be correct on average if individuals are to remain satisfied with their mechanism of expectations formation' (Begg, 1982, p. 29). Hahn is unimpressed by this learning-from-experience argument.

Rational Expectations themselves are justified by the argument that rational agents will learn what is the case. The argument is ill-founded in theory for it must be shown that agents could learn. Just as classical general equilibrium theory has never been able to provide a definitive account of how equilibrium prices come to be established, so rational expectations theory has not shown how, starting from relative ignorance, everything that can be learned comes to be learned. (Hahn, 1984, p. 82)

10. It should be noted that the size of the difference between predicted and actual outcome is no guide to whether the prediction was correct but randomly displaced or a systematic error. According to the rules of the REH, random deviations from correct predictions will be normally distributed around a mean of zero, but the 'tails' of the normal distribution have no upper or lower bounds.

11. Shaw is quite clear about this, 'Assuming [the REH agent] uses [his] information efficiently, his prediction or expectations will be identical to the mean value of possible outcomes generated *by the relevant theory.*' (Shaw, 1984, p. 58, emphasis added.)

12. It should be added that only in recent years has the ability to foretell the future been granted to econometric models. The previous view involved the more limited and scientifically justifiable claim that these models could provide unbiased estimators of hypothetical alternatives to observed (i.e. past) events, and that the models did not necessarily say anything about the future.

13. Shaw writes (1984, p. 55), '. . . much of rational expectations theory is concerned with the behaviour of labour in negotiating formal wage contracts', and this can be verified by reference to the seminal REH literature. See Thomas J. Sargent and Neil Wallace, 'Rational Expectations, the Optimal Monetary Instrument and the Optimal Money Supply Rate', *Journal of Political Economy* (April 1975); and the original

source, J. Muth, 'Rational Expectations and the Theory of Price Movements', *Econometrica* (July 1961).

14. Akerlof provides a clear summary of the model, referring to the work of Sargent (George A. Akerlof, 'The Case Against Conservative Macroeconomics: An Inaugural Lecture', *Economica* (August 1979)).

15. 'New classical market clearing models gain greatly in elegance and tractability by assuming a one-product economy . . .' (Shaw, 1984, p. 74).

16. '. . . [T]he trade union leadership will pay very close attention to crucial economic variables in the economy. They will possess a highly sophisticated model of how the economy behaves and employ highly qualified economic advisors . . . Through the proxy of trade unions many economic agents are acting in accordance with the rational expectations postulate.' (Shaw (1984) p. 55) This, of course, presumes that the true model is known and agreed upon by 'highly qualified economic advisors'.

17. 'When we say that the labour market clears, we do not mean that *measured* unemployment is literally zero. Rather, we mean that no individuals are voluntarily unemployed in the sense that they are prepared to work at the going wage, but cannot find employment. Friedman has termed this full employment rate of unemployment the *Natural Rate of Unemployment*' (Begg, 1982, p. 136, first emphasis added).

18. Shaw, whose book is quite balanced in its judgement on the REH, explicitly recognises the hypothetical nature of the 'natural rate'.

19. Hahn calls 'the natural rate of unemployment' an 'unproven assertion' (Hahn (1980); and F. H. Hahn, *Money and Inflation* (Oxford: Basil Blackwell, 1982)).

20. Shaw writes, 'The rational expectations thesis departs from the classical equilibrium framework [Walrasian general equilibrium] in one very important respect. It does *not* assume that all economic agents possess perfect knowledge of all market conditions.' (Shaw, 1984, p. 67.) This is incorrect.

21. Begg demonstrates that the REH produces a solution that converges to general equilibrium which is formally equivalent to the PFH. The proof has no relevance for *actual* predictions of future variables, however, since it presumes that the parameters of the correct model remain unchanged over many time periods. This is a perfectly legitimate procedure for an abstract model, but will not serve to justify market-clearing in the real world in which each time period heralds a new and unique event.

22. Begg (1981) p. 137. The last clause in the quotation is misleading. Since the story being told is about static equilibrium states, the precise statement would be, 'the effect on the *level* of real output will be nil'.

23. It is no accident that REH–new classical economics stories are frequently told using the model of the simple quantity theory (see Shaw, 1984, pp. 3–7). Such examples prove nothing, even in the abstract, because they incorporate the false dichotomy.

24. The inclusion of the phrase, 'no matter how we define the rest of the model', seems to be a slip of the pen on Begg's part. Elsewhere he argues cogently that introduction of the wealth effect cancels the 'remarkable'

conclusion of the new classical economists: 'Provided there remains a real balance effect on consumption, systematic monetary policy will feed back through into the goods market, thereby affecting the level of investment required for market clearing,' and 'if monetary policy can alter the real steady state [full employment equilibrium] it will generally have real effects' (Begg, 1981, pp. 149, 147).

25. '. . . [P]eople who base policies for real economies on the belief that citizens form their expectations rationally and the invisible hand . . . will guide us to a rational expectations equilibrium without much delay cannot, I think, be taken seriously.' (Hahn, 1984, p. 123.)

26. Even before the end of the war, Modigliani provided the summary statement which would become the keystone of the neoclassical synthesis.

> It is usually considered as one of the most important achievements of the Keynesian theory that it explains the consistency of economic equilibrium with the presence of involuntary unemployment. It is, however, not sufficiently recognised that . . . this result is due entirely to the assumption of 'rigid wages' . . . (Franco Modigliani, 'Liquidity Preference and the Theory of Interest and Money', *Econometrica*, vol. 12 (January 1944)).

The thinly-veiled disdain here ('usually considered', 'due entirely to', and rigid wages in quotes) indicates the low esteem in which Keynes's contribution was held by some even before he died in 1946.

27. But not too much heterodoxy, at least in the United States. In the 1950s there were only two Marxist economists at a major American university, Paul Baran of Stanford and James Becker of New York University. After Baran's death Becker was the only one for several years.

28. The difficulties in maintaining an interventionist position while accepting general equilibrium theory is well treated in Murray Milgate and John Eatwell, 'Unemployment and the Market Mechanism', in Eatwell and Milgate (eds), *Keynes's Economics and the Theory of Value and Distribution* (New York: Oxford University Press, 1983) pp. 260–61.

10 FULL EMPLOYMENT AND MULTI-COMMODITY PRODUCTION

1. Keynes explicitly accepted what he called 'the first classical postulate', which he summarised as follows, 'the wage is equal to the marginal product of labour' (Keynes, 1936, pp. 5ff).

2. The term 'output/income function' was used to refer to $y = y(k, l)$. This term was used because in neoclassical models y equals total value added. In this chapter we revert to the conventional term, 'aggregate production function', because the debate summarised in the next section is over whether $y = y(k, l)$ can be treated as summarising production relations.

3. In the last decade the identifying terms have become quite confused. Eichner and Kregel, for example, claim the term 'post-Keynesian' for an

analytical model which derives its inspiration from Joan Robinson and Nicholas Kaldor (Eichner and Kregel, 1975). *The Journal of Post-Keynesian Economics* seems to include the Robinson–Kaldor school in its title. This is unfortunate, for long before the term post-Keynesian came into general use, these two economists and like-minded theorists were referred to as neo-Keynesian. See Geoffrey Harcourt, *Some Cambridge Controversies in the Theory of Capital* (Cambridge: The University Press, 1972).

4. Some economists, particularly those disposed to the Robinson–Kaldor school, would object to the use of the word 'Keynesian' to identify this second group. Brothwell, for example, prefers calling them 'neo-Walrasians', for reasons that should become clear in the next chapter. See John Brothwell, 'Rejoinder', *Bulletin of Economic Research*, vol. 28 (2) (November 1976).

5. In this respect, the neo-Keynesians have much in common with the 'neo-Ricardians'. The latter, however, place their analysis of distribution within a *gross product* framework (i.e. they consider intermediate costs as well as value added). See P. Sraffa, *The Production of Commodities by Means of Commodities* (Cambridge: The University Press, 1960). On the other hand, those we call disequilibrium Keynesians have little in common with the neo-Ricardians.

6. Following closely on this conclusion is the argument that the distribution between profits and wages is technically determined, a position first worked out in detail by John Bates Clark in the 1890s in his book, *The Distribution of Wealth*. If one takes as given the aggregate production function, the supply schedule of labour, and the capital stock, and if money is strictly neutral, then the profit share and wage share are uniquely determined in full employment equilibrium. Aggregate distribution will not be treated here. For an excellent discussion of the implications of the Capital Controversy for the theory of distribution, see Ben Fine, *Economic Theory and Ideology* (London: Edward Arnold, 1980) pp. 109–113.

7. The production function and marginal product schedule are made up of line segments and not merely four points because at levels of employment in between points $l(a)$ and $l(b)$, for example, a combination of techniques A and B can be used.

8. The point of intersection corresponds to the commodity wage which is equal to the marginal product of the technique intersecting from the right in quadrant 10.2(d). It is to be recalled that for each technique the marginal contribution of labour is constant (though lower for technique B than A, C than B, etc.).

9. *The Pocket Oxford Dictionary of Current English* (compiled by F. G. Fowler and H. W. Fowler) (Oxford: the Clarendon Press, 1964) p. 572.

10. The critique presented here has also been developed in great detail by the neo-Richardian–Sraffian school. Our discussion follows the neo-Keynesian version.

11. The debate is so called because its two sides tended to coincide with the two Cambridges, Cambridge, England, and Cambridge, Massachusetts.

This particular designation indicates that the protagonists represented the élite of the élite of the economics profession at the time.

12. Hahn writes, referring to the Sraffian version of the critique,

> What is at risk [in the debate over the aggregate production function] is a simplified neo-classical comparative static equilibrium analysis and a simplified neo-classical dynamics. Sraffa's point was a fine technical insight into neo-classical economics but . . . [the critics] have not exploited it.
>
> . . . [O]n the manner in which an equilibrium is supposed to come about, neo-classical theory is highly unsatisfactory . . . The remarkable fact is that neither [Sraffa] nor the Sraffians have made anything of this. (Frank Hahn, *Equilibrium and Macroeconomics* (Oxford: Basil Blackwell, 1984) pp. 383, 384. This article was first published as 'The Neo-Ricardians', *Cambridge Journal of Economics*, vol. 6 (1982).)

13. What follows treats only one aspect of what is called 'the Capital Controversy'. The definitive work on the various ramifications and implications of the debate is Harcourt (1972), where it is presented with insight and wit. The core of Harcourt's analysis is found in G. Harcourt, 'Some Cambridge Controversies in the Theory of Capital', *Journal of Economic Literature* (June 1969), and reprinted in O. F. Hamouda (ed.), *Controversies in Political Economy: Selected Essays of G. C. Harcourt* (Brighton, Sussex: Harvester Press, 1986).

14. For those familiar with trigonometry this is obvious. Equations (10.8) indicate that $K(a)/l(a)$ is the tangent of the angle formed at the horizontal axis by a straight line beginning at point a' and passing through the relevant wage-rate of return coordinates. For example, $K(a)/l(a)$ at $w(a)$ is measured by the tangent of the angle formed on the r axis by the extension of the line $a'a$. Applying a ruler to the diagram proves the point without trigonometry. Measuring and substituting into (10.8), one finds that $K(a)/l(a)$ for $w(a)$ is $[12 - 5]/0.05 = 140$, and at $w(b)$ it is $[12 - 1.5]/0.15 = 70$. The choice of units is arbitrary, for only the relative distances matter.

15. In the Marxian and neo-Ricardian literature, the variation of relative prices with the profit rate is referred to as the transformation process, or transformation problem. See Weeks (1982) ch. III.

16. The mathematics of an economy-wide factor price frontier for a multi-commodity system are complex and tedious. See Fine (1980, p. 101), where the shape of the curve is briefly discussed, and for a more detailed presentation, Harcourt (1986, pp. 173ff).

17. Charles E. Ferguson, *The Neoclassical Theory of Production and Distribution* (Cambridge: Cambridge University Press, 1969).

18. Any econometric test using time series data requires that the aggregate demand for labour schedule be estimated with a production function specified to distinguish between returns to scale and technical change. As is widely recognised, this is not possible without assuming what is to be

tested. Were this problem somehow solved, correct identification of the demand for labour schedule requires simultaneous estimation of the demand schedule for capital (though this is hardly ever attempted). This part of the estimation encounters the problem that if factor price frontiers are not linear, then the value of the capital stock varies with the wage and profit rate and cannot be taken as an independent variable. Since the empirical test is for reswitching, it would be invalid to assume linear factor price frontiers, which exclude reswitching. Some writers have sought to test for reswitching in an indirect way, by looking at the factor intensity of commodities traded between two countries. This way of approaching the problem requires one to make a number of rather arbitrary assumptions specific to trade theory. It is interesting to note that some of these studies sustain the hypothesis that reswitching is a significant phenomenon. B. S. Minhas, 'Homohypallagic Production Function, Factor Intensity Reversals and the Hecksher–Olin Theorem', *Journal of Political Economy* (April 1962); W. Leontief, 'An International Comparison of Factor Costs and Factor Use: A Review Article', *American Economic Review* (June 1964); and D. P. S. Ball, 'Factor Intensity Reversals: An International Comparison of Factor Costs and Factor Use', *Journal of Political Economy* (February 1966).

19. Paul A. Samuelson, 'Rejoinder: Agreements, Disagreements, Doubts, and the Cause of Induced Harrod-Neutral Technical Change', reprinted from the *Review of Economics and Statistics* in M. Merton (ed.), *The Collected Scientific Papers of Paul A. Samuelson* (Cambridge, Mass.: MIT Press, 1972) p. 174.

11 FULL EMPLOYMENT AND DISEQUILIBRIUM

1. To quote from Clower,

> Walras' Law, although valid as usual with reference to *notional* market excess demands, is in general irrelevant to any but full employment situations. *Contrary to the findings of traditional theory, excess demand may fail to appear anywhere under conditions of less than full employment.* (R. W. Clower, 'The Keynesian Counter-Revolution: A Theoretical Appraisal', in Frank Hahn and F. P. R. Brechling (eds) *The Theory of Interest Rates* (London: Macmillan, 1965))

2. 'Actual income' can be defined in many ways. The generality of the discussion which follows is not affected if one takes the simple case in which actual income is that income which accrues to the agent during the period when the expenditure is made.

3. The argument is set forward in Chapter V of Leijonhufvud (1968), and in Leijonhufvud (1981) pp. 56–8.

4. In the later chapters of *The General Theory* one encounters strong suggestions of a 'secular stagnation' thesis, with Keynes placing stress upon the alleged investment-depressing effects of slow population growth and a slow pace of technical change.

5. 'The traditional diagnosis of depressions which lays the "blame" of unemployment on the obstinate behavior of labor is based on a *partial equilibrium analysis* . . .' (Leijonhufvud, 1968, p. 337).
6. See Hahn (1984) ch. 4, 'Some Adjustment Problems'.
7. Hahn, an eloquent and sometimes polemical defender of the usefulness of general equilibrium theory in economics, is quite clear in his warnings about the theory's improper use.

> The most superficial acquaintance with game theory is enough to convince one that competitive instantaneous market clearing is not an axiom one wants to adopt. . . . What one must . . . not do is to claim that it comes from a deep 'universal' of economics or that there are profound philosphical reasons for its employment. (Hahn, 1984, p.13)

8. Leijonhufvud (1968, p. 37) asked only that the 'strong assumption of instantaneous price adjustment' be relaxed.
9. Hahn (1984, p. 88) writes,

> The achievements of economic theory in the last two decades are both impressive and in many ways beautiful. But it cannot be denied that there is something scandalous in the spectacle of so many people refining the analyses of economic states which they give no reason to suppose will ever, or have ever, come about.

10. Hahn writes,

> A consequence of [the use of general equilibrium theory in macro models] . . . has been . . . to designate all economic states with Keynesian features (e.g. involuntary unemployment) as disequilibria with the further implication that they will, if they exist at all, also soon disappear. Those who have been somewhat more sympathetic to Keynes . . . have none the less quite supinely agreed to having their endeavors called 'disequilibrium economics'. They have also much to their cost gone along with the vacuous proposition that there could be no Keynesian problems if prices and wages were 'flexible' (Hahn, 1984, p. 9)

Hahn's accusation that the Disequilibrium Keynesians accept in principle the existence of a general equilibrium full employment solution finds support in the following passage from Leijonhufvud.

> '[R]econciling competition with unemployment' appears as a 'riddle' only when 'competition' is implicitly equated with 'perfect information'. When a more realistic view is taken of the information problem . . . the emergence of unemployed resources is a predictable consequence of changes in demand. (Leijonhufvud, 1968, p. 102)

11. Because of the neoclassical method of the disequilibrium Keynesians, their approach would seem to yield the same conclusion as that reached

by a distinguished practitioner of general equilibrium theory, 'Certainly, macroeconomics serves as a good "simple" model which many economists feel is what we need . . . But how one is to give it a theoretical foundation, I do not know.' (Hahn, 1984, p. 193.)

12. Fine and Murfin argue that the disequilibrium Keynesians abandon macroeconomics and therefore should be considered as generalising general equilibrium theory rather than as critiquing it. See Ben Fine and Andy Murfin, *Macroceconomics and Monopoly Capital* (Brighton: Wheatsheaf Books 1984) ch. 2.

13. 'The idea that there would be no unemployment in a barter economy is grotesque.' (Hahn, 1984, p. 192.)

14. Chick summarises the argument well (Chick, 1983, p. 141).

15. This argument is pursued further in the final chapter and in the companion volume to this book, *Capital and Circulation*.

16. On monopoly, he writes, 'We have argued that Keynes' theory constitutes an attack on, not an elaboration of, those explanations of depressions which stress monopolistic restraints on the movement of prices'. Warming to his topic, he goes on to say,

> If the wealth distribution which the automatic working of the system brings about is accepted, behaviour that interferes with the adjustment of relative prices is dysfunctional to the system and can be condemned on ethical grounds. Academic economists have been the high priests of this ethic. (Leijonhufvud, 1968, pp. 107–8)

12 NEOCLASSICAL INFLATION: AGGREGATE SUPPLY

1. 'Inflation is always and everywhere a monetary phenomenon.' (Milton Friedman, 'Inflation: Causes and Consequences', reprinted in *Dollars and Deficits* (Englewood Cliffs, NJ: Prentice-Hall, 1968) p. 39.

2. Reference will also be made to Keynesian Neoclassical treatments, in which inflation is consistent with unemployment ('stagflation').

3. In previous chapters 'the price level' was used in the context of one commodity models. The objection is raised now and not before because it is at this point that a precise term for this concept becomes important. Had the objection been raised earlier it would have seemed nit-picking.

4. For example, see Michael Parkin, *Macroeconomics* (Englewood Cliffs, NJ: Prentice-Hall, 1984) ch. 12, where much is made of this distinction.

5. It should be stressed that the discussion here refers to the distinction as a tool of abstract analysis. For policy purposes it is obviously important to separate usual from unusual events, with the oil-price increases of the 1970s being an example of the latter. While a separation of events into these two categories has theoretical implications, it is an empirical not a theoretical distinction.

6. 'So-called' because for a generation of neoclassically trained economists, 'aggregate demand' meant a function of the type, $AD = c(y) + i(r) + g$, with g the level of real government expenditure; and aggre-

gate supply simply $y = y(k*, l)$. Largely as a result of monetarist influence the new usage refers to aggregate expenditure and the supply of the single commodity as a function of the price of the single commodity ('price level').

7. Let the output of a firm be q. If the firm is a price taker, then its net revenue is given by the following expression with p constant, $(q = q(k, l)$ being the firm's production function).

$$NR = pq(k, l) - (Wl + rk)$$

NR is maximised (or –NR minimised) when the partial derivatives of this expression with respect to l and k are set to zero. In the short run k is fixed, so one can deal with the derivative $y'(l)$ only.

$$p[y'(l)] = W, \quad \text{and} \quad p = W/y'(l)$$

W is what the marginal worker costs the firm (assuming perfect competition in the labour market), and $y'(l)$ is what the marginal worker produces. Their ratio is marginal cost.

8. As was noted in Chapter 2, Gordon makes the mistake of saying, 'The aggregate supply curve is just the horizontal sum of the supply curves of the individual firms . . .' (Gordon, 1981, p. 176).

9. 'In the classical case, the aggregate supply curve is vertical . . . The classical supply curve is based on the assumption that the labor force is always in equilibrium with full employment . . .' (Dornbusch and Fischer, 1984, p. 356). 'The aggregate supply curve shows the amount of output that the economy will supply at each different price level, given that firms are maximizing profits, households are maximizing utility, and the labor market is in equilibrium.' (Parkin, 1984, p. 116)

13 NEOCLASSICAL INFLATION: AGGREGATE DEMAND

1. Indeed, this treatment of aggregate demand *is* the false dichotomy model, as shown momentarily.

2. If the aggregate demand curve has an elasticity of unity, then there can be no real balance effect operating. Were there a RBE, then a fall (say) in the price level would shift the saving function (and perhaps the investment function, depending upon specification of agents' behaviour). The shift in the saving function would shift the IS curve, with the result that any particular level of $i = s$ would occur at a level of income/output greater than in the absence of the RBE. As a result, the aggregate demand curve would have an elasticity greater than unity. To make matters more complicated, the RBE is usually assumed to affect the demand for money and thus the LM curve. Such aggregate demand curves are considered below.

3. Passing judgement upon contemporary treatments of inflation, Parkin writes, 'There are a variety of alternative particular "stories" that lead to the same conclusions. . . . The "story" used here [the New Classical Theory] is, in my view, the simplest one' (Parkin, 1984, p. 350). In

neoclassical usage, to be identified as a 'simple' or 'the simplest' theory is a high compliment.

4. Recall from Chapter 6 that if there is an interest-elastic demand for money, then an increase (say) in output requires an increase in the interest rate to induce money holders to reduce their idle balances, thus increasing the transactions supply of money.

5. This is a point that requires the textbook reader to be on his or her toes. Dornbusch and Fischer (1984, p. 352) are careful to point out that the aggregate demand curve requires IS–LM equilibrium, while Parkin (1984, ch. 9) is not.

6. The IS curve is (see Chapter 3):

$$y = \frac{i^* + c^* - dr}{1 - b}$$

The false dichotomy LM curve is:

$$y = M*/vp$$

For IS and LM equilibrium,

$$\frac{M*}{vp} = \frac{i^* + c^* - dr}{1 - b}$$

If r varies, then either (1) the price level is a function of the interest rate, or (2) income is a function of the interest rate; but y is not a function of p.

7. This point reflects the logic of the neoclassical general equilibrium model that the system can be at a state of rest at less than full employment only if there is a rigid money wage. In other words, income is wage constrained, not demand or price constrained.

8. One presumes that all authors would treat the equilibrium of the money and commodity markets as simplifications for isolating the impact of price without asserting that markets are actually in equilibrium in practice. Not so. Parkin argues that the money market is always in equilibrium in practice.

> Although we have just conducted a conceptual experiment to analyze what would happen if the amount of money that people wanted to hold was different from the amount supplied, a moment's reflection will reveal that in the ordinary course of events these situations will not be observed. Individuals will not ordinarily be holding an excess or a deficiency of money . . . Rather, they will vary their expenditures in order to eliminate either a money balance deficiency or an excessive amount of money holdings. (1984, p. 132)

> He goes on to argue that the supply and demand for money can be treated analogously to Lake Tahoe 'arbitrarily divided by a straight line running north–south midway along its length.' Just as the water on one side of the imaginary line maintains a level more or less the same as on the other side, so functions the money market. The example is singularly

inappropriate. First, the division between the supply and the demand for money is not imaginary, but the result of there being borrowers and lenders who are different people. Further, careful neoclassical writers point out that money market equilibrium requires perfect foresight or the rational expectations equivalent.

9. Solving for r:

$$r = 1/j[h - M*/P + vy(d) \quad \text{(LM curve)}$$
$$r = 1/d[c* + i* - \{1 - b\}y(d)] \quad \text{(IS curve)}$$

Setting these equal to each other:

$$\frac{c* + i*}{d} - \frac{[1 - b]y(d)}{d} = h/j - \frac{M*}{jp} + \frac{vy(d)}{j}$$

Solving for y:

$$y(d) = \frac{1/d[c* + i*] - h/j}{1/d[1 - b] + v/j} + \frac{M*}{[j/d\{1 - b\} + v]}[1/p]$$

Let the first term on the right be a_1 and the denominator of the second be a_2. Then one obtains,

$$y(d) = a_1 + \frac{M*}{a_2}[1/p]$$

$$p = \frac{M*}{a_2[y(d) - a_1]}$$

A similar derivation for IS–LM equilibrium is found in Gordon (1981) pp. 145–7.

10. The economic logic of an elasticity less than unit is explained in the text. Algebraically, the elasticity of nominal demand with respect to price can be written as:

$$E = \frac{a1p}{Y(d)} = \frac{a1p}{a1p + M*/a2}$$

Since $M*/a2$ is positive, E must be less than unity.

11. With the inclusion of the real balance effect the elasticity of nominal demand with respect to price is greater than before because,

$$E' = \frac{a1p}{a1p + [a3/a2]M*}$$

The term $a3$ in general is less than unity, which makes E' less than E (see equivalent expression in note 10).

12. An aggregate demand curve of this type is found in Dornbusch and Fischer (1984) ch. 11.

14 EXPECTATIONS, INFLATION AND FULL EMPLOYMENT

1. Irving Fisher, 'A Statistical Relation between Unemployment and Price Changes', *International Labour Review* (June 1926); and A. W. H. Phillips, 'The Relation between Unemployment and the Rate of Change of Money Wages in the United Kingdom, 1861–1957', *Economica* (November 1958).
2. Dernburg uses the less judgemental term 'non-accelerating-inflation rate of unemployment' rather than the normative 'natural rate' (Dernburg, 1985, p. 298).
3. The implausibility of such a bargaining goal was discussed in Chapter 9 and will not be repeated here.
4. The rest of the story is that price stability can only be achieved by generating unemployment in excess of $u*$. If $SFC1$ is the prevailing expectations curve and the inflation rate is reduced to zero, the real wage will rise, increasing unemployment to $u2$.
5. '. . . the long-run Phillips Curve is vertical, or, *in substance, that in the long run money is neutral* . . .' (F. Modigliani, 'The Monetarist Controversy, or Should We Forsake Stabilization Policies?', reprinted in Konlinas and Thorn (eds), *Modern Macroeconomics* (New York: Harper & Row, 1979), p. 119). Emphasis added.
6. Assume that the money wage is flexible and workers predict correctly and capitalists err. In Figure 14.2 the demand for labour curve would remain at $l(d)$, po. When price falls, the labour supply curve would shift out since every money wage would be associated with a higher real wage. Point J is a possible intersection of $l(s)$, p_2 with the demand for labour. If the price rises, labour supply shifts to the left, and an intersection with $l(d)$, p_o would be a point such as K. In this case excessive inflationary expectations by capitalists result in a *rise* in employment and underestimations of inflation in a *fall*. The aggregate supply curve would be negatively sloped.
7. Keynesian Neoclassicals are impatient with this approach,

> If we assume a self-regulating economy that tends to equilibrate at full employment, an inflation that is not supported by sufficient monetary demand has to come to an end eventually, and full employment and price stability will be restored. But these facts do not constitute sufficient information. Great concern also attaches to the process of adjustment. . . . The economist who tells us that eventually we will achieve noninflationary equilibrium at full employment. . . . is telling us very little. (Dernburg, 1985, p. 295)

8. Parkin states the interpretation clearly,

> If the price level turns out to be lower than that which is expected [by workers], then there will be a cut in the employment level and a higher

real wage – there will be *unemployment* . . . In the institutional setting of the United States, such a cut in employment will usually be recorded as a rise in unemployment since the individuals involved will be 'available for' and 'able and willing to' work. They are not, however, willing to work at the wage that is available. The unemployment survey does not ask questions in sufficient detail to establish that fact [i.e. that there is no involuntary unemployment]. (Parkin, 1984, p. 360)

9. Parkin writes,

The key ingenuity of the rational expectations [New Classical in this case] theories lies in their ability to account for the autocorrelated movements of output and the procyclical co-movements of prices and interest rates. (Parkin, 1984, p. 439)

10. Also crucial is the assumption of a positively sloped supply curve for labour for all relevant money and real wage levels. This is an empirical question, since leisure is not an inferior good, and at high real wage levels the supply curve may become vertical or negatively sloped ('the backward-bending supply curve for effort').

11. This inconsistency has been recognised by New Classical economists and dealt with in a revealing manner. Barro argues from a priori grounds that fixed money wage contracts are inconsistent with profit-maximising and utility-maximising behaviour, and are therefore irrational. Being a priori irrational, they should be ignored in theoretical analysis even though they are commonplace in practice. This approach, rejecting what actually occurs in favour of arbitrary idealised behaviour, is consistent with an approach that refers to actual market behaviour as 'false trading'. See Robert J. Barro, 'Long Term Contracting, Sticky Prices, and Monetary Policy', *Journal of Monetary Economics*, vol. 3 (July 1977).

12. Parkin summarises the argument in his New Classical textbook,

Firms are not being supposed, in some sense, to be smarter than households. Rather, the asymmetry arises from the fact that firms sell a small number of goods, so they and their workers are specialized in information concerning the prices of those goods. In contrast, households buy a large number of goods and services and are not specialized in information concerning the prices in all of those markets. *It is this asymmetry . . . that provides the basis for a modified theory of aggregate supply that is capable of explaining the observed relationship between output (employment and unemployment) and inflation.* (Parkin, 1984, p. 353.) Emphasis added.

The argument was first made in Milton Friedman, 'The Role of Monetary Policy', *American Economic Review*, vol. 58 (March 1968). The importance of the asymmetry stressed by Parkin is often not noted in textbook presentations. See, for example, Edgmand, who says only '. . .

if people's expectations are incorrect, the aggregate supply curve will be positively sloped.' (Michael R. Edgmand, *Macroeconomics: Theory and Policy* (Englewood Cliffs: Prentice-Hall, 1987) third edn, p. 252.)

13. It is to be noted that random errors cancelling each other out is relevant in two different ways in this discussion. In a rational expectations world, the predictions of agents will tend to be correct on average for a large number of predictions of precisely the same event. It is in this sense that the predictions of a single price are correct on average. In addition to this sense in which errors cancel, the prediction of many prices, the entire set predicted only once, tends to benefit from the cancelling of random errors. If workers have more prices to predict than capitalists, then they benefit from the second type of error-cancelling more than capitalists do.

14. Referring to the positively sloped aggregate supply curve he has presented, Gordon writes,

> It is possible to illustrate the determination of the equilibrium real wage on a supply-demand [for labour] diagram, but this is a needless distraction for our purposes. (Gordon, 1981, p. 179)

A student would find this statement extremely difficult to verify. First, the aggregate supply curve is drawn for a fixed money wage (the diagram on page 178 of Gordon's book is entitled 'The Aggregate Supply Curve with a Fixed Nominal Wage'). Since the money wage is fixed, the real wage cannot possibly be in equilibrium except at one point (the 'natural' rate of unemployment). Second, if the labour market implications of this aggregate supply curve were investigated, the curve would have to be redrawn as in Figure 14.4.

15. Perhaps it is in implicit recognition of the labour constraint that Gordon defines his aggregate supply curve as 'the amount of real GNP firms will *be willing* to produce at different levels of the aggregate price index' (Gordon, 1981, p. 183), emphasis added. The additional output implied by an unemployment rate less than $u*$ remains an unrequited hope, however, unless there is a shift in the supply of labour curve.

16. Gordon writes,

> Friedman has had the satisfaction of seeing many of his long-held beliefs adopted as part of the mainstream . . . [He] introduced the then heretical natural-rate hypothesis of unemployment, which has since been accepted by most economists. (Gordon, 1981, p. 366)

15 THE NATURAL RATE, NEUTRALITY AND MONETARY INFLATION

1. Gordon describes a similar process,

> In reality the actual economy is divided into numerous separate labour markets differing in location, working conditions, and skill require-

ments. If aggregate spending increases when the overall unemployment rate is 20 or 30 percent, then unemployed workers are available in almost every skill category and location, and firms do not have to raise wage rates to attract applicants. But . . . at a 5 or 6 percent unemployment rate, any increase in aggregate spending generates job openings in some labor markets while many people remain unemployed in other markets. (Gordon, 1981, p. 307)

2. It must be stressed that Phillips measured the relationship between unemployment and inflation, not as some suggest the relationship between output and inflation. The latter need not strictly correspond to the former because of the rate of growth of productivity.

3. A generation of Keynesian neoclassicals has drawn such a curve relating the price level to the level of output, indicating 'demand-pull' inflation.

4. A particularly clear presentation of the Neoclassical Keynesian view augmented by expectations is found in the now out-of-print textbook by Barrett (Nancy Smith Barrett, *The Theory of Macroeconomic Policy* (Englewood Cliffs, New Jersey: Prentice-Hall, 1975) (first edn) pp. 284ff).

5. The natural unemployment rate is a 'danger zone' that sets a lower limit on the level of actual unemployment that can be attained without accelerating inflation . . . In the late 1960s most economists misunderstood the inflationary consequences that alternative paths of output would bring about. They thought unemployment could be pushed down to 3.5 or 4.0 per cent with only minor inflationary results. . . . A major achievement of the monetarist counterrevolution was to show that any attempt to hold unemployment below the natural rate of unemployment would cause ever-accelerating inflation. Before this contribution of the monetarists had been accepted by economists, *the damage had been done* . . . (Gordon, 1981, pp. 15–16, 21–2, emphasis added).

6. A clear exposition of this argument is found in Dernburg, (1985) pp. 299ff. In Figure 15.1 point *F* could be interpreted as a 'stagflation' position, though the argument should be represented with inflation rates on the vertical axis rather than levels of price.

7. Inflation creates no problem in the abstract if one moves to open-economy one commodity models. If money is strictly neutral, then adjustment of the exchange rate compensates for inflation and keeps the external account in balance.

8. Neutrality and super-neutrality are treated in Robert J. Barro, *Macroeconomics* (New York: John Wiley, 1987) (2nd edn) pp. 194–209.

9. Barro would seem to agree: 'Corresponding to the increase in expected inflation and the reduction in real cash, people expend more resources on transactions costs. *Although we regard these costs as small in normal times*, we cannot neglect them during extreme circumstances.' (Barro, 1987, p. 208, emphasis added)

10. In 1947 [in the United States] the nominal interest rate was about 3 percent; holdings of money amounted to a very large 48 percent of

GNP. In 1979, when the nominal interest rate on bonds was a much higher 9.6 percent, people economized on their holdings of money to earn the lucrative interest paid on bonds; holdings of money in that year amounted to only 15.8 percent of GNP. (Gordon, 1981, p. 336)

This is an example of an invalid invoking of the *ceteris paribus* assumption. No conclusion can be drawn about causality without including other factors affecting the demand for money. One might begin, for example, by accounting for why the nominal interest rate in 1979 was over three times the rate in 1947, even though the rate of inflation was almost the same in both years (8 and 9 per cent, respectively). This is hardly consistent with the argument that the nominal rate of interest should be the real rate plus the rate of inflation.

11. Barro writes,

[W]e neglected any effects of transactions costs on households' choices of work effort, consumption, and saving. If we took account of these effects, then we would find that an acceleration of money might influence the real interest rate, the real wage rate, and the quantities of output and employment. The independence of these real variables from the path of money is only an approximation, which is satisfactory when transactions costs are small. (Barro, 1987, p. 201)

12. 'The resulting fall in real cash balances is one real effect of the change in monetary behavior [accelerating inflation]. Therefore, money is *not quite super-neutral* in the model.' (Barro, 1987, p. 201)
13. As pointed out in Chapter 10, Samuelson used the word 'parable' to describe the relationship between the aggregate production function and actual functioning economies. (P. A. Samuelson, 'Parable and Realism in Capital Theory: The Surrogate Production Function', *Review of Economic Studies* (June 1962).)
14. See the discussion of this point in Chapter 8.
15. Bonds are obviously a characteristic of actual economies. Their inclusion is unavoidable in an abstract model if there is an interest rate.
16. One way of avoiding non-neutrality is to assume that new bonds are issued at the same rate as money is expanded.

16 THE CRITIQUE OF NEOCLASSICAL MACROECONOMICS SUMMARISED

1. One such curiosity is the excellent attempt at a neo-Keynesian/neo-Ricardian text by Robinson and Eatwell. (Joan Robinson and John Eatwell, *An Introduction to Modern Economics* (London: McGraw-Hill, 1973).)
2. Nicholas Kaldor. After Joan Robinson, Kaldor is probably the most distinguished economist of his generation not to receive the Nobel Prize. His approach to macroeconomics is shown in Nicholas Kaldor, 'A Model

of Economic Growth', *Economic Journal*, vol. 67 (1957); which is developed further in Luigi L. Pasinetti, 'Rate of Profit and Income Distribution in Relation to the Rate of Economic Growth', *Review of Economic Studies*, vol. 33 (1962).

3. Almost without exception Kaldor and others of the NeoKeynesian school (e.g. Robinson) go unmentioned in textbooks entitled 'Macroeconomics' while these texts are rife with references to lesser figures in the profession. A truth-in-advertising law might require most texts to be renamed, 'Neoclassical Macroeconomics'.

4. An important exception is Colander, in which the aggregate production function is used only to explain pre-Keynesian models and not subsequently. David Colander, *Macroeconomics* (Glenview, Illinois: Scott, Foresman, 1986).

5. The 'structuralist' school in the literature on Latin American inflation has stressed this possibility. For those interested, a good place to begin is the seminal article by Seers. (Dudley Seers, 'A Theory of Inflation and Growth in Under-developed Countries Based on the Experience of Latin America', *Oxford Economic Papers* (June 1963).)

APPENDIX: KEYNES AND AGGREGATION

1. Leijonhufvud provides a humorous critique of the tendency of economists to ignore their theoretical forebears in his satirical essay, 'Life among the Econ' (Leijonhufvud, 1981).

2. Speaking of the economics profession, Keynes wrote,

> [A]lthough the [theoretical] doctrine itself has remained unquestioned by orthodox economists up to a late date, its signal failure for purposes of scientific prediction has greatly impaired, in the course of time, the prestige of its practitioners. For professional economists . . . were apparently unmoved by the lack of correspondence between the results of their theory and the facts of observation; – a discrepancy which the ordinary man has not failed to observe, with the result of his growing unwillingness to accord to economists that measure of respect which he gives to other groups of scientists . . . (Keynes,1936, p. 33)

3. A balanced and highly-readable assessment of Marx's contribution to the understanding of capitalism is found in two books by Heilbroner: Robert L. Heilbroner, *Marx: For and Against* (New York: W. W. Norton, 1980); and *The Nature and Logic of Capitalism* (New York: W. W. Norton, 1985).

4. Keynes did not shy away from ridiculing his opponents:

> The celebrated optimism of traditional economic theory, which has led to economists being looked upon as Candides, who, having left this world for the cultivation of their gardens, teach that all is for the best in the best of all possible worlds provided we will let well alone. . . . It

may well be that the classical theory represents the way in which we should like our Economy to behave. But to assume that it actually does so is to assume our difficulties away. (Keynes, 1936, pp. 33–4)

5. It could be called the *aggregation* problem. While we have no desire to contribute to the proliferation of unnecessary terms, the 'aggregation problem' is a phase commonly used in mainstream economics in a quite narrow and restricted sense. Our use of an alternative term avoids potential confusion.

6. The problem is not one of finding a common unit of measure. Wheat and beer could be weighed and added together, but the resultant 'aggregate' measure would be nonsense except for purposes such as ensuring a vehicle was not overloaded.

7. Derivation of community indifference curves is unnecessary for the current discussion. The simplest conceptualisation is to assume that all economic agents have the same utility function, so a community of people can be treated as an individual.

8. Theoretical objections to the apparent incompatibility of macro- and microeconomics resulted in the 'micro foundations' literature. This literature sought to construct a macro theory consistent with microeconomics (and certainly not the reverse), and can be seen as a precursor to the new classical economics. Particularly influential was Edmund S. Phelps *et al.*, *Microeconomic Foundations of Employment and Inflation Theory* (New York: W. W. Norton, 1970).

9. The rest of this chapter draws upon a longer treatment of Keynes's views on valuation and aggregation. See John Weeks, 'Value and Production in the *General Theory*', in John Hillard (ed.), *J. M. Keynes in Retrospect: The Legacy of the Keynesian Revolution* (Upleadon, England: Edward Elgar, 1988).

10. Keynes writes,

> So long as economists are concerned with what is called the Theory of Value, they have been accustomed to teach that prices are governed by the conditions of supply and demand. . . . But when they pass . . . to the Theory of Money and Prices, we hear no more of these homely but intelligible concepts . . . (Keynes, 1936, p. 292)

11. Referring to 'real' variables and using the terminology of his time, Keynes wrote,

> The National Dividend, as defined by Marshall and Professor Pigou, measures the volume of current output or real income, and not the value of output or money income. . . . But it is a grave objection to this definition for such a purpose [use in economic models] that the community's output of goods and services is a non-homogeneous complex which cannot be measured, strictly speaking, except in certain special cases, as for example when all the items of one output are included in the same proportions in another output. (Keynes, 1936, pp. 37–8)

12. Keynes (1936), p. 43. In a typical display of his rather wry sense of humour, Keynes writes,

> To say that net output to-day is greater, but the price-level lower, than ten years ago or one year ago, is a proposition of a similar character to the statement that Queen Victoria was a better queen but not a happier woman than Queen Elizabeth – a proposition not without meaning and not without interest, but unsuitable as material for the differential calculus. Our precision will be a mock precision if we try to use such partly vague and non-quantitative concepts as the basis of a quantitative analysis. (Keynes, 1936, p. 40)

13. He also rejected the closely-related concept of the 'general price level' (Keynes, 1936, p. 39).
14. There are no units (including units of labour) which will produce well-behaved aggregate capital-labour substitution (i.e. no re-switching) in response to changes in the real wage. A relatively non-technical explanation is found in Fine (1980) ch. 5.
15. The chapter in which Keynes discusses aggregation and valuation is called 'The Choice of Units', but would better be entitled 'Choice of Method'.
16. Keynes (1936) pp. 53–4. In the discussion which follows a simplified version of Keynes's procedure will be presented in order not to raise unnecessary complications.
17. Devaluation of the capital stock as a consequence of technical change plays a major role in Marx's treatment of demand failures. See the discussion in Weeks (1982) chs vii and viii.
18. Keynes discusses devaluations of the capital stock as one aspect of measuring net income to the enterprise (Keynes, 1936, pp. 56–7).
19. When neoclassical economists do empirical studies at the firm or industry level they may include intermediate commodities on the supply side and treat output in the usual sense. The point is that the abstract theory of price teaches one to think of price determination in general as if each firm produced only value added.
20. Use of labour as the basic ingredient of value theory involves certain analytical difficulties which has led some non-neoclassical economists to abandon it in favour of a price theory based upon inputs (including labour) which cannot be directly aggregated. This approach, sometimes referred to as 'the production of commodities by means of commodities', involves measuring total output in terms of a concept called 'the standard commodity'. The standard commodity is a collection of commodities such that when it is introduced into an input–output system as an input, yields an output precisely like the input with regard to the proportions of each commodity in the collection. See Sraffa (1973).
21. Keynes concludes the paragraph quoted in the text by saying that his sympathy for the doctrine that everything is produced by labour 'partly explains why we have been able to take the unit of labour as the sole physical unit which we require in our economic system [i.e. model], apart from units of money and time' (Keynes, 1936, p. 214).

22. To quote Keynes,

> [I]n so far as different grades and kinds of labour and salaried assistance enjoy a more or less fixed relative remuneration, the quantity of employment can be sufficiently defined for our purpose by taking an hour's employment of ordinary labour as our unit and weighting an hour's employment of special labour in proportion to its remuneration. . . . We shall call the unit in which the quantity of employment is measured the labour-unit . . . (Keynes, 1936, p. 41)

23. For example, the late Joan Robinson (as said before, the greatest economist who could have received the Nobel Prize but did not, with the possible exception of Nicholas Kaldor) agreed with Keynes about neoclassical 'real' aggregates, '*The* volume of output and *the* purchasing power of money are metaphysical concepts.' However, in her famous book on growth theory, she does not use the labour unit, but assumes that consumption and investment commodities are always produced in the same proportions. (Joan Robinson, *The accumulation of Capital* (London: Macmillan, 1969), third edn, p. 22.)

24. The way Keynes defines Z is quite confusing: ' . . . where Z is the return the expectation of which will induce a level of employment N' (Keynes, 1936, p. 44). If nothing else, this syntax suggests that one should write, $N = N(Z)$.

25. The supply curve for the firm under perfect competition is the marginal cost curve above the 'break-even' point. The industry supply curve is the sum of all firm supply curves. See Chapter 12, note 7.

Select Bibliography

BOOKS

Gardener Ackley, *Macroeconomics: Theory and Policy* (New York: Macmillan, 1978)

R.G.D. Allen, *Macro-economic Theory* (London: St. Martin's Press, 1968)

Nancy Barrett, *The Theory of Macroeconomic Policy* (Englewood Cliffs, New Jersey: Prentice-Hall, 1975)

Robert J. Barro, *Macroeconomics* (New York: John Wiley & Sons, 1987)

William J. Baumol, *Economic Dynamics* (New York: Macmillan, 1959)

David K. H. Begg, *The Rational Expectations Revolution in Macroeconomics: Theories and Evidence* (Oxford: Philip Allan, 1982)

David Bohm, *Causality and Chance in Modern Physics* (London: Routledge & Kegan Paul, 1957)

H. Bondi, *Assumption and Myth in Physical Theory* (Cambridge: The University Press, 1967)

Max Born, *Natural Philosophy of Cause and Chance* (Oxford: Clarendon Press, 1949)

William H. Branson, *Macroeconomic Theory and Policy* (New York: Harper & Row, 1977)

Martin Bronfenbrenner, *Macroeconomic Alternatives* (Arlington Heights, Illinois: AHM Publishing Company, 1979)

Victoria Chick, *The Theory of Monetary Policy* (Oxford: Basil Blackwell, 1979)

Victoria Chick, *Macroeconomics after Keynes* (Oxford: Philip Allan, 1983)

Alan Coddington, *Keynesian Economics: The Search for First Principles* (London: George Allen & Unwin, 1983)

David Colander, *Macroeconomics: Theory and Policy* (Glenview, Illinois: Scott, Foresman & Company, 1986)

G. Debreu, *Theory of Value* (New York: John Wiley & Sons, 1959)

Thomas Dernburg, *Macroeconomics* (New York: McGraw-Hill, 1985)

Rudiger Dornbusch and Stanley Fischer, *Macroeconomics* (New York: McGraw-Hill, 1983)

John Eatwell and Murray Milgate (eds), *Keynes's Economics and the Theory of Value and Distribution* (New York: Oxford University Press, 1983)

Michael Edgmand, *Macroeconomics: Theory and Policy* (Englewood Cliffs, New Jersey: Prentice-Hall, 1987)

Charles Ferguson, *The Neoclassical Theory of Production and Distribution* (Cambridge: Cambridge University Press, 1969)

Ben Fine, *Economic Theory and Ideology* (London: Edward Arnold, 1980)

Ben Fine and Andy Murfin, *Macroeconomics and Monopoly Capital* (Brighton: Wheatsheaf Books, 1984)

Robert J. Gordon, *Macroeconomics* (Second Edition) (Boston: Little, Brown & Company, 1981)

J. G. Gurely and E. S. Shaw, *Money in a Theory of Finance* (Washington: The Brookings Institution, 1960)

Frank Hahn, *Money and Inflation* (Oxford: Basil Blackwell, 1982)

Frank Hahn, *Equilibrium and Macroeconomics* (Oxford: Basil Blackwell, 1984)

Frank Hahn and F. P. R. Brechling (eds), *The Theory of Interest Rates* (London: Macmillan, 1965)

D. F. Hamouda (ed.), *Controversies in Political Economy: Selected Essays of G. C. Harcourt* (Brighton: Harvester Press, 1986)

Geoffrey Harcourt, *Some Cambridge Controversies in the Theory of Capital* (Cambridge: Cambridge University Press, 1972)

Laurence Harris, *Monetary Theory* (New York: McGraw-Hill, 1981)

Robert L. Heilbroner, *Marx: For and Against* (New York: W. W. Norton, 1980)

Robert L. Heilbroner, *The Nature and Logic of Capitalism* (New York: W. W. Norton, 1985)

J. R. Hicks, *Value and Capital* (Oxford: Oxford University Press, 1939)

John Hillard (ed.), *J. M. Keynes in Retrospect: The Legacy of the Keynesian Revolution* (Upleadon: Edward Elgar, 1988)

Harry G. Johnson, *Macroeconomics and Monetary Theory* (Chicago: Aldine Publishing Company, 1972)

Harry G. Johnson, *Essays in Monetary Theory* (London: George Allen & Unwin, 1974)

J. M. Keynes, *The General Theory of Employment, Interest and Money* (London: Macmillan, 1936)

Axel Leijonhufvud, *Keynesian Economics and the Economics of Keynes* (Oxford: Oxford University Press, 1968)

Axel Leijonhufvud, *Information and Coordination: Essays in Macroeconomic Theory* (New York: Oxford University Press, 1981)

M. Merton (ed.), *The Collected Scientific Papers of Paul A. Samuelson* (Cambridge: MIT Press, 1972)

Michael Parkin, *Macroeconomics* (Englewood Cliffs, New Jersey: Prentice-Hall, 1984)

Don Patinkin, *Money, Interest and Prices: An Interpretation of Monetary and Value Theory* (New York: Harper International Editions, 1965)

B. P. Pesek and T. R. Saving, *Money, Wealth and Economic Theory* (New York: Macmillan, 1967)

Edmund S. Phelps *et al.*, *Microeconomic Foundations of Employment and Inflation Theory* (New York: W. W. Norton, 1970)

A. C. Pigou, *The Veil of Money* (London: Macmillan, 1941)

Radcliffe Committee, *Committee on the Working of the Monetary System: Report* (London: Her Majesty's Stationery Office, Cmnd 827, 1959)

Joan Robinson, *The Accumulation of Capital* (Third Edition) (London: Macmillan, 1969)

Joan Robinson and John Eatwell, *An Introduction to Modern Economics* (New York: McGraw-Hill, 1973)

Edward Shapiro, *Macroeconomic Analysis* (Third Edition) (New York: Harcourt Brace Jovanovich, 1974)

G. K. Shaw, *Rational Expectations: An Elementary Exposition* (Brighton: Harvester Press, 1984)

P. Sraffa, *The Production of Commodities by Means of Commodities* (Cambridge: The University Press, 1960)

Stephen Toulim and June Goodfield, *The Fabric of the Heavens* (New York: Harper Torchbooks, 1961)

John Weeks, *Capital and Exploitation* (Princeton: Princeton University Press, 1981)

John Weeks, *Capital and Circulation: Macroeconomics after Marx* (London: Macmillan, forthcoming)

ARTICLES AND ESSAYS

George Ackerlof, 'The Case Against Conservative Macroeconomics: An Inaugural Lecture', *Economica* (August 1979)

K. J. Arrow and G. Debreu, 'Existence of an Equilibrium for a Competitive Economy,' *Econometrica* (1954)

D. P. S. Ball, 'Factor Intensity Reversals: An International Comparison of Factor Costs and Factor Use', *Journal of Political Economy* (February 1966)

Robert J. Barro, 'Long Term Contracting, Sticky Prices, and Monetary Policy', *Journal of Monetary Economics*, 3 (July 1977)

John Brothwell, 'Rejoinder', *Bulletin of Economic Research*, 28, 2 (November 1976)

R. W. Clower, 'The Keynesian Counter-Revolution: A Theoretical Appraisal,' in Frank Hahn and F. P. R. Brechling (eds), *The Theory of Interest Rates*

Alfred Eichner and J. A. Kregel, 'An Essay on Post-Keynesian Theory: A New Paradigm in Economics', *Journal of Economic Literature*, XIII, 4 (December 1975)

Irving Fisher, 'A Statistical Relation between Unemployment and Price Changes', *International Labour Review* (June 1926)

Milton Friedman, 'Inflation: Causes and Consequences,' in *Dollars and Deficits* (Englewood Cliffs, NJ: Prentice-Hall, 1968)

Milton Friedman, 'The Role of Monetary Policy,' *American Economic Review*, 58 (March 1968)

Frank Hahn, 'Monetarism and Economic Theory', *Economica* (February 1980)

Nicholas Kaldor, 'A Model of Economic Growth,' *Economic Journal*, 67 (1977)

W. Leontief, 'An International Comparison of Factor Costs and Factor Use: A Review Article', *American Economic Review* (June 1964)

B. S. Minhas, 'Homohypallagic Production Function, Factor Intensity Reversals and the Hecksher-Olin Theorem', *Journal of Political Economy* (April 1962)

Franco Modigliani, 'Liquidity Preference and the Theory of Interest and Money', *Econometrica*, 12 (January 1944)

Panayotis G. Korliras and Richard S. Thorn (eds) *Modern Macroeconomics: Major Contributions to Contemporary Thought* (New York): Harper & Row)

John Muellbauer and Richard Portes, 'Macroeconomic Models with Quantity Rationing', *Economic Journal*, 88 (December 1978)

J. Muth, 'Rational Expectations and the Theory of Price Movements', *Econometrica* (July 1961)

A. W. H. Phillips, 'The Relation between Unemployment and the Rate of Change of Money Wages in the United Kingdom, 1861–1957', *Economica* (November 1958)

Paul A. Samuelson, 'Parable and Realism in Capital Theory: The Surrogate Production Function', *Review of Economic Studies* (June 1962)

Paul A. Samuelson, 'Rejoinder: Agreements, Disagreements, Doubts, and the Cause of Induced Harrod-Neutral Technical Change,' in M. Merton (ed.), *The Collected Scientific Papers of Paul A. Samuelson*

Thomas J. Sargent and Neil Wallace, 'Rational Expectations, the Optimal Monetary Instrument and the Optimal Money Supply Rate', *Journal of Political Economy* (April 1975)

Dudley Seers, 'A Theory of Inflation and Growth in Underdeveloped Countries Based on the Experience of Latin America,' *Oxford Economic Papers* (June 1963)

Warren L. Smith, 'A Graphical Exposition of the Complete Keynesian System', *Southern Economic Journal*, 23 (December 1956)

John Weeks, 'Value and Production in the General Theory', in John Hillard (ed.) *J. M. Keynes in Retrospect*

Index